THE GOOD GIRL'S
— GUIDE —
TO NEGOTIATING

THE GOOD GIRL'S
—— GUIDE ——
TO NEGOTIATING

*How to Get What You Want
at the Bargaining Table*

LESLIE WHITAKER AND
ELIZABETH AUSTIN

Little, Brown and Company
BOSTON | NEW YORK | LONDON

First Edition

Library of Congress Cataloging-in-Publication Data

Whitaker, Leslie.
    The good girl's guide to negotiating : how to get what you want at the bargaining table / by Leslie Whitaker and Elizabeth Austin. — 1st ed.
        p.   cm.
    Includes bibliographical references.
    ISBN 0-316-60105-5
    1. Women — Psychology. 2. Negotiation. I. Austin, Elizabeth. II. Title.

    HQ1206.W63 2001
    302.3'082 — dc21   00-062445

10 9 8 7 6 5 4 3 2 1

Q-FF

Book design by Giorgetta Bell McRee

Printed in the United States of America

With love to my daughter, Alexandra, my sister, Sarah, and my nieces, Liza and Melissa

— L.W.

To Madeline and Claire, my two best girls

— E.A.

CONTENTS

❧

AUTHORS' NOTE

People in the book who are identified solely by first name have been given fictitious names and characteristics; in some cases their stories are based on the composite experiences of more than one person. Any resemblance to real persons, living or dead, is purely coincidental.

ACKNOWLEDGMENTS

Good girls try to acknowledge every act of kindness with a polite "thank you." However, simple thanks hardly begin to express our gratitude to the many kind people who have helped us as we worked on this book — everyone from friends who suggested potential sources to administrative assistants who helped us get in touch with their busy bosses. If we inadvertently neglect to mention any of the gracious and helpful people who made this book possible, please accept our sincere apologies as well as our appreciation.

First and foremost, we'd like to express our gratitude to the dozens of successful, dynamic women who agreed to be interviewed for the book — both those who have been identified and those who wished to remain anonymous. We'd also like to thank the many academics and professional negotiators who shared their expertise with us.

Many people offered invaluable suggestions and assistance along the way, including Mary Maples Dunn, Jean Allard, Rick Casilli, Andrea Sachs, Micheal Frances, Suzanne Becker, Steve Parker, Peter LeBrun, Sam Nejame, Judith Lichtman, Carol Bellamy, Ruth Ayisi, Ellen Seidman, Kari Ytterhus, Persephone Zill, Ann Winters Bishop, Susan Klonsky, Wendy Cole, Giovanna Breu, Dr. John Hartmann, Chris Tavolacci, Hedy Ratner, Larry Msall, Lesley Spencer, Patty Abramson, Mary Rowe, Anastasia Toufexis, Helen Thomas, Sandy Soule, Erin Peters, JoLyn Matsumuro, Jack Jost, Mary Heidkamp, Gio Gutierrez, Tom McCullough, Jason Tom Klower, Pam Baird, Lilly Black, Amy Stillwell, Nicole Wild, Nick Bullat, Mary Conners, Judith Martin, Elaine Williams, Alison Nelson, Lisa DiMona, Rafe Sagalyn, Jane von Mehren, Beth Bland, Terry Murphy, Bobby Worth, Kimberly Charles, Clare Smith, Marie Kisiel, Brian Reardon, Al Lowman, Terri Woolsey, Pip

Denhart, Willa Reiser, Jeanette Oxford, Dave Lackey, Robert Stains, Greg Patterson, Dirk Johnson, Ann Patruno, Jane Wiedenman, and Robert Hargrove.

Heartfelt thanks are due to our agent, Alice Martell, and to former Little, Brown editor Jennifer Josephy, who believed in this book from the start. We also must thank many others at Little, Brown, including Deborah Baker, Peggy Leith Anderson, Marilyn Doof, Madeleine Schachter, Linda Biagi, Heather Kilpatrick, Bridgette Rodgers, Chika Azuma, Peggy Freudenthal, Beryl Needham, Karen Auerbach, Farrah Newbold, Beth Davey, and Matthew Ballast. We appreciate the hard work of Kathy Glidden and her colleagues at Stratford Publishing Services.

Very personal thanks to Roxie Glasco, Laurie Swanson, Colleen Mohyde, Curt Pesmen, Nancy Drew, Catherine Fredman, Rebecca Levin, Teresa Barker, Marina Justice, Michelle Wheeler, Deborah Gillespie, Elizabeth Taylor, Charlotte Lyons, Carla Forster, Beth Howard, Lydia Wozniak, Betsy Gardner, Paula Kamen, Bernadine Whitaker, Orin Whitaker, Sue Gordon, Jane Austin, and baby-sitter par excellence Maryshia Skretkowski. Love from Mom to Benjamin. Thanks to Dad for cheese and sympathy. We'd also like to thank our husbands, Randy and Michael, who constantly inspire us to become better negotiators.

THE GOOD GIRL'S
—— GUIDE ——
TO NEGOTIATING

INTRODUCTION

I wrote a *New York Times* bestseller.

I got paid $12,400 for it.

Don't let this happen to you.

As a sadder but wiser woman, I'm here to tell you that there's nothing like making a bad deal to inspire you to do better the next time. Since I made that perfectly awful deal, I've mastered some valuable lessons about negotiating. And I'd like to share my learning experiences with the many women (perhaps even you) who are in danger of repeating some of the mistakes I made.

Do you get paid too little for your work? Do you pay others too much? Do you get queasy thinking about negotiating for a big-ticket item, like a car or a new house? Do you pick up more dirty socks than anyone else in the family?

If you answered yes to any of the above, you're in good company. Millions of wonderful, intelligent, professionally skilled, and do-mestically adept women have lousy bargaining skills. Partly that's because we're simply mystified by the negotiation process, so we avoid it whenever possible. But more significantly, many of us were raised to be what I call "good girls" — which means we can't stop being nice, even if it kills us financially or robs us of our fair share of the proverbial pie. *This book is for every woman who ever made a bad deal because she was too nice or too naive to negotiate effectively.*

If you're looking for proof that just about any polite pushover can learn how to improve her winning percentages at the bargaining table (without having a total personality transplant or sex change), you can stop your search. In this book, my friend Beth and I will reveal all the bad deals we ever made — and how we finally figured out how a couple of good girls can negotiate for their fair share of the pie.

A SAD (BUT TRUE) STORY OF A VERY BAD DEAL

When I sat down to sign my first book contract, my head was full of warm, fuzzy thoughts of how lucky I was to have such a great opportunity. I had just been hired to ghostwrite for the Beardstown Ladies' Investment Club, to tell the story of how they used their down-home good sense to invest in the stock market. A friend recommended me to the book's New York–based packager because I had been a reporter for *Time* and a columnist for *Modern Maturity*. He had hired me over the telephone, then flew to meet me, contract in hand. I felt so special that he'd go to all that trouble just for me.

In my excitement, it didn't occur to me that I might need a lawyer to review the contract, or that I had no idea what professional ghostwriters usually got paid. I just wanted to see my name on the cover of a book. So my main goal was to make this high-powered stranger like me.

He did. Who wouldn't like such a nice, friendly woman — especially one who was so willing to help him get rich? I signed the contract with a big smile, and ended up with no claim to royalties, hardcover or paperback, for what turned out to be a hugely successful book. It spent three months on the *New York Times* bestseller list — with the packager's name on the list, not mine. That's when I finally realized I might need a little help with my negotiating skills.

My coauthor, Elizabeth Austin, was an equally proficient deal-maker. When she saw her first house, it was love at first sight; she immediately offered the sellers their full asking price. (She says she really liked the porch swing.) Later she realized she had paid nearly 20 percent above market value.

When I began complaining to Beth about my fabulous book deal, we put our journalistic heads together and realized we could do ourselves, and millions of our sisters, a service by figuring out how to negotiate competently. Don't misunderstand. We still pride ourselves on being do-gooders; Beth is a Girl Scout leader, I'm a frequent volunteer at my children's schools, and we've both driven in more car pools than we care to remember. But we didn't enjoy feeling like chumps, and we bet you don't either.

So we set out to learn how to be better negotiators. At first our hearts sank; to us, the best-known dealmakers, people like Donald Trump, seemed like ruthless jerks. To negotiate successfully, it looked like there were two basic requirements: First, be mean. Second, be male.

But after some more digging, we found there are plenty of successful negotiating styles that work for good girls like us. It turns out that legions of admirable women (and men) are advancing their causes and careers by sitting down at the bargaining table with the goal of solving problems in tandem with the people on the other side. And guess what? Those types of negotiations often end up yielding creative settlements that provide both sides with more than they ever expected.

Now, after several years of poring over the bestselling negotiating books and the latest academic articles, interviewing researchers in the field, and seeking out women who have succeeded at the bargaining table, we've actually used what we've learned to negotiate much more equitable deals on subsequent book contracts and home purchases — not to mention the great deal Beth got on her new car.

Moral: Don't give up just because you weren't raised to be a shark. You don't have to choose between being a good person and getting a good deal. A negotiation is truly successful when both sides feel they've struck an equitable bargain, one that feels good to you the day you make it, and when you look back years later. Like us, you can learn how to make better deals — and still feel like a good girl, too.

CHAPTER 1

❧

GOOD GIRLS 'R' US

Interior designer Alexa Hampton learned her business from a master — her dad. When his daughter was still a teenager, legendary designer Mark Hampton started bringing her into his Madison Avenue studio. There, Alexa watched as her father dazzled well-heeled clients like former president George Bush and Texas philanthropist Anne Bass with his legendary elegance. Her early introduction into the high-flying world of interior design held her in good stead in 1998, when her father died of cancer.

At the age of twenty-seven, Alexa had inherited the impeccable taste and style she needed to take over as CEO of her father's company, Mark Hampton Inc. But when it came time for the young designer to talk money with her clients, she realized she'd also inherited the family curse — her father's chronic reticence about financial matters. "My father was very proper. He didn't like to discuss money. He found it awkward and embarrassing. He would never sit down with a client and discuss a bill."

Alexa realized that if she couldn't find a way to broach the awkward subject of how to meet her clients' champagne expectations on their proposed Merlot budgets, she'd end up squeezing her subcontractors and shaving her own fees. She owed it to herself, and to her employees, to learn to make better deals. So she learned how to handle those overnight millionaires who don't blink at plunking down $40,000 for an exquisite English antique desk but balk at paying master artisans to put a faux leather finish on their office walls. "I make it clear I'm not running a sweatshop," Alexa says firmly. "It's a balancing act, and I've gotten better at it."

She's also learned not to flinch at putting a hefty price tag on her own work. Before she puts a proposal in the mail, she calls her clients to let them know what to expect. "I ask them to respond at that moment," she says. "I could do it through the mail, which would function as a shield for me, but it's easier for them to push you around if they're not speaking directly to you." If her prospective customers suffer from sticker shock, she's always willing to offer more economical furniture and fabric options. But she doesn't cut her fee, even when a customer tells her she's charging too much. "I'll say, 'I understand your position,'" she says. Then she details the many design services included in that fee, services her clients may not have considered. She's firm but cordial. "There's no acrimony. They don't take offense. I'm not a pit bull."

By holding her ground, Alexa buys herself the freedom to give her clients the stylish, sumptuous rooms they love and that she loves to create. "My favorite part of the job is when everything comes together," she says. "The carpeting is down, the curtains are up, and the client is about to come in. It's like Christmas morning."

Not every trip to the bargaining table ends in a neatly wrapped package. But those of us who dread the very thought of negotiating (probably because we expect to wind up with the equivalent of a piece of coal in our stockings) should be cheered by Alexa's early success. It shows we all can learn — and must learn — to negotiate.

Negotiating is what you have to do when you can't get what you want simply by asking Dad or Santa Claus. We all have to make trades, strike deals, and forge compromises every day, over the telephone and via e-mail, in office meetings and at the water cooler, at family gatherings and around the dinner table, in the showroom and even in the bedroom.

"Everyone needs to learn to negotiate," insists Sheila Wellington, president of Catalyst, a not-for-profit think tank that works with businesses to advance women.

That statement is even more true today than it was ten years ago, adds Harvard professor Rosabeth Moss Kanter, author of *Men and Women of the Corporation*. "Very few things are fixed today. Prices are negotiable. At work, people often don't have clear authority over others, so they must influence and persuade them. And with so many independent contractors having to negotiate their terms of employment, I don't see how anyone can survive who doesn't know how to negotiate."

It's part of the fabric of our daily lives, agrees Marsha Johnson Evans, national executive director of Girl Scouts of the U.S.A. "In your family, it could be as simple as deciding to go to the movie I want to go to this week, and the one you want to go to next week," she says. If that seems too trivial to discuss, it's not. The world is full of women who've spent years simmering with suppressed resentment over being dragged to all those *Rocky* sequels. But where were those guys when we wanted to see *The English Patient*? Those seemingly minor issues, the ones you decide aren't worth fighting (or negotiating) about, can poison your relationships.

Let's be honest. Not every negotiation has a storybook ending. No matter how good your dealmaking skills are, you still may end up ruffling somebody's feathers (or mussing some plumage of your own). You may not get the raise, or a fabulous deal on a shiny new car. Doors may still slam in your face. But if you learn how to negotiate, you may find new ways to open doors that can dramatically change the course or quality of your life. You'll find you can do more than bargain your way to a promotion or a raise. You can use those same skills to solve the annual "Whose house for Thanksgiving?" dilemma, or to figure out how to put together funding for a cutting-edge reading program at your children's school.

The good news is that the number of fearless female negotiators is on the rise — and they weren't all born that way. In fact the notion that good negotiators start honing their haggling skills in the cradle is a myth, says Leigh Thompson, author of *The Mind and Heart of the Negotiator.* "Good negotiators are self-made," she writes. "Effective negotiation depends on practice and study."

The bad news is that many more of us bring our "good girl" personalities to the bargaining table, sweetly and obligingly giving away far more than we ever get in return. "A lot of women are polite, and they confuse asking for what you want with conflict. They confuse assertiveness with aggressiveness and hostility. They think asking for things means you are taking advantage of others. Or they just don't know what they are entitled to, so they don't ask," says Bernice Sandler, of the National Association for Women in Education.

It's even more discouraging to see women who have been trained to negotiate on the job turn into overly accommodating invertebrates when it comes to getting what they need on the home front. "I've never bought a car," confesses Gun Denhart, cofounder of

Hanna Andersson, the mail-order clothing company. "I send my husband or my son. I don't know very much about cars, so I'm easy to take advantage of. Car dealers talk around you, and you feel stupid." And one longtime union negotiator admits: "I hate personal confrontations, and I'm not very good at them."

THE FUZZY SIDE OF THE LOLLIPOP

If you expect to lose, you will inevitably wind up with the short end of the stick. Historically, that means most women are almost predestined to make crummy deals. We still bring home less money than men do — 76 cents for every dollar a man earns. And if you compare the take-home pay of female and male managers, the gap is even greater — 68 cents in our cute vinyl pocketbooks for every dollar in their leather wallets, according to a 1999 study by the Bureau of Labor Statistics. After women break through the glass ceiling, they still feel some pain on payday. The median total compensation (not including stock-option awards) for the top five female executives in 1996 was $981,000, little more than half the median of $1.9 million earned by CEOs at the largest five hundred public companies, the *Wall Street Journal* reports.

Many underpaid female execs are hampered by the same feminine trepidations that hamstring their secretaries. "There's a question of, 'Will I jeopardize getting the offer if I insist on too much?' " Joseph Bachelder, a lawyer who specializes in executive compensation, told the *Wall Street Journal*. "When a female is trying to break through and get an important new job, there may be something in her saying, 'Don't push it.' " Rosemarie Greco, the highest-ranking woman in American banking before she quit as president of CoreStates Financial Corporation, confesses that it took years before she learned to negotiate forcefully on her own behalf. "After my first promotion, it's a good thing I never asked for a certain amount of money — because I probably would have asked for less than I got."

Divorce is another arena where women who don't have negotiating skills may suffer. Mediation, a process in which a settlement is worked out directly between the husband and wife with the assistance of a neutral third party, is increasingly popular. But women who are less assertive than their husbands may be at a disadvantage if they don't have an attorney advocating for them. "If your partner is pursuing a very aggressive strategy and you are shy and retiring, you can't expect a mediator to correct the imbalance," explains Charlotte Adelman, a retired divorce attorney.

Not only do we make less money and control fewer resources, we also end up paying much more than we should for the big-ticket necessities of life. The book *Women Pay More (And How to Put a Stop to It)* cites a Chicago-area study that found car dealers offered better prices to white men than to white women and African Americans. Black women got a double-whammy, paying markups three times those paid by white men. To Ian Ayres, who directed the study, that means car salesmen see women customers as "suckers."

Well, suckers end up with the fuzzy side of the lollipop. And that's scary for women who find themselves being dragged to the bargaining table more and more often these days. As we move into this new century, women can expect to change jobs — and even careers — several times during our lifetimes, and many of us will be making those moves without a man nearby to hold our hands or watch our backs. If we're going to survive, we have to learn to negotiate, and then teach our daughters, our friends, and even our mothers. It's never too late to get a better deal in life.

HOW GOOD GIRLS GO BAD

It's easy to assume that good negotiating requires a heavy dose of testosterone. That's just not true. After years of study, most scientists have concluded that females match males in verbal ability, math ability, spatial ability, moral reasoning, and leadership skills — all the attributes necessary to successful negotiating. So why do so many women wimp out at the bargaining table?

One likely culprit is social conditioning — that "be a good little girl" training we get from the moment the nurses strap on those little pink wristbands in the delivery room. Generally, we girls are rewarded for our social skills. We win applause when we share our toys or help Mommy in the kitchen. Even if a feisty female toddler gets Mom's approval, she soon learns in nursery school that being

King (or Queen) of the Hill doesn't earn high marks from the teacher. Instead, girls learn to yield power for the common good, through games like jump rope and playing house. By the time we're out of elementary school, most girls are well on the way to becoming nurturing team players — great assets for community building and child rearing, but not much use when it comes to buying a new house. "We're conditioned to provide," says Sue Yellin, a New York City–based business development coach. "We're not used to asking for things."

"It's completely understandable that women are uncomfortable with negotiating," says Carol Watson, a professor of management and organizational behavior at Rider University in Lawrenceville, New Jersey. "We tend to think of negotiating as a competitive situation, in which winning is not something women are supposed to do. Women are in a bind. Should we be tough like guys and have everyone hate us, or be nice and let everyone walk all over us?"

Feminist psychologists contend that women feel pressured to get along, to the point that we'll sacrifice almost anything — especially our own needs — to win the approval of others. "Many girls are 'empathy sick,'" psychologist Mary Pipher says in her bestseller about adolescent girls, *Reviving Ophelia*. "That is, they know more about others' feelings than their own." Girls are particularly uncomfortable about stating their needs to boys and adults, Pipher says. "They worry about not being nice, or appearing selfish."

There is recent evidence that girls start getting pressured to button their lips as early as nursery school. In her eight-month study of five preschool classes, University of Michigan sociologist Karin Martin found girls were generally quieter than boys, reports *Allure* magazine. Yet their teachers told the girls to speak softly or use a "nicer" voice nearly three times as often as they shushed the boys. The discrepancy was even clearer when the children were trying to settle disputes: The teachers discouraged loudness in girls, but not in boys. When the girls toned down their voices, they toned down their physical movements, too. So while the rowdy boys were doing jumping jacks, the quiet girls were playing jacks. By muffling the girls' self-expression, Martin concludes, teachers were telling them that their voices shouldn't be used for arguing and fighting back.

For many women, speaking softly and carrying no stick eventually becomes routine. By the time the average girl reaches adulthood, she has spent years surrounded by visions of women as self-sacrificing saints. Movies constantly pit the tough, cold business bitch against the warm and wonderful Mom — and guess who we always root for in the last reel?

Women's magazines approvingly tell heartwarming stories of corporate females who desert the fast track in favor of those non-financial intangibles, like the smell of chocolate chip cookies baking in the oven when the kids get home from school. (Three pages later, you'll find the heartbreaking story of a different woman left impoverished by her double-dealing husband. But it's considered too negative to remind smiling, saintly Mommy A that a runaway truck or a runaway blonde could wipe out her husband's support and leave her in the same sad straits as Mommy B.) In the popular press, Bill Gates may win grudging admiration for his canny, self-serving dealmaking. But when Princess Diana held out for a bigger slice of the (immense) royal pie, she was reviled as a grasping gold digger. Only her untimely death left her halo intact.

NEGOTIATING OPHELIA-STYLE

Very few of us are blessed with natural negotiating savvy. Instead, we mostly learn to negotiate from the same women who taught us to sit down and shut up. It's no wonder we turn into sweet-tempered mush when we're pressured by real estate agents and car salesmen. We're all desperate to be liked, and we'll pay almost anything to buy a new (temporary) friend. (Although, as Beth points out, "in my life, I've bought a total of five cars from five different car dealers. And I've never run into any of those five salesmen ever again. So why on earth did I care what they thought of me?")

Since we're such deplorable negotiators, we often end up accepting the first offer just to avoid the whole ordeal. Then we come up with creative "good girl" rationalizations to mend our sagging self-esteem. One classic example comes from a friend of ours whose daughter was flailing in the job market. Finally the daughter got a lead on a promising new job. At the first interview, she was told the salary range was $22,000 to $28,000. When she landed the job, she was offered a starting salary of $24,000. Her mother advised her to accept immediately, without a counteroffer. "That way, she doesn't get stuck at the top of the pay scale," her mom reasoned. "This leaves her some space to move up the ladder." Doesn't that sound like good maternal advice? Think about it this way: If she'd held out for $26,500 and got $500 raises each year, she'd hit the salary maximum after four years. Over five years, her salary would amount to $137,000. But by following Mom's advice and taking their first offer, even $1,000 annual raises will only bring her up to $130,000 over the same period. So Mom's well-intentioned advice to keep quiet, not rock the boat, and leave room for dessert cost her daughter a cool $7,000 — the price of a decent used car.

To whitewash over our desire to avoid negotiating and keep the peace at any price, we end up downplaying our own abilities. This was one of my great-aunt's well-polished techniques. She would say she didn't know how to get somewhere rather than admit that she didn't want to go, or claim she couldn't possibly learn how to operate a new gadget she had no interest in mastering. This ploy avoided unpleasant confrontations — but at the price of providing an example of feigned female incompetence.

The result of all this good girl modeling? By the time we reach adulthood and need to bargain on our own behalf, we have a well-developed set of internal deal-breakers:

- I don't really deserve much.
- I don't want to be manipulative.
- I don't want to brag.
- It's only money.
- They'll think I'm a bitch.

If you listen carefully to your inner voices as you approach a negotiating session, you're likely to hear one or more of these negative messages quietly undermining your ability to advocate for yourself. I know this from bitter personal experience. As I was preparing to sign the contract for the Beardstown Ladies' book, my inner voices were all working for the other side. "You don't deserve much," the voices said. "You've never written a book before, and you're lucky they're even considering you." When the book packager said, "This book has the best chance of any of the ones I've done so far to become a bestseller," my inner voices laughed themselves sick: "Leslie? Writing a bestseller? Ha! Take the money and run!" When the book packager offered me a $2,000 bonus if the book hit the

New York Times bestseller list, I almost laughed, too. Later I told my husband I should have asked for another $2,000 if the book won a Nobel Prize. It all seemed really, really funny. Until the packager's prediction came true, and the book went on to make a bundle.

(A couple of years after the book was published, the Ladies' calculations of their stock market profits were publicly challenged, much to my dismay. My assignment as the Ladies' ghostwriter hadn't involved auditing their numbers, but I still wished my inner voices had offered some practical advice, like "Call an agent before signing anything, you dummy.")

GENDER BENDER

In hindsight, it's easy to see how those nasty little voices leave us unable to strike a smart deal. When Beth offered way too much for her first house, she was propelled by her soft heart, not her hard head. She was enraptured by a vision of sitting on the porch swing with her husband, holding hands and rocking slowly while their children played in the front yard on soft summer nights. So when the house failed to appraise out at the price she'd agreed to pay, she didn't consider walking away, or even renegotiating with the sellers. Entranced by the house, she convinced her husband to agree to a personal loan to make up the difference in the down payment. What was a few thousand dollars compared with that idyllic porch vision? After all, "It's only money." She learned her mistake the hard way, when the house needed substantial repairs and they didn't have enough home equity to get a construction loan.

Research comparing men's and women's bargaining styles suggests it may be those inner voices that really do us in. Point by point, we seem to have the same basic skills that men do; we just don't use them effectively. "The research so far hasn't found any differences of any great substance," says Professor Watson. "You can find data to support whatever view you want, but the differences are inconsistent and small." Those research findings have set Watson on a personal mission to fight the widespread belief that there are innate differences in men's and women's ability to negotiate.

Other researchers blame the difference in men's and women's

success at the negotiating table on women's relative lack of power. It's hard to insist on win-win negotiating when you feel like you have little to win, and everything to lose.

Why are there no simple explanations for women's difficulties at the bargaining table? For one thing, each negotiating situation is unique and complicated. It's hard to measure all the emotional baggage, personal history, and individual needs that come into play in any particular deal. It's also hard to figure out just how much laboratory studies that pit male business students against female business students reflect what goes on in the real world.

So while the academic experts study the issue, the rest of us have to figure out how to cut a fair deal the next time we have to negotiate for a new car or a new division of household labor.

One thing is clear: All the research shows that you don't have to be a man — or a jerk — to succeed in negotiating.

We're not here to tell you how to "fix yourself" with a few quick injections of macho attitude guaranteed to turn you into the distaff version of Donald Trump. Instead, we want to reshape your notions of what successful negotiating really is — and what it isn't. No matter what those voices in your head may whisper, negotiating isn't an aggressive, win-lose competition that you can never master. Negotiating is really a joint problem-solving session helping both sides get what they need to reach a lasting settlement. And that's the kind of thing we good girls really do best.

It's time to call in your mental moving van and get rid of your vision of an unfriendly bargaining table, that big rectangular block with the sharp corners and hard, wide surface keeping the two sides far apart. Instead, envision sitting down at a round, low coffee table — or even on a love seat, where the two negotiators can sit comfortably side by side. Picture yourself sitting there, happily proposing solutions and reaching agreements between sips of tea.

UNTIL THE LOVE SEAT ARRIVES

Unfortunately, in the time it takes for your imaginary furniture store to deliver your friendly little love seat, you may have to negotiate with an unhappy client, a husband who wants to take off for a week-long conference in sunny Santa Fe, and a baby-sitter who's just announced she's cutting her hours to attend a series of real estate seminars. So what can you do to get what you need from the people who have the biggest impact on your life?

We wish there were a clear program guaranteed to make you a winner in every major (and minor) negotiation of your life. Sadly, there's not. But there are clues that can help you identify what you may be doing to undercut your own bargaining position. So take a seat and answer (honestly) the following questions.

➡ *Do you put a lower value on your work than your male colleagues put on theirs?*

"I used to cut my fees like crazy," admits Melinda Brody, an Alta-monte Springs, Florida–based sales trainer who specializes in the home-building industry. "I lacked confidence. If conference orga-nizers said they didn't have the budget, I'd say okay and lower my fee. I wanted to come out looking like the nice person."

If that sounds a little dopey, don't be too hard on poor Melinda; there are a lot of women out there just like her. Back in the 1980s, Brenda Major, a psychology professor at the University of Cali-fornia–Santa Barbara, put together a series of studies designed to compare the dollar value men and women put on their work. She asked a group of undergraduates to take on a piece of busywork, such as counting the dots on a page. Then she asked the students to put a price tag on their work. She found that female students worked longer hours, made fewer mistakes — and consistently charged less than their male counterparts. When the students were told their "salary requests" were being reviewed by outside ob-servers, the women's requested wages went down even further. Sadly, that self-imposed wage gap remains in place; researchers at major universities in Canada and the United States recently con-ducted similar experiments, with similar results. (There's one ray of hope, however; when women were told what others were charging, they boosted their salary estimates to give themselves a fair deal.)

Melinda, the sales trainer, is a single mother with an eleven-year-old daughter. Yet she spent eight years buckling every time one of her clients whined about her bill. Then she attended a National Speakers' Association workshop that changed her life. "Fee, Free, or

Flee was the mantra," she recalls. "It means either stick to your fee, donate your services, or walk away. That was three years ago, and I'll never forget it." Since then, she's kept her rates high — along with her self-esteem. "Now I feel very confident," she says. "I'd rather walk away than jeopardize my rate." To make sure she's charging the right amount, she now tracks the rates of her top ten competitors (including two women) and charts her place in the pecking order. "Right now I'm number two," she says proudly.

➤ Do you underestimate your negotiating skills?

Incredible as it may seem, you may be better at negotiating than you think. Professor Watson says women managers made far more disparaging remarks about their negotiating abilities than their male peers, even when they used similar methods and came out with equal results. Gun Denhart says she shied away from negotiating with suppliers when she and her husband started Hanna Andersson. "I always thought I was a bad negotiator in that male sense," she recalls. "I have a hard time anticipating what the other side will say. I can't scheme about things like that." Then she realized that her own open personality could work to her advantage. "I have found that I'm up front and honest, and I'm not afraid to say what my needs are. I also try to find common ground."

Susan George, the town manager of Woodside, California, says she had a similar experience. "My introduction to negotiating came as an entry-level financial analyst. I wasn't invited to the table, but I heard people in the hallway bragging about their big business deals. To hear them talk about it, it sounded as though you had to be tough. There was a veil of power surrounding it."

It wasn't until she became part of a negotiating team that she realized she was just using skills she'd been honing her whole life. "Negotiating actually comes easily," she learned to her amazement. "It dawned on me that people negotiate every day of their lives; there's nothing mysterious about it at all. Shoot, I used to negotiate with my mother."

She realized she'd become a master negotiator during her first government post, when she had to represent Santa Clara County's interests in negotiating the deputy sheriffs' salary contracts. "At first I thought it would be dominated by testosterone, and there were some tense moments. But after we got through the initial posturing, it was just people dealing with people." Susan, a petite woman with short brown hair and bright green eyes, admits she got a slight kick out of watching one of her colleagues try to "act like a big gorilla. I noticed that we seemed to lose ground every time he tried to push his weight around," she says. "Since I'm not a big gorilla, I was pleased to see that tactic didn't work." Now, she says, "I realize that negotiating is really just people trying to come to some agreement with which they can all be satisfied."

→ *Do you give away all the Popsicles?*

Anybody who thinks men invented the win-win strategy should watch a mother trying to divide one Popsicle between two greedy toddlers. When it comes to tending relationships, women are experts at the often-delicate tasks of smoothing feathers and mending fences. From a negotiating standpoint, that's not all bad; a healthy, longstanding relationship can help to hold things together when a deal starts to dissolve. The trouble is, women can worry too much about keeping everybody else happy. We've all seen mothers solve an angry dessert dispute by handing over their own treats, just to keep peace in the family. Maybe that's not so bad as a picnic-table strategy. But when it comes to negotiating with the outside world, Mom needs to remember to keep at least one Popsicle for herself.

Consider Margaret, a caterer who hates to take other people's money. As a sales representative for a major catering company, she found she couldn't bear bringing up the thorny issue of payment when she sat down with dewy brides and their mothers to talk about wedding menus. "People would actually have to ask me how much things were going to cost," she says, sometimes after they had already spent an hour nailing down a buffet menu. If the sticker shock proved overwhelming, Margaret then had to deal with a tearful bride whose heart was set on beef tenderloin but whose purse could only stretch to chicken tenders. "It causes unpleasant situations," Margaret acknowledges. "I would minimize the money discussions, even though the entire gist of what we're doing boils down to, 'You give us money for food.'"

Over time, Margaret has learned to negotiate on her employer's behalf. But when she recently did a catering job on her own, her money phobia proved crippling. The problem started when one of her mother's friends asked her to cater a golden anniversary party. Even though the friend is a millionaire, Margaret was reluctant to send her a bill. "I love the food," she explains. "I want to shop for the food, taste the food, stay up all night making the food, because that's what I loooove to do," says this smart, capable woman. "But when it comes to price, it's like, 'Oh, do we have to talk about this?'" So the normally energetic and well-organized Margaret procrastinated madly about sending a bill.

Finally her kindly, well-to-do client called to remind Margaret gently that her invoice was overdue. So Margaret sat down to tally the cost of the ingredients — which were about one-quarter the cost of a normal catered meal, since she got everything wholesale. With her husband's encouragement, she agreed to add a couple hundred dollars to account for the hours and hours she had spent shopping, cooking, and serving the food for some sixty people.

Luckily for Margaret, her client realized the total was lower than it should have been. So when she paid the bill, the friendly millionaire added a few hundred extra dollars to Margaret's requested amount. "She had obviously seen that I had not charged enough to cover my time," Margaret says. "I could have charged her any amount and she would not have batted an eye. I don't know why I needed to cause myself all that internal trauma."

The thing that's so astonishing about Margaret's negotiating debacle is that nobody was asking her to give up anything. Her client was more than happy to pay whatever Margaret asked; it's just that Margaret insists on giving away the store. The problem, she says, is that she goes into a negotiation imagining all the possible negative things people might say: "The food wasn't good." "The menu was boring." "You didn't clean up properly." She's willing to pay any price to avoid hearing those negative comments — and who's mean enough to insult someone who's working for free?

➼ Do you overcompensate and try to act too much like a man?

To avoid coming off like a doormat, some women take the opposite tack and model themselves on sharklike men. But this can backfire, warns Dallas attorney Courtenay Bass. "First, if you're not being natural, people will sense your insincerity and distrust you," she writes in *The Woman Advocate*. "Secondly, by adopting an unnatural style, you are throwing away your natural talents in a self-defeating effort. Why should Streisand want to sing like Pavarotti? Remember, the first rule of successful negotiation is to be yourself."

Scholastic Inc. executive vice president Deborah Forte, a persuasive dealmaker with a pleasant smile, advises striking a tone "that suits your style." So while some women get a kick out of assuming an angry, loud, or bullying posture, she notes, "if it's not something you are comfortable with, it doesn't work."

➥ Do you tiptoe around the tough issues?

Ask a man how a negotiation went, and he'll likely tell you whether he met his target. But ask a woman, and she might tell you where they went for lunch. In one of Professor Watson's studies, she found that women rated their negotiations a success if everybody got along, even if they never actually talked about the main points of the deal. "I see this much more frequently with women," says Sue Yellin, the business development coach. "They tend to postpone closing a deal. They will take a prospect to lunch, but they won't ask for what they want. 'What will I do if they say no?'"

➥ Do you give up too easily?

In one 1994 academic study, male business school students outfoxed females every which way — whether they were buying or selling, and whether they were negotiating against men or women. The researchers concluded that the men came out better because they were more active bargainers, offering more proposals and coming up with more ways to make the deal work. However, women who recognize that negotiating is an endurance sport say they've learned to hang in there and come out with a winning deal.

"I'm persistent. I won't take no for an answer," says Cordia Harrington, a Dickson, Tennessee–based entrepreneur who has successfully concluded negotiations with McDonald's over the terms of a joint business venture. "It's very important to know what I want before I go in. But if one proposal doesn't work, then I approach it from lots of different angles."

"No doesn't mean no," agrees Whitney Johns Martin, immediate past president of the National Association of Women Business Owners. "No means 'not this way,' which means you have to try something else. I try to 'embrace the no,' because it tells me I'm going down a path that's not going to work. Rather than wallow in rejection and waste time, I realize I know more than I did before."

"The way we win is we keep it up," adds Teresa Johnson, an Arizona mom turned environmental activist. She has found that women in her group are actually more persistent than men. If one woman's husband tells her to stop demonstrating in front of the TV cameras because it jeopardizes his job, "she'll call us and say, 'I can't go out, but I can baby-sit so others can go out, or I can make copies, or whatever you need.'"

➨ *Do you expect everyone to be as nice as you are?*

Just because you may go out of your way to be nice, don't expect everyone to be equally altruistic. "I thought if I made friends with the people I was dealing with, they'd treat me nicely," says an Atlanta-based business consultant. "It doesn't shake out that way at all. Everyone has an agenda they're pursuing, and it's never the one that's in your best interest. They're always coming from a different corner of the box — and we're not getting together to have a tea party."

Suellen Long, fifty-seven, says her younger associates are often taken aback when older women play hardball. But Long, president of her own public relations firm, Long Promotional Group, in Chicago, says those young women are mistaken in expecting their elders to be motherly mentors. "Some older women in business got up there the hard way," she says. "They're tough, and they're mean."

Just because you're fair-minded or inexperienced, don't assume all other women are, too. Never assume the woman sitting across the table is a good girl, too (unless, of course, you're negotiating with Beth or me).

GETTING STARTED: UNTYING
THE KNOT IN YOUR STOMACH

Look — in a perfect world, we know you'd rather avoid negotiating altogether. We know that your stomach hurts every time you think about asking your boss for a raise, and that you get nauseated whenever it's time to work out a new contract with a supplier. Well, rest assured that you're not the only one. Even the most seasoned negotiators can get that I'd-rather-do-anything-else feeling.

But believe it or not, negotiating can actually be an intellectually stimulating, creative, even exhilarating experience. "I like to negotiate when the end result has made both sides happy and I'm the one who found the key," says Jeanette Wagner, an Estée Lauder executive who strikes deals all over the world. Catalyst president Sheila Wellington agrees. "I love negotiating because it calls for an array of talents and abilities. It's challenging. And if you believe in your position, you are trying to figure out some way you can advance some cause you think is right."

Once you're familiar with the basics, you can view each negotiating situation as another opportunity to improve on your personal best. You'll win new points you wouldn't have considered in your old good days. You'll figure out which basic negotiating ploys work best for you. And although you don't believe it right now, you'll even leave a couple of car salesmen gasping in the dust.

Let's face it. That prenegotiation knot in your stomach may never go away completely. It's like the stage fright that energizes even the most accomplished actors before they step in front of an audience. But with time and practice, you may start to see negotiating as an exciting process that generates new ideas and strengthens old relationships. You won't believe the boost it gives your self-confidence when you negotiate $50 off the price of your new washing machine. (Beth's husband is still bragging that his savvy wife got 10 percent off the price of their new TV, just by asking the clerk whether there was a sale coming up.) And in the negotiations that really count, the ones with the most important people in your life, you'll enjoy some creative problem-solving sessions that may help you uncover unexpectedly great solutions. "I always listen for something new," says one professional negotiator. "Frequently, I'm surprised by some completely new idea I never would have thought up on my own." Sure, you won't always reach the win-win agreements of your dreams and end up with everything you want. But if you learn to negotiate more effectively, you'll always know you've done your best to get the things you really need.

Life Is a Garage Sale

If you're feeling shaky about your negotiating skills, hop in a car some bright Saturday morning and head out to a grassroots negotiating seminar — or in layman's terms, a garage sale. This incredible insight came to us after we talked with Cindy Skrzynecki, a garage sale consultant in Minneapolis. As it turns out, her advice on running a successful garage sale closely follows our advice on running a successful negotiation — with the difference, of course, that we don't advise sticking little price tags on all the boardroom furniture.

The real trick in a garage sale (as in life) is doing your homework and figuring out your bottom line.

The homework part is fairly forthright. To get people to buy, you have to price your merchandise properly — generally, in garage sales, at somewhere between 10 and 20 percent of its original retail price. If you think an item is worth more than that, sell it somewhere else, Cindy says. Take it to a consignment shop, or put a little ad in your local paper or on your company's employee bulletin board.

Be realistic. Your "treasures" are worth more to you than they are to the general public. So don't get your nose out of joint when someone offers three bucks for your prom dress. "You have to be clear about your objectives," Cindy says. "It's a very emotional process to get rid of your stuff. If you want to sell a high school letter jacket, pick a price that makes it worthwhile to sell it. It's all about deciding what you want ahead of time, so that when you get to the negotiating part, you know your bottom line."

As for the other odds and ends you're selling, don't be greedy. "Basically, you want people to come up and give you money for things you don't want or need anymore, and that you would throw away anyhow. So you're ahead of the game, getting money for stuff you don't want."

Never take anyone's negative comments about your merchandise personally. Usually it's just a ploy to get you to lower your prices; don't fall for it. "You can just walk away," Cindy says.

Life Is a Garage Sale (cont.)

Don't get caught off guard by people who ambush you by showing up ahead of time. "I warn my classes that these people count on your being very naive. They want a private showing and the pick of the litter. So when buyers come early, be prepared. Have a sign that says, 'If you want to buy something before the start time, all prices are double.' "

Take time to talk to your customers when you're negotiating. If you understand why they want a particular object, you'll have a better idea of your bargaining power. "Ask, 'How do you plan to use it?' If they say, 'I don't know, I just thought it would be nice to have around,' that's one thing. But if it's, 'I've looked all over town, and they don't have these anymore,' then you're in a better position to negotiate."

When you're the buyer, Cindy says, use your empathy to get what you want. If you've ever had a garage sale, you know there's nothing as discouraging as putting away all the stuff that didn't sell. So gather up all the treasures you've found and offer a "nice round number" for them. After that, Cindy says, "the first one who speaks usually loses. If they refuse my offer, then I can decide if I really want to pay full price for this stuff." But Cindy says she doesn't always bother to dicker. "Sometimes I don't negotiate. If I really want something and it's not overpriced, I'll just buy it."

(For more garage sale insights, you can buy Cindy's booklet, *50 Ways to Make the Most Money on a Garage Sale,* by sending $5 to CMS Publishing, P.O. Box 23448, Minneapolis, MN 55423.)

CHAPTER 2

❦

GETTING TO YOU

It was a typical week. On Monday, Lynn agreed to take on a rush project left hanging by a coworker whose elderly father had broken his hip. Her supervisor, also a personal friend, explained helplessly that there was no budget to cover Lynn's overtime, but that she really appreciated the extra effort. On Tuesday, Lynn found out that her daughter's children's choir itinerary had been changed; instead of flying from Chicago to Dallas, they would be making the 950-mile trip by bus — nonstop. "We wanted to save the airfare, and I figured nobody would mind sleeping on a bus a couple nights," the choir director said with a winning smile. "You're still willing to chaperone, aren't you?" On Thursday, she got a desperate call from her sister: Their baby-sitter had just canceled, and she needed someone to watch her two-year-old for a week while she and her husband took a long-planned second honeymoon. "I wouldn't ask, but we've really been going through a rough patch lately," her sister said tearfully. "I'm just desperate for some time away."

Facing four muggy days on a bus with thirty-two bored little choristers, hours of frantic unpaid overtime, and then a week of chasing after a not-quite-toilet-trained toddler, Lynn called Beth to unload some of the Parent-Teacher Organization assignments she'd agreed to take the week before.

Beth, ever the good girl, said she'd be glad to help out with publicity for the school talent show. But hearing the panic in her friend's voice, Beth thought it was time for a gentle lecture on the benefits of learning to negotiate. "Why don't you take *Getting to Yes* to read on the bus," Beth suggested.

"Ha!" Lynn shrieked. "I don't need help getting to yes. Everybody knows I start at yes. That's my whole problem!"

She's not alone. The world is full of good girls who can't say no.

You see, saying "No" (or even "Let me get back to you") runs completely contrary to the whole good girl ethic. We're friendly and helpful, kind and self-sacrificing, and always available in a pinch. We'll do anything to help a friend, or even a friend of a friend.

Sometimes that's great. It's the good girl brigade that organizes the family's meals when the woman next door is stricken with breast cancer. We put together layettes for impoverished inner-city mothers. We Run for the Cure, Trick-or-Treat for UNICEF, and give to the United Way. If it weren't for us, the world would be a much colder, crueler place.

The trouble is, we don't know when to stop. We're so good-hearted and so easily persuaded that we fall for every sad story we hear. It's one thing to volunteer at a soup kitchen; it's quite another to get stuck with doing all the cleanup after Christmas dinner because your sister-in-law just got her nails done and doesn't want to mess up her expensive manicure.

Maybe we're afraid people only like us for the good deeds we do, not the good women we are. Maybe we've been bamboozled into thinking we don't deserve equitable treatment. Or maybe we're stuffed so full of pent-up frustration that we fear one small act of rebellion might trigger a furious avalanche of self-assertiveness. And then who would make the bok choy costumes for the kindergarten's Good Nutrition pageant?

So we say yes. Yes, I'll train the inexperienced guy you brought in to take the supervisor's job I deserved. Yes, I'll leave work early on Fridays to drive the car pool so you don't have to miss your yoga class. Yes, I'll overpay to have the house painted because the contractor's pregnant wife is on bed rest. Sure. Okay. Fine. No problem. I'll work it in. Don't worry about it. In the Land of the Good Girls, we have 657 ways of saying yes.

So it's no wonder that Lynn flinched when she heard the title of *Getting to Yes*. When the concept of win-win negotiating was first popularized by this 1981 negotiating classic, authors Roger Fisher and William Ury were trying to convert tough-guy negotiators from their old, aggressive view of dealmaking as a zero-sum game,

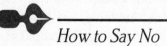

How to Say No

Beth is a huge fan of Judith Martin (better known as Miss Manners). In fact, Beth's WWJD bracelet stands for What Would Judith Do? So when Beth needs advice on how to deal gracefully with a tough situation, she turns to *Miss Manners' Guide to Excruciatingly Correct Behavior.*

Miss Manners, a pretty good girl herself, understands how hard it can be to protect yourself from marauding friends and colleagues who want you to buy cases of Girl Scout cookies or sell dozens of raffle tickets. Impolite people can just tell those folks to buzz off, but Miss Manners realizes "the real need in the lives of civilized people is to say, 'No, thank you.'"

Since good girls can't always bring themselves to say the N-O word, Miss Manners offers this alternative: "I'm so terribly sorry, I just can't." If somebody asks you why not: "Because I'm afraid it's just impossible."

And if the pressure to join the committee, chair the benefit, type the term paper, paint the gym, or picket the power plant gets too unbearable, she recommends this all-purpose response: "Oh, dear, thank you so very much, I would simply love to if there were any way I were able, but it's absolutely impossible, and what a terrible shame that is because I would so have enjoyed to, and you were so very kind to have asked me."

where I win only if you lose. In *Getting to Yes,* they promoted what was then (for their male readers, at least) the radical notion of reaching settlements that benefit everyone at the table. When they wrote that their purpose was to help their readers "obtain what you are entitled to, and still be decent," they were closing in on the good girl wavelength. Unfortunately, they didn't realize how many of us confuse decency with martyrdom.

We good girls need a different type of instruction if we want to get to yes — a good, healthy yes, not that automatic yes we hand out so mindlessly. We're talking about negotiating here, not rolling over and playing dead. And the whole point of negotiating is getting what you need.

To do that, you have to be honest with yourself. What do you need, and what do you desire? Those can be tough questions for good girls to answer, because we're so used to thinking about the needs and desires of others. But if you're aiming for a win–win solution, the first step has to be figuring out what you really want. Where are you going? What do you wish for? What would make you happy? What do you want from life?

Before you can get to yes, you have to get to you.

Deep in your heart, you may think that putting yourself first and meeting your own needs is going to turn you into one of those New Age, Me Generation, Self-Actualized jerks. Trust me, it's not. In fact, your friends and family might be secretly relieved if you stopped saying yes to every request and started giving them a better idea of what would really make you happy. As communications consultant Kare Anderson told *Nation's Business:* "It's a lot easier to deal with a jerk who knows what he wants than a nice person who doesn't."

If you don't figure out what you want, you'll consistently cut yourself short of time, money, recognition, credit, and everything else that makes your life workable and enjoyable. Our friend Molly learned that lesson the hard way. An intensely creative California artist, she took a job working for one of her friends, Kevin, a well-known graphic designer. When she started, she told herself she was just looking to express her creativity, make a little money, have a little fun, and generally "follow her bliss." It took a long time for her to admit that her ambitions were aimed far higher.

"It always starts out, 'We're going to have such fun,'" Molly says in retrospect. "But after we've had all our fun, you have to set aside the fantasy and take a hard look at what we're talking about here. Don't pretend you're just there for the fun of it, if that's not the case."

As time went on, she became more and more frustrated when her friend-employer didn't share the credit (and the financial rewards) Molly thought she deserved. The moment of truth came when Molly realized she wasn't working for the sheer joy of creating beautiful images to make the world a prettier place. She was a skilled artist, and she wanted money and public recognition. "You have to be realistic about your true objective — the reason you're at the table to begin with," she advises. In her own case, she asked herself a basic question: "Do you want to design things just for other people to take home and enjoy, or do you want to create things with your name where everybody sees it?"

Once she acknowledged just how important it was to her to see her own name on her work, she started looking at her career in a different way, thinking about whether the projects and related deals would further her goal of becoming a nationally known designer. She realized she hadn't been asking for what she really needed. And it suddenly became clear that what she wanted — artistic independence — was something Kevin simply couldn't offer. But because she wasn't honest with herself about her deep-rooted ambitions, she spent years in her comfortable but artistically stifling old job before she struck out on her own.

Whether you're facing formal salary negotiations or a surprise inspection from your mother-in-law, you have to break the habit of that automatic yes.

PLEASE DON'T APPEASE

Instead of saying no, too many good girls adopt a strategy of appeasement — what Beth calls the "yes-yes-yes-yes-yes-yes-yes-yes-yes-yes-yes-I'm outta here" approach. That was the "strategy" that nearly cost Linda Calafiore a million-dollar investment.

Linda, a former state bureaucrat, dreamed of opening a cooking school. So she quit her secure job, took out a bank loan, and in 1983 launched the Cooking and Hospitality Institute of Chicago — known locally by its stylish acronym, CHIC. Under Linda's leadership, the school is thriving, with eight hundred students.

Part of CHIC's success is due to its location in Chicago's trendy River North neighborhood. To attract top-quality students (and to lure the luncheon crowd), Linda has invested more than $1 million in the school's state-of-the-art kitchens, high-tech equipment, and cozy eatery. Yet whenever it came time to negotiate with her landlord, Linda transformed from successful entrepreneur to good girl par excellence. Wary of losing her modish location, she simply shrugged and agreed to just about every request her landlord made. "For many years I cooperated to the extreme," she sighs.

Finally, after years of yes-yes-yes-yes-yes, she decided she'd had enough. It dawned on her that she was paying the biggest rent bill in the building, and that ought to buy her some extra privileges. When it came time to negotiate her next lease, Linda's landlord resisted her requests — probably, Linda thinks, because he figured she'd never walk away from her huge investment in building improvements. But Linda had reached the slow rolling boil stage. So she started looking at some possible alternative locations — and made sure her landlord knew it. Realizing he might lose a valuable tenant, he hastily backed down. "When you finally say no, that freaks them out," Linda comments wryly. "This time I let my strength be known."

Linda's lucky. Her high-stakes gamble paid off. But if her strategy had backfired, it could have cost her a fortune. If only she'd realized earlier that her landlord needed the status and style her school brought to the building as much as she needed the high-profile location; they could have been crafting win-win solutions years ago.

The trouble with appeasement is that it doesn't pay off the way we think it will. When we give in to request after request, we expect we'll eventually get some goodies as a reward. Someday our landlords, our bosses, or our partners will add up the many concessions we've made and realize what swell human beings we really are. They'll be so overwhelmed by our goodness that they'll reward us in kind.

Yeah. Right. And then they'll hop on their magic pigs and fly us off to Neverland.

More likely, you'll get the same response Beth got from her six-year-old after a special mother-daughter trip to Walt Disney World. The day after they got home, Beth was still basking in a warm maternal glow as she returned to her desk. Then her daughter walked in and demanded a trip to the shopping mall. "Sorry, Mommy has work to do," Beth said with a smile. "Aww," her daughter whined. "We never do anything together." Indignant, Beth exclaimed: "What about Disney World?" Her daughter paused, then responded, "Well, we haven't done anything today."

It's too bad, but the more you do for some people, the more they expect — and the less they give in return. Giving in "may do nothing more than convince the other side that you can be taken for a ride," warn Roger Fisher and William Ury in *Getting to Yes.*

The Little Red Hen Doesn't Live Here Anymore: Negotiating Housework

Remember the Little Red Hen? One day she discovered a little sack of wheat. Energetic and optimistic, she decided to plant a wheat field. "Who will help me plant the wheat?" she asked her friends. "Not I," said the cow. "Not I," said the duck. "Not I," said the pig. "Not I," said the goose.

"Then I'll do it myself," said the Little Red Hen. And she did.

And so it went. Every time Little Red asked for a helping hand, she was solidly ignored. But when she asked, "Who will help me eat the bread?" she suddenly found herself surrounded by a helpful team of her nearest and dearest. In classic good girl fashion, Little Red smiled sweetly and handed out the fresh, crusty little loaves. They all enjoyed a tasty meal and lived happily ever after. At least, that's how Beth's aunt Kathleen always told it.

But Beth thinks the real end of the tale went something like this: "Investigators have found the remains of four farm animals in a shallow grave in a suburban forest preserve. Forensic specialists are examining little red feathers found near the scene. . . ."

I'm more optimistic. I like to think that Little Red went on to establish a small chain of artisan bakeries, featuring breads and cakes made from her hand-ground wheat. Now she no longer clucks plaintively, "Who will help make the bread?" She just delegates.

Home Truths

When it comes to housework, good girls often end up feeling just like the Little Red Hen. There are never any volunteers offering to wash the kitchen floor or vacuum the stairs. But when it's time to enjoy the pleasure of eating a home-cooked meal in a pleasant, tidy house, family members magically appear out of the woodwork. Left to toil alone, we sigh deeply, square our shoulders, and head downstairs to fold yet another load of laundry — until we finally get fed up and explode in a fireball of fury. Then there's a temporary flurry of activity, followed by our loved ones' stealthy retreat from the domestic front.

So we're stuck in a typical good girl bind: Either we transform into screaming harridans, browbeating family members into performing a few basic chores, or we resign ourselves to spending every spare minute hard at work while the others are out enjoying themselves.

Negotiating Housework (cont.)

But there is a third option. If you can put a lid on your simmering resentments and find a few quiet minutes to think things through, you can probably negotiate your way into a more equitable division of household labor.

Let's be honest. There are plenty of jerks out there who flat do not care how their wives feel. If there's dinner on the table and clean underpants in the dresser, who cares if Mom cries herself to sleep every night? But more often, I think, these domestic stalemates develop when generally well-meaning spouses get knotted up by all the emotional and symbolic baggage we attach to housework. "We come to marriage with different domestic languages," says Cheryl Mendelson, author of *Home Comforts: The Art and Science of Keeping House.* To you, a room with a few books scattered on the sofa and a throw pillow on the rug may look comfortably "lived in." So you're taken off guard when your husband storms in, throws his briefcase on the floor, and bellows, "Why is this place always a pigsty?"

Even if you basically agree on the definition of a "clean enough" house, you may still find that the housekeeping equation tips out of balance over time. I've experienced this problem firsthand. When my husband and I were first married, we had no problems sharing the housework in our snug New York apartment. Without any bickering, we both pitched in and got the job done.

It was only after our son was born and we moved to our house in the Chicago suburbs that housework started to become a chronic source of conflict. My husband loves to garden; I don't. So he started spending his weekends happily digging in the backyard — leaving all the indoor maintenance to me. Our work schedules changed as well. I started working from home, so I could spend more time with the kids, while Michael spent more and more time at the office. That left me burdened with an ever-increasing share of the daily chores.

Frankly, I started to resent it. Yes, I was at home all day. But from 9 to 3, I was trying to pack a full day's work into the six short hours our son was in school. And from 3 to 6, I was dashing from one car pool to another, getting the kids to their soccer games and music lessons, etc. By the time Michael got home, I was exhausted — and in no mood to hear him complain that the house, which I considered comfortably mussed, was unbearably disorganized. As you can imagine, a series of rather testy discussions ensued.

"It's a big issue," agrees Barry G. Ginsberg, Ph.D., director of the Center for Relationship Enhancement in Doylestown, Pennsylvania. "The basic question is, how do we go about organizing and managing our life together?"

Things to Do

The first step is to sit down together (in a more pleasant location than your chaotic family room) and figure out exactly what it takes to keep your household running, on a daily, weekly, monthly, and yearly basis. Start by listing the nitty-gritty tasks, Cheryl Mendelson advises, such as basic cleaning, grocery shopping, meal planning and preparation, and laundry. Don't forget the household administration responsibilities, such as paying the bills, plus lawn mowing, snow shoveling, and other essential outdoor duties.

Then set up a quiet time to go over the list with your spouse. Make sure you're both very clear on the difference between home maintenance, which is required, and home improvement, which is voluntary (and generally a lot more fun than doing dishes).

Once you've agreed on your list of necessary chores, you need to figure out how often each task needs to be done. Try to be a little flexible. When you were growing up, your persnickety mother may have insisted on vacuuming the rugs every single day, while your husband's harried mom believed the long pile of shag carpet was precision engineered to contain dust for at least a month. If you're trying to transfer vacuuming from your chore list to his, you'll have better luck if you package it as a weekly task, not a daily duty. Figure out a Plan B that allows you to live comfortably in your own home without feeling like a domestic drudge.

Consider the example of my friend Danielle. After years of struggling, her husband finally got the job of his dreams as a partner in a big accounting firm. That meant he'd be spending lots more hours at the office — but he'd also be bringing home a substantially larger paycheck. Danielle was more than happy to take up the slack on the home front, even though she was still working full-time, too. But then she noticed that her husband was turning from Felix Unger into an unbelievably sloppy Oscar Madison. "He completely stopped doing anything around the house," she says. "Instead, he'd leave his dirty underpants on the kitchen counter. It was disgusting." When Danielle fussed and fumed, her husband merely brushed her off, claiming he was now too busy to worry about such things.

Then one day, as Danielle was scooping up the pizza sauce her husband had slopped onto the dining room rug, she had a sudden vision. She called Oscar Madison at his office and calmly laid out her Plan B. Thanks to his new job, she pointed out, they finally had enough money to take a family vacation to Hawaii — or even a romantic trip to Tahiti without the kids. But while a

Negotiating Housework (cont.)

couple of weeks in the South Seas sounded pretty tempting, she felt that in the long run she'd be happier spending fifty-two weeks in a tidy house. "I know you work hard every day, and I really appreciate it," she said. "But I'm working hard, too, and I'm not willing to spend all my leisure time picking up after you. So if you can't find a few hours for basic cleanup each week, I'm going to hire a full-time housekeeper. That will eat up most of the extra money you're bring-ing in, but I think it will save our marriage. What's it going to be?" Once her accountant husband tallied the cost-benefit ratio of his inconsiderate behavior, he started tossing his dirty laundry in the hamper. And the two of them are now planning an anniversary cruise to the Caribbean.

Most people don't have the means to hire full-time help, of course. But if you sit down and think about it calmly, you might be able to figure out a way to solve your housekeeping conflict. Could you cut back on your work hours, or hire a cleaning lady once a week? Your partner may feel more motivated about folding laundry if he realizes his recalcitrance is going to hit him in the wallet.

Neat Tricks

Don't overlook the cheap labor you may have right under your own roof. Children can — and should — help to keep their homes running smoothly. At first it may take more energy to persuade the little darlings to pitch in than it would to just do it all yourself. But it's worth the effort, Cheryl Mendelson believes. "Think how valuable it will be when they go out into the world," she says. "They'll be able to make homes for themselves."

Don't waste your time and emotional energy complaining about all the extra work you've done in years gone by. Families are grounded in love and respect; if you make your case clearly and unemotionally, you may be sur-prised at your family's willingness to improve your lot in life. (However, you may want to discuss some likely consequences for slackers. When one of Beth's kids fails to clean her room, the maternal taxi service quietly stops run-ning. So if you want to play in the softball championships, you'd better make your bed.)

Over time, you may find that certain jobs aren't getting done on schedule. Again, don't waste your time nagging. Instead, call another family conference, and come up with some alternative solutions. Remember that your family's schedule changes over time. When your teenaged son fails to scrub the kitchen floor two weeks in a row, ask him what's going on. If he's in the thick of the soccer season, he may really be too physically exhausted to wield a scrub brush when he gets home. So maybe he could load the breakfast plates into the dishwasher and put the laundry away in the mornings, at least until the season is over. (Just make sure he doesn't trade all his jobs to his trusting little sister. She may wind up scrubbing the toilets from now until 2007.)

In the first few weeks, as you're laboring to convince your grudging family members to lend a hand, you may wonder whether it's really worth the effort. It's true; initially it's easier to give up and do it yourself. But you're not doing them any favors if you're seething with anger and resentment as you go about your never-ending duties. Keep your eyes on the long-term goal. If you persist in making housekeeping a family affair, your children will learn necessary skills and feel more competent and confident. Even more important, you'll stop feeling like an unpaid household underling, and start seeing yourself as a valued partner in making — and keeping — a loving home.

NOT EVERYTHING IS NEGOTIABLE

Before you get to yes, you have to realize that some things simply aren't negotiable. The trick is figuring out where you draw your own line in the sand. For Grammy award–winning songwriter Lucinda Williams, it was one lyric of a song.

Although Williams has yet to become a household name, she's legendary among music insiders for her uncompromising perfectionism. Characteristically, she sent her impatient fans into fits when she decided she didn't like any of the tracks on her latest CD, *Car Wheels on a Gravel Road,* and insisted on rerecording them — twice. Her pickiness paid off when *Car Wheels* went gold — her first big hit. In fact, *Rolling Stone* magazine named it one of the "essential recordings of the '90s."

Finding herself an overnight success after two decades in the business, Lucinda got a call from *Good Morning America,* asking her to sing on the show. Her managers suggested she perform "Right In Time," a passionate song of lost but keenly remembered love. The producers had just one little request: Could she please leave out the verse with the line, "Lie on my back and moan at the ceiling." It might be a little, well, intense, for morning television audiences.

To put it in context, it wasn't such an unusual request. TV producers have been asking musicians to edit their material ever since the Rolling Stones appeared on Ed Sullivan and sang that well-known raunchy favorite "Let's Spend Some Time Together." For Lucinda, it could have been a decisive moment. After twenty years of looking for a crossover hit, this national TV appearance might put her over the top. So she mulled for a second. If getting a shot at the spotlight meant pruning one of the songs she had crafted so lovingly, it just wasn't worth it.

She sang the whole song on *Good Morning America* — with no reports of Williams-related viewer fatalities. Now Lucinda relishes telling the story during her concerts, the tale of the lone artist who defied the networks and won.

Lucinda won out for a simple reason — those producers needed to book a hot, interesting new talent as much as she needed to promote her record. That's a simple fact that many women just don't understand: All negotiators are interdependent. If your opponent didn't need something from you, he wouldn't be sitting across the table, or hanging on the other end of the telephone line. You may be desperate for an apartment — but if the landlord doesn't find a reliable tenant, she'll be stuck with a crushing mortgage payment. You want a pay increase and more vacation time; your boss wants to avoid the expense of training a replacement if you walk away.

Nobody negotiates just for fun — at least, nobody we know. People sit down to make deals because there's something they need that they can't obtain on their own. So you have to be honest with yourself about what you are (and aren't) willing to give up.

YOU'RE WORTH IT

Paradoxically, a little negative feedback can make you realize how valuable you really are. Jenny, the owner of a Seattle marketing firm, prides herself on delivering stellar client service. So she was flabbergasted by a client's letter stating that he thought the quality of her work was slipping and he wanted to renegotiate her fees.

Near tears, she called a business-savvy friend for advice. His counsel was to "crush them with the facts" — write a lengthy memo detailing how much high-quality work she had delivered for the client over the last six months.

As she labored over her response, Jenny discerned that Mr. Disgruntled was by far the most difficult and time-consuming (and therefore least cost-effective) client she had. Her fees were indeed unfair — to her. So her memo ended: "I would like to resign from the account."

When he received her fax, the astonished client immediately called to try to restore the relationship. Apparently, his whole disgruntlement letter had been a negotiating ploy that backfired. He had wanted to cut his cost, but he hadn't bargained on losing her.

That put the ball back in Jenny's court. Although she felt like telling him to take a leap into Puget Sound, her calmer second thoughts prevailed. Thanks to the failure of his little cost-cutting maneuver, she was now in an enviable bargaining position. She realized that the current contract didn't meet her own needs, and he'd already admitted that he wanted to retain her services. So she took a deep breath, called him back, and renegotiated a contract that made sense for her.

Don't wait for a crisis to figure out how much you're worth to the rest of the world. Every once in a while, take stock of all your strengths, from your sunny disposition to your Phi Beta Kappa key. You'll be surprised at how much you have going for you.

Sandra Pesmen, author of the syndicated column "Dr. Job," says compiling her personal inventory used to be an annual event. As a junior editor at *Crain's Chicago Business,* she quickly realized that the budgets were put together in August — but the salary reviews weren't done until December. To make sure her section's budget included room for her raise, she sat down every summer and "put together a package of all my accomplishments, all the awards I'd won that year, everything I'd done that was wonderful." She then sent the packet to all the executives above her on the masthead, starting with Mrs. Crain herself. "I always said something like, 'I hope you will take notice of these accomplishments, and treat them

Tit for Tat

Tit for tat is a simple, highly successful strategy in which you can be nice without becoming a pushover. Here's how it works.

Let's say you're negotiating with your big sister over how to divide up your grandmother's best china. You start out with a cooperative gesture and offer to let her choose the first item. If she shows some goodwill, passing over the teapot you've always cherished and taking a lovely antique pitcher instead, you respond in kind: When your turn comes, take the teapot but offer her an extra piece in return for her kindness.

On the other hand, if she uses that first choice to snap up the teapot, take revenge on your next turn and nab that handpainted platter she's always wanted. (If she's brokenhearted, you've got a bargaining chip; offer to swap the platter for the piece you really want.)

Admittedly, with tit for tat, you may not end up with your grandmother's teapot. As anybody who's been through a bitter heirloom battle can tell you, an aggressive strategy can sometimes pay off. (There's always the Bad Girl option of coming in early and snagging all the good stuff before your sister even shows up.) But outflanking your opponent is not what tit for tat is all about. Instead, it's a "nice" strategy that's often effective in eliciting a little friendly cooperation from the other side. "Aggression often begets aggression," observes Northwestern professor Leigh Thompson in *The Mind and Heart of the Negotiator*. The tit-for-tat strategy avoids the costly mutual escalation trap that can end up with both parties engaged in the emotional version of thermonuclear war.

accordingly when you plan your budgets.'" The strategy paid off; in January, she always received a little note from her boss approving a nice-sized raise.

When you list your personal assets, give it some thought. Come back to it over a few days. You'd do your homework if you were working for someone else; put that same effort into advocating for yourself. Don't forget all those good girl traits you bring to the table — things like well-maintained client relationships, plenty of patience, and a fathomless well of good humor. Those are attributes that other people — and perhaps you yourself — may not always appreciate. But they are worth real money in the marketplace, because they make you a pleasure to work with.

For once in your life, don't be modest. You don't have to post this list on your personal Web site. Just keep it close to your heart, to help you win the deals you deserve.

THE POWER OF PASSION

Okay. So we don't see many women in Girl Scout uniforms on the covers of romance novels. But fluttering beneath our gingham aprons are hearts filled with passion — and that's one of the greatest assets good girls have to offer.

Take Sarah Hoit, who at thirty was an entrepreneur armed with a business plan and a heartfelt desire to make the world a better place for working mothers. Her idea was to create a company, Explore Inc., to provide high-quality before- and after-school care nationwide. She just had to persuade investors to give her the start-up cash she needed. "It was me and a piece of paper," she recalls. "It was a daunting thing. I had student loans and if I didn't make it work, I wasn't going to make the bills."

Sarah was so passionate and convincing in presenting her idea that she put together her funding in a matter of months. "I believe strongly in the things that I do," she says. "That's a very strong negotiating position."

Passionate advocates often come out winners, in part because their belief in their mission sustains them during difficult, drawn-out negotiations. "I always do best when I feel strongly about something," confirms former Colorado congresswoman Pat Schroeder. That's especially true when you're fighting for a cause you believe in. But you can bring that passion to more mundane matters, such as buying a car, if you tap into a principle that fires you up. The next time you walk into a car showroom, write down the sticker price in a special notebook. Then pledge any savings you negotiate to a cause dear to your soul — your children's college nest egg, your synagogue's building fund, even your Christmas club account. When you sit down to haggle, you'll be fueled by the courage of your own convictions.

JUST TELL ME WHAT YOU WANT

Once you are waxing confident about the value you bring to the table, it's time to start listening to the Spice Girls. The Spice Girls may not fit the classic good girl stereotype — most of us wear extremely sensible shoes — but they do give excellent advice in their song "Wannabe": "Tell me what you want, what you really, really want." (As it happens, the Spice Girls say they just want to "zig-a-zig-ha!" But that doesn't mean it's bad advice.)

Because we're such amateur negotiators, we sometimes come to the table with our cards so close to our vests nobody (including us) can see them. We're afraid if we let our passionate desires be visible, the other side will know how badly we want something and take advantage of our eagerness. Or maybe we think our objectives are so clearly obvious that there's no point in discussing them.

Well, that kind of thinking might work if you're renegotiating your contract with the Psychic Friends Network. But nobody else can read your mind. And if you're clear on what you want and why you want it, you may come up with some win-win solutions that you never imagined.

THE BATTLE OF THE ORANGE

There's a classic negotiating example of two sisters battling over a single orange left on the kitchen table. After a fair amount of sibling bickering, they decide to cut the orange in half.

A fair solution? No, a stupid solution. What Sister Ann didn't know was that Sister Sally was planning to bake some orange scones; all she needed was the peel. Meanwhile, Sister Ann had decided she was coming down with a cold and needed some fresh orange juice.

Bedtime Stories: Negotiating in the Boudoir

Imagine this: Your boss has just posted the summer vacation schedule, and you're really steamed. For the third year in a row, he's ignored your request for two weeks off in mid-July. This time you're going to let him know exactly how you feel.

So when he walks into your office, you grunt slightly, shrug your shoulders, give a barely perceptible shake of your head, then stalk off into the bathroom — certain that you've made your outraged feelings crystal clear.

Strategically, does that response seem a tad oblique? Even downright obscure? Then why on earth are you using it in bed?

As you might imagine, good girls are often terrible negotiators in the bedroom. First of all, many of us have trouble admitting even to ourselves that we'd like someone to do various naughty (but nice) things to us, which makes it almost impossible for us to ask our partners to fulfill our inmost fantasies. And even less inhibited good girls are paralyzed at the thought of hurting our partners' sensitive feelings by asking them to do a little less of this and a little more of that. So too many of us end up with a nice, friendly, but not particularly thrilling sex life.

Well, it doesn't have to be that way. If you can learn to negotiate in a car showroom, you can certainly learn to negotiate in the bedroom. (At least in the boudoir, you won't have to worry about getting talked into unnecessary undercoating.) And if you learn effective ways of asking for what you want — and declining what you don't — you'll end up with a truly win-win solution that will improve your relationship, both in bed and out.

Linda Perlin Alperstein, a licensed clinical social worker, certified sex therapist, and associate clinical professor in the department of psychiatry at the University of California—San Francisco, has led workshops on "Speaking Up While Lying Down: Being Assertive in Intimate Relationships." She says many women are sexually hamstrung by their belief that men instinctively know how to give pleasure to their partners. "The myth that a man ought to know how to please you, and what to do for you, is a burden — for men as well as women."

Think about it. You don't expect your real estate agent to magically intuit whether you're looking for a three-bedroom ranch or a one-bedroom condo. You don't make your painting contractor guess whether you prefer oil to latex.

Negotiating in the Boudoir (cont.)

It's simply unfair to leave your partner in the dark about what makes you swoon and what leaves you cold, especially if you pout when he guesses wrong. "Remember — in sex, by your silence, you lead the other person to believe that what he or she is doing is okay," Alperstein comments.

What seems like a perfectly clear nonverbal communication to you may mean absolutely nothing to your partner. Frankly, that little grimace you make every time he touches you there instead of here means nothing if the lights are off. And let's face it: Your subtle little bits of body language may not be the focus of his attention at that particular moment. "It may be peripheral to him, not because he doesn't care, but because his mind is somewhere else," Alperstein says.

Taking the Quantum Leap

Since you wouldn't be reading this book if you weren't a good girl, we're assuming that you have some kind of emotional bond with your bed partner. He's not whisking you off for a romantic weekend because he wants to make you miserable. If he's like most men, he really wants to be the lover of your dreams — and he may be scared to death that he's not going to perform to your specifications. Do the poor guy a favor and let him know what you want. "What's really required of the good girl is to speak up," Alperstein stresses.

Of course, that's easier said than done. If you're just embarking on a new relationship, you don't want to start criticizing his technique during your first night of mad, passionate lovemaking. And if you've been together forever, any helpful hints are going to lead him to the inescapable conclusion that he's been doing it wrong for the last few decades. One way or the other, you're running the risk of hurting his feelings.

Don't underestimate the guts it takes to renegotiate your sex life, Alperstein says. "You're risking being laughed at, ridiculed, or ignored," she says. "You have to give yourself kudos for even a small improvement. Even though some of these things sound so easy, to actually say them requires a quantum leap."

But before you open this particular can of worms, you need to do a little bit of honest thinking. Too often, the bedroom serves as the silent battleground of a relationship, where you express all the resentment and bitterness that you keep bottled up during the day. Are you frustrated solely by his tendency to zig when you want him to zag — or is it really his failure to replace the $18,000 he took out of your retirement savings to buy that fancy new car?

Think about when this problem first started to bother you, and why you've now decided you can't take it anymore. If you hate it when he kisses your elbow, why did you wait until your silver wedding anniversary to mention it? Or if there's something new that's troubling you, check whether the problem coincided with some nonsexual conflicts.

If the overall climate of your relationship is sunny and warm, then your bedroom difficulties aren't likely to be impossible to resolve. But if you're really sore over his personality or spending habits, it's hateful to use sexual complaints as a weapon to wound him in his most vulnerable spot.

Is That a Franklin Planner in Your Pocket, or Are You Just Happy to See Me?

Once you've figured out precisely what you want, and why you want it, think about where and when to have this conversation.

"You need to make an appointment to talk about this outside the bedroom," Alperstein says. "You don't just come in and say to your boss, 'I want a raise.' If you're a good negotiator, you say, 'I'd like to make an appointment to talk with you about my salary.' It's the same with negotiating about sex. You have to say, 'I really want to have a talk about our sexual life. When would be a good time for us to do that?' "

Don't expect your partner to respond by pulling out his Franklin Planner and penciling you in for 7:30 P.M. on the twenty-third. If he's like many men, the prospect of a heart-to-heart talk about a sensitive emotional issue may spur him into scheduling back-to-back oral surgery appointments from now until next November. "You need to think about your capacity to talk about difficult subjects with each other," Alperstein says. "If you have a history of tackling difficult subjects, your partner might groan but be willing to bite the bullet. However, if you're with somebody who has a really hard time sitting down and having a discussion, you might need to go have some professional help."

Expect him to express some anxiety, and try to reassure him as much as you can. "You could say, 'I want to let you know some things about my body that I haven't really been clear about,' " Alperstein suggests.

Pick a private, comfortable time and place. You need to give each other your uninterrupted attention. And don't even think about having this talk in bed. You're both likely to feel more confident and unemotional if you're sitting up with all your clothes on.

Negotiating in the Boudoir (cont.)

Build in some comforting ground rules when you make your appointment. "One thing that sometimes works is to guarantee a time-limited discussion: 'I'm willing to take only twenty minutes, and then we don't have to talk about it again until next week. We can put it on a shelf until we are both calm.'"

Although it may be difficult for you to express your desires out loud, try to say exactly what you want. But say it as gently as possible. "The ancient skills of tact and diplomacy go a long way in these negotiations," Alperstein says. Focus on how you feel. Tell him that your sexual connection is stretched to the limit and you want to rescue it before your relationship is irretrievably damaged. You can be honest without being adversarial.

Once you've told him how you feel, you need to button your lip and listen. Use "active listening," allowing each person to talk without any interruption. Once your partner finishes his piece, repeat back to him what you just heard, to make sure there are no misunderstandings. "You don't have to agree," Alperstein explains. "You only have to let him know you heard what he said."

Be prepared to hear a few unsettling comments yourself. If you've been unable to tell each other what you want, it's probable that neither of you has been enjoying your sex life to the utmost. Just try to listen without losing your temper or backing down on your resolve to fix this problem.

When you've both stated exactly what you want, try to find a little common ground. Is there anything you both agree that you'd like to try, or to avoid? You may be surprised to find that your sexual routine of Saturday nights at 11:15 is as boring to him as it is to you.

One common minefield is the question of who decides that tonight is the night. "How do you know that you're going to have sex?" Alperstein says. "Does your husband say, 'Let's have a date tonight, honey?' Is it automatic when Grandma and Grandpa have the kids on Wednesday night? Is it built into the schedule, or is it something that has a lot of anxiety connected to it?" If one partner is always the initiator, you've got a situation that's ripe for conflict, Alperstein believes. "The person who always initiates often feels like a beggar, while the person who never initiates often feels put-upon, or feels guilty if they don't feel interested at that time."

If your partner has been doing something that turns you completely off, don't be shy about saying so. There may be a surprising reason behind his behavior. "I once worked with a very well educated, highly sensitive guy who was a chronic crotch-grabber," Alperstein recalls. No matter how many times his wife said, "I hate it when you start there," he would frequently "forget" and grab his wife between the legs as a signal of his sexual interest. "She was just furious at him," Alperstein says. "He would grab, she would shut down, and he would sense her lack of interest and give up."

Eventually the two sought Alperstein's help. Over time, the husband realized that his unpredictable grabs made him feel lusty and vigorous, like a swashbuckling pirate. But his Long John Silver fantasy was putting his wife in the position of a female commuter under attack by a groping subway pervert. Once they were able to talk frankly about why he was behaving this way, and how it made her feel, they were able to come up with some sexy substitutes that fed his fantasies without making her feel attacked and abused.

As you're talking about these sensitive subjects, remember that men often feel a tremendous load of performance anxiety. Some men rely on a sexual sequence of events that hasn't varied since prom night. If you ask them to adjust their routine, they fear, they might not be able to get aroused at all. Try offering some alternatives. Maybe you could ask him to try it your way one night and go back to his preferred routine the next time. Let him know that you're considering his feelings; you just want him to consider yours, too.

Don't expect to completely redesign your sex life in one twenty-minute chat. Your partner is deeply invested in his old habits, and he's likely to "relapse" a few times before he changes his ways. Don't get upset; just stick to your guns, and keep talking about what you want. "You're making it clear that you're not going to suffer silently and just tolerate it anymore," Alperstein says. "Hopefully you're partnered with someone who realizes when an injustice is being done. Some husbands will realize they've been getting away with murder, and they'll stop. If you're at your bottom line and he can't comply, you need to be prepared to put your money where your mouth is."

Negotiating your sex life isn't simple. You may find it profoundly liberating to look a man in the eyes and tell him exactly what you want in bed — and your partner may find it profoundly unsettling. "You need to be aware that you're changing the rules, that you're setting a boundary you never set before," Alperstein notes. "When you instigate change in a relationship, in the bedroom or anywhere, you are creating both a danger and an opportunity." (In some cases, sadly, the danger may be very real. If your partner is abusive, broaching these sensitive subjects may trigger a violent outburst. When your safety is in jeopardy, you need to call your local shelter for battered women and get expert help.)

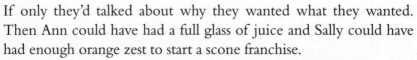

Negotiating in the Boudoir (cont.)

Thankfully, however, the risks of speaking out usually are not as great as you fear, and the opportunities can be tremendous. Just stay calm and brave, and keep on reminding yourself that there's nothing wrong in asking your partner for what you want. You may find that this first awkward conversation marks the beginning of a new and fulfilling phase in your relationship.

If only they'd talked about why they wanted what they wanted. Then Ann could have had a full glass of juice and Sally could have had enough orange zest to start a scone franchise.

In technical terms, they didn't understand the difference between their interests and their positions. Your position is the stand you take; your interest is what you really want from the deal. So the squabbling sisters both took the stand "I want the orange," which put them directly at odds. They'd have done better if they had put their interests clearly on the table, next to the disputed orange.

"Often you think you are in competition when you're not, and people make premature concessions," warns Professor Leigh Thompson, who uses the scone story in her classroom. "Win-win does not mean everyone should compromise to an equal degree." The trick is to figure out who wants which piece of the orange and to start shooting for a plan that works for everybody.

In 1997, basketball star Sheryl Swoopes learned how to turn her orange into a big pitcher of orangeade when she discovered that she and her husband were expecting a baby. Unfortunately, the timing couldn't have been worse, professionally. The baby was due in June, just as the inaugural season of the WNBA was set to begin. And from the baby's point of view, the schedule was nonnegotiable.

Apprehensively, Sheryl called to share the good news with her agent, Tom George, senior vice president of Virginia-based Octagon Athlete Representation. Not surprisingly, he was shocked. She had a special contract that paid her more than any other player. Would the league think that price tag covered maternity leave? Sheryl also had an endorsement deal with Nike; how would the company react to the news that its high-flying star was going to be temporarily grounded by pregnancy? "We thought it was awful and horrible for about two hours," says Tom. "Then we figured out that it was workable and wonderful."

How did they turn a very personal and precious liability into an asset? They backed off their positions and looked at everybody's interests. And they realized that an Olympic gold medalist with an adorable new baby was a highly marketable commodity.

First, Sheryl pledged to make her WNBA debut as soon after the birth as possible. The dates were tight; the league's season was only ten weeks long. But Sheryl's a tough woman. Her son, Jordan, was born on June 25; Mom was back on the court practicing with the team on July 30. Just two months after Jordan's birth, she scored a season-high 20 points against the Charlotte Sting, helping to propel the Houston Comets to victory in the first WNBA championships.

Did her negotiations pay off? Absolutely. The WNBA realized that Jordan's birth helped to draw a whole new audience to the game. Thanks to Swoopes, women's basketball wasn't just for athletic, energetic teenagers; working moms could identify with her, too. Her stellar performance, as a player and as a new mother, caught the attention of major marketers. Kellogg's and Sears clamored to sign up "the quintessential working mother." Nike, which had named the Air Swoopes shoe after Sheryl, gave Jordan a starring role in his mom's commercials. Orangeade, anyone?

You can't expect to score a slam dunk every time. But think about Sheryl the next time you're filled with negotiation trepidation. If you back off your position and start looking at everybody's interests, you may find the situation isn't as conflict-ridden as you thought.

JUST WALK AWAY, RENE

Sometimes there aren't enough Popsicles to go around. Or one of the other kids insists on grabbing more than his share. When that happens, don't accept a cherry-stained stick with just a smidgen of sugary juice clinging to it. If a deal doesn't work for you, walk away.

We know, we know. You feel bad because the salesman was so nice and spent so much time with you. You're afraid you will hurt your aunt's feelings after her friend suggested you apply for the job. You think your sister will get mad if you don't buy your storm windows from her boyfriend.

Listen up. None of those things matters. At the end of the day, you're going to be the one making those payments, or cashing that paycheck. And if all those people you're so worried about offending aren't willing to make up the difference out of their pockets, why are you so concerned about what they'll think?

Remember Sarah Hoit, who decided a few years ago to take her business to the next level. She started looking for venture capital and decided her best bet was the Women's Growth Capital Fund, a fund that invests in women-owned businesses. The fund's directors were impressed by Sarah's passion, as well as her track record. In two years, she'd opened programs in sixty-five schools. But when they offered to buy into her company, their proposed price per share was only half what she had in mind.

Objectively, Sarah knew that it's hard for outsiders to estimate a new company's value. She also really wanted to have the women's fund as a partner. But she stepped back and looked at the big picture. She wasn't desperate for cash, and she had other interested investors. "I believed enough in what I was asking for that I didn't want to back down," she says. So she declined their offer.

Two weeks later, Sarah got a call from the fund's director. They'd thought it over, and they were willing to pay her price. Sarah got the partners she wanted at the price she considered fair.

The ability to walk away is the ultimate source of power in any negotiation. It is more powerful than money or position or resources. If that sounds exaggerated, think about it. Suppose you're a novice waitress and want the weekend off to attend your best friend's wedding. You're quivering at the thought of asking for two days off. But if you're doing a good job, you're in a powerful position. Suppose your boss threatens to fire you if you don't come in. What's harder — finding someone to cover two shifts, or going through the whole process of finding and training another worker? Your boss may have a more impressive job description than you do, but that doesn't mean she holds all the cards.

Beth took a walk of her own last year. On a warm Sunday afternoon, she and her husband stopped at an open house. The moment they walked in the front door, they felt right at home. The house had everything they needed, and a few amenities they'd never dreamed of. The room Beth chose for her home office even had a wood-burning fireplace. She could just see herself curled up on a little sofa in front of the crackling flames, sipping tea and scribbling the Great American Novel.

But this time, she remembered there's more to a real estate purchase than your Martha Stewart fantasies of gracious living. Before they made an offer, Beth asked their agent to check the price of a much fancier house across the street that had sold the week before. Comparing the two properties, Beth came up with their opening bid, which was a little over 90 percent of the owner's asking price. The owner turned them down flat. Beth's husband shrugged his shoulders. "You know," he said, "it would be tight, but we could qualify for a mortgage for the asking price." The agent encouraged them to go for the full amount. "Prices are soaring in that neighborhood," she said. "If you wait for another house to come on the market, you may not be able to afford it."

This time Beth held firm. She'd done her research, and she knew she'd offered a fair price. Maybe prices would skyrocket. But maybe they wouldn't. She wasn't about to repeat her old mistake and put herself in a potentially desperate financial position because she'd fallen in love with a fireplace. So they walked away.

Apparently Beth's market sense was right on the money. The home's owner never found a buyer willing to pay full price and eventually took the house off the market.

AND NOW, PLAN B

Of course, it's easy to walk away from a house deal if you've got somewhere else to live. It's quite another thing to negotiate calmly if you're seven months pregnant, you've just been transferred to the Portland office, and you've got one brief weekend to find a house and make a deal.

When you approach the table with a feeling of desperation clutching your chest, it probably means you believe your opponent can walk away and you can't. You can't afford to lose your medical coverage, and your boss has a stack of applications from eager workers

Look Homeward, Good Girl: Buying a House

Just like Dorothy, good girls believe there's no place like home. Unfortunately, in today's real estate market, you can't expect to click your heels together and wind up with the house of your dreams. If you don't rein in your nesting impulses when you're buying a new home, you could end up like the Wicked Witch of the East — crushed by an overpriced house.

Remember, that suburban three-bedroom ranch or beautiful downtown brownstone is more than your haven in a heartless world. It's an investment, perhaps the biggest one of your life. Don't let that perfect picket fence or cozy fireplace blind you to the importance of the financial decision you're making. You need to calm down, read up, and make the best deal you can. Here are a few basic hints to help you avoid making some classic good girl mistakes.

Do your homework.

We both know from sad experience just how discouraging house hunting can be. You wander from shack to shanty, wondering if you'll ever find a place to call home. The only places you'd even consider cost precisely twice what you can afford. The last thing you want to do is immerse yourself in the depressing details of your local real estate market.

Well, get over it. You'll feel much better once you get your hands on some facts.

Ignore those depressing friends and family members who share tales of toolsheds selling for a mere $200,000. And don't let a real estate agent brain-wash you into thinking you can't find shelter for less than $5,000 a month. Instead, call the local county or township office to find out about recent purchase prices in your desired neighborhood. Local newspapers may also periodically publish listings of recent sales of residential properties. Find out how long the average house stays on the market, and how the average sale price compares with the average asking price. Realtors love to tell stories about houses selling two hours after they're listed. But even in a hot market, most houses take a while to sell. Don't panic.

Before you head for that first open house, pick up a couple of how-to books on home buying. (We like *Tips and Traps When Negotiating Real Estate,* by Robert Irwin, and *100 Questions Every First-Time Home Buyer Should Ask,* by Ilyce R. Glink.) The more you know, the more confident you'll feel.

Take a good look in your financial mirror.

I have a dear friend, Margot, who is desperately seeking a new house. Her husband got transferred to Chicago, and they're living in his parents' basement until they find their own place. So when a house in our neighborhood went on the market, I called Margot to give her the inside track. "What's your price range?" I asked. "Oh, I don't know," Margot sighed. "I can't bear to pull out all those numbers. I'm sure we'll never be able to afford anything decent."

Margot's not alone. It can be incredibly painful to dig out your records, get a copy of your credit history, and figure out how much house you can afford. But you've got to do it. Otherwise, like Margot, you'll spend every Sunday tramping through open houses with your stomach tied up in knots.

As a first step, get a copy of your credit report by calling or writing Equifax, TransUnion, and Experian, the three credit reporting agencies. Report any mistakes to the agency. (When Beth did this, she found her old car loan had been reported twice. Although she'd paid it off years before, the clone loan was still listed as an unpaid debt.) Then sit down with a mortgage banker to figure out exactly what you can afford each month and how much house that amount will buy. Getting prequalified will make your sales contract look much more attractive to the sellers.

Don't share your top dollar.

Never reveal exactly how much you're willing (or able) to spend. In many states, the agent's first responsibility is to the person who pays her fees — the sellers. So she's duty-bound to represent them, not you. If she knows you're willing to go up to $185,000, she's not going to encourage them to leap at your bid of $173,500. Even if she's legally representing you, a higher purchase price means a higher commission for her. So when talking with your agent, tell her you're looking for something "in the $200,000 range." She doesn't need to know your mortgage lender has given you the green light for anything up to $225,000. A good agent won't press you on this; if she keeps asking for your top-dollar amount, go elsewhere.

Don't let a real estate agent choose you.

When you walk into an open house, do you feel like you've just been adopted? The friendly agent follows you around, smiling and complimenting your children. Then she calls you at home a day or two later, just to check

Buying a House (cont.)

whether you have any questions about that house. Pretty soon she's sitting on your living room sofa, handing you a stack of papers. And suddenly, mysteriously, you have a real estate agent, whether you wanted one or not.

Stop being such a wimp. You're the customer here, and you need to carefully select your own agent. You don't have to be rude. Just be straightforward and say, "I'm still in the process of interviewing agents. I'll get back to you if we decide to work with you. Thanks so much for your help."

Ask some pointed questions. Find out how long the agent has been working in your area. Ask for some recommendations from former customers. Talk to her about the way she does business. Legally, in your state, does she represent you or the sellers? Find out whether your state allows you to hire a buyer's agent who strictly represents your interests for a fee. If so, you might consider that option. (The Consumer Federation of America estimates that misunderstanding who represents their interests in a residential real estate transaction costs buyers up to $10 billion a year in higher home costs.) Before you make a bid, you'll need to see the listings of the last ten homes that sold in your desired neighborhood; is she willing to gather that information for you? And finally, look for someone who is willing to work all day every day, if necessary. Don't commit yourself to someone who's planning to spend every sunny weekend up at her lake cottage.

In real estate, everything is negotiable, including commissions.

Suppose you've signed a contract to buy a $225,000 house. Then your home inspector comes through and finds that the house needs a new roof — for a mere $6,000. The sellers absolutely refuse to fix the roof themselves, and you're neither willing nor able to come up with that amount before the rainy season. At this point it's everybody's problem. So you might propose this division of the pie: You agree to pick up $2,000 of the cost, the sellers pledge to hand over $4,000 at closing, and to ease the seller's plight, each of the agents agrees to reduce her slice of the 6 percent commission — paid by the seller — by $1,000. You'll walk away with your roof problem solved — and the real estate agents still split $11,500.

Hire a lawyer and shut your mouth.

Whatever you do, don't sign anything before your lawyer looks at it. And don't agree to anything orally. Get it all written down, then run it past a lawyer with plenty of experience in real estate. That lawyer's fee may be the best investment you'll ever make. If she says you're making a bad deal, listen thoughtfully to her advice; it could save you from some serious regrets later on.

Don't forget your Plan B.

It's easy to whip yourself into a frenzy of homebuyers' despair: "Oh, we're going to end up out on the street!"

No, you're not. And if you allow yourself to overdramatize this situation, you could end up making a boneheaded decision. Instead, think of Beth's admirable neighbor Melissa. After fixing up their house to a fare-thee-well, Melissa and her husband realized their marriage couldn't survive the sudden lack of home improvement projects. So Melissa started looking for a new house to conquer.

After researching the overheated local market, she realized she'd have the best shot at her dream house if she could come in with a wad of cash and no house to sell. So she put her own house on the market, and it sold in four days, for $10,000 over her asking price. She happily signed the sales contract — then found, to her chagrin, that her dream fixer-upper simply wasn't available. Instead of having an extended nervous breakdown, she put together a Plan B: she found a nice apartment building in her neighborhood that offered short-term leases. "No matter what happens, we've got a place to live," she said with enviable calm. "Moving twice in a year certainly isn't the worst thing that could happen to a family. And when the dream home finally comes onto the market, I'll be sitting on a pile of cash." Three months later, she found that perfect house. And thanks to her clever Plan B, she got it.

Keep your cool.

Don't lose your cool in the homestretch. We know how nerve-wracking this whole process can be. But your pleasant good girl personality can be one of your greatest assets throughout the ordeal — so long as you don't let your emotions get the better of you.

One of your biggest worries may be the home inspection. If you can, find your own home inspector. (Call the American Society of Home Inspectors at 1-800-743-ASHI, or go to their Web site at www.ashi.com.) An inspector recommended by your real estate agent may have a conflict of interest; if his negative reports kill too many deals, she's not likely to keep on recommending him. Brace yourself for some unpleasant surprises — carpenter ants chewing

Buying a House (cont.)

on the crossbeams, or an underground stream flowing a half-inch below the basement floor. Often, buyers can use the home inspector's report as an opportunity to renegotiate the purchase price. But before you do that, figure out which of these unpleasant surprises is a deal-breaker. If the sellers won't address a serious problem, then walk away. But if they say, "Take it or leave it" — and you take it — your pouting over the unmended crack in the driveway is just going to sour the experience.

Similarly, stay composed when you take your final walk-through, just before the closing. This is your last chance to make sure the kitchen appliances are all still in place and the light fixtures haven't disappeared. If you spot something major, call your lawyer immediately. But if it's minor, let it go.

Finally, don't get flustered during closing. You can reduce the stress if you ask the title company to prepare the documents a day in advance, to give you time to check and recheck all the key information. If the sellers try to throw you a curve at closing, that's your cue to unleash your lawyer.

on his desk. Or your car is on its last wheels, and there's only one Volkswagen dealer in the three-county area. Or you're madly in love, but your boyfriend can't decide if he's ready to commit.

Girlfriends, stop right there. Anytime you feel this desperate as you enter into a negotiation, it means you want it — whatever it is — way too much. You need to call a halt, take a breath, and figure out Plan B.

In the world of professional negotiations, Plan B is known as a BATNA. We know, that sounds like a superhero's sidekick. But it's the unwieldy acronym for Best Alternative To a Negotiated Agreement, a concept created by *Getting to Yes* authors Fisher and Ury. And there's nothing like a well-thought-out BATNA to put you in a power position when it's time to negotiate.

To develop your Plan B, answer the following question: What will I do if I don't reach agreement? If you've got a list of reasonable alternatives hidden in your purse pocket, you'll feel empowered to walk away instead of settling for less than you deserve.

Suppose you're in the market for a new VW Beetle. You drive 100 miles round-trip to work each day, and you've heard they're safe, gas-efficient little cars. Then the lady at the beauty shop tells you her brother-in-law heard those cars are so hard to come by that dealers are getting $5,000 over the sticker price. Goodness knows, you can't afford to pay that much. So you'll either have to go deeply into debt or try to convince your old pile of junk to hang together for another year or two.

Or you could stop fretting and figure out Plan B. Even if the cars are outside your price range, you've probably got a few options you haven't considered. Are you skittish about buying a used car? Find a reliable mechanic and ask him to check it out before you buy. Are all the car dealerships in your area owned by one notorious family? Plan a weekend car-shopping trip to the nearest big city, where prices are more competitive. Maybe the smartest idea would be to keep your old car and move somewhere closer to your workplace. Walk into the dealership with all those options in your back pocket, and you may find their prices more negotiable than you thought.

Negotiating without your BATNA can reduce you to a vulnerable, quivering pile of anxieties. "If you have not thought carefully about what you will do if you fail to reach an agreement, you are negotiating with your eyes closed," Fisher and Ury warn in *Getting to Yes*. Again, a BATNA isn't a magic talisman that can protect you from a harsh, pragmatic world. But it can keep you from accepting a deal that's not good enough — or from turning down a deal that's better than any of your alternatives.

Tennessee native Cordia Harrington got some BATNA practice a few years ago when she negotiated with executives from the McDonald's Corporation. Cordia was the owner of three McDonald's franchises when she heard that the fast-food company needed a new bun supplier in her area. Her franchises were flourishing, but she dreamed of running a larger business. So she applied for the opportunity to open a new bun bakery. McDonald's responded by offering to match her up with two partners who had experience in the food supply field.

Before she started negotiating with her prospective partners and the McDonald's Corporation, she figured out Plan B. "It's very important to me to know what I want before I go in," she says. In this case, she wanted to hang on to at least 51 percent of the bun business. If she didn't get that, she resolved, she would stick with running her franchises.

When her partners pressed for a controlling interest, Harrington mulled it over. Then she reaffirmed her initial demand, even though she knew she might be walking away from a small fortune. "In my heart of hearts, I knew if I gave them control, I'd never be able to make any of the decisions," she said. "Not getting it was a deal-breaker for me."

But Cordia didn't give up. During a meeting with McDonald's executives about the prospective partnership, she pulled out her BATNA. "I've never worked for anybody, and I don't want to start now," she told the McDonald's executives. "You seem to want an employee. You've obviously got the wrong girl."

Those were magic words. The burger giants knew Cordia could do the job. "That's when they brought me back," she says with satisfaction. They left the room and then returned with an offer. McDonald's agreed that she should have 51 percent ownership of the bakery business; her partners would own the rest.

A similar ploy worked for Yvonne Thornton, now a New Jersey obstetrician and clinical professor of obstetrics and gynecology at the University of Medicine and Dentistry of New Jersey. The daughter of a ditchdigger and a cleaning lady, she recalls: "I was raised to be a lady and be quiet." But her parents' admonitions to be a good girl were teamed with a quiet determination to see all six of their daughters succeed. In her book *The Ditchdigger's Daughters: A Black Family's Astonishing Success Story,* Yvonne tells how her loving parents encouraged her and her sisters to aim high. With courage and determination, they could do anything.

At first, soft-spoken Yvonne didn't rock the boat. "But in medical school I found myself sitting next to men who were not my intellectual equals — yet they were thought of as serious and I was ignored. I just wasn't going to stand for it. My father had taught me never to let anyone define who you are. I rose up and became my father's daughter."

By the time a major medical school started courting her to join its faculty, she had learned to assert herself big-time. Early in the interview process, she submitted a list of requests. When she was told they couldn't accommodate her, she was polite but direct: "If you can't meet my requests," she said, "perhaps you don't have the right person." Suddenly, the school decided her requests weren't quite so outlandish after all.

For Yvonne, every negotiation gets down to her personal bottom line: "You don't need to love me, just respect me."

NEVER THINK PETITE

Yvonne's parents instilled her with an extraordinarily important message: Never underestimate yourself. But as good girls, we find that advice incredibly difficult to follow. We're always the ones who carry umbrellas in case of rain. We tuck sweaters in our children's backpacks. We stick an extra ten dollars into our makeup kits, just in case. We're always thinking about what might go wrong, and what we'll do to fix it. (Beth has declared herself the International Vice President in Charge of the Worst-Case Scenario.) We're all old Girl Scouts, and we intend to Be Prepared.

But why are we only prepared for things to go wrong? In negotiating, you need to look at the whole picture, and that can include a whole universe of incredible success. So don't think petite when you're heading to the bargaining table.

Professor Leigh Thompson sees that mistake all the time. When her business students conduct simulated negotiations, they dutifully establish their BATNAs. Then they jump at any deal that beats the worst-case scenario by more than a nickel. "Some of my students get so focused on their BATNA that they forget about their aspirations," she says.

Try envisioning every deal through rose-colored glasses. What would you like most? What would make you swell with pride? How high could you possibly go? What would it mean to shoot for the moon?

No matter what you're doing, you should always consider the best-case scenarios. Think about those second-string major league ballplayers whose contracts call for six-figure bonuses if they lead the league in home runs. Those guys aren't keeping Sammy Sosa awake at night. But if lightning should strike, they'll cash in.

Always ask for bonuses for extraordinary performance. If you're supplying raw materials to an eager manufacturer, ask for a share of the savings if you deliver the goods a week early. What's the harm? If you win, they do, too. If you don't, they don't lose anything and neither do you.

GO WITH YOUR GUT

Finally, follow your instincts. We're not endorsing some mystical concept of women's intuition. But when you get a gut feeling during a bargaining session, pay attention. You just might be right. "If you are beginning to get a vibe that something is not right, go slower," says Anna Lloyd, president of the Committee of 200, an organization of America's most influential businesswomen. "Too many women don't recognize or trust what our gut is telling us. Our intuition is wonderfully effective. Use it, rely on it, trust it."

When you feel what's right for you, you'll make the right decision. That's what finally happened with our friend Lynn, the one stuck on the bus with thirty-two cherubs screaming out "100 Bottles of Beer on the Wall." That fifteen-hour trip gave her plenty of time to think about the ways she was spending her days, and the things that were important in her life. By the time she got to Dallas, she'd also gotten to Lynn — what she really wanted to do. So she went to a pay phone, called her sister, gave her the name of two reliable baby-sitters, and wished her bon voyage. Then she dialed American Airlines and booked a one-way flight from Dallas to Chicago. "I realized there were plenty of adults on hand without me. So I chaperoned the trip to the rodeo, stayed on through the last concert, and got all the kids rounded up and on the bus. Then I flew home — which gave me a free day to get that extra work done. Since then, I've resigned from two school committees and I've told my boss I'm not available for overtime for the rest of the school year. That trip made me realize I desperately needed some breathing room. And now I've got it. I've always thought of myself as a yes person. But sometimes, I think you just have to say no."

CHAPTER 3

◆

GOOD GIRL POWER

One summer day a few years ago, Amy Barzach and her husband, Peter, took their two little boys to a neighborhood playground near their home in West Hartford, Connecticut. The two parents cuddled their baby, Jonathan, while they watched their three-year-old, Daniel, romp with the other kids. Then Amy noticed a beautiful little girl sitting in a wheelchair, rolled up all the way to the edge of the playground. The child's chin was quivering, and there were tears shining in her eyes. Amy's heart went out to the child, sitting so very close to her playmates but unable to join them.

The picture of that little girl at the playground's edge lingered in Amy's memory, gaining special poignance soon afterward when she and Peter learned that Jonathan had spinal muscular atrophy. He died at the age of only nine months. But had he lived, Amy realized, Jonathan might have been in a wheelchair just like that little girl, alone at the edges of the other children's fun.

When a counselor suggested that Amy and Peter create some kind of memorial to Jonathan, she thought of that little girl and decided to build a truly accessible playground, where no child would be excluded.

Within a few months, Amy had put together plans for a 25,000-square-foot playground. Although it was a massive project, she had the skills to put it all together. As vice president of marketing for a real estate management firm, she had organized community relations programs, trade shows, and special events. But the trait that drew 1,200 volunteers to the project and persuaded local business owners to donate a quarter of a million dollars' worth of services and materials was Amy's extraordinary capacity for empathy — her ability to put herself in someone else's shoes.

Empathy is just one of the many good girl traits that can give you an edge in negotiating. We're also good at listening to what people are saying, and picking up on those subtle cues that reveal what others really feel. Think about it. Can you tell if your best friend had a fight with her husband, just from the way she says "Hello" when she picks up the phone? Can you remember the exact words your son's teacher used at your last school conference? Do you get a little tearful when you watch pictures of refugees on the evening news?

Personally, I value people with eager ears and warm hearts for themselves alone. But I've also learned that those skills are critical to putting together a win-win deal.

You may be thinking, "Those aren't skills. I'm just being nice." Well, that's partially true. But we good girls need to realize that our niceness (properly applied) can give us some real advantages when it comes to dealing with other human beings. I always chuckle a bit when I read negotiating textbooks that basically try to explain how to stop being a jerk. For some guys, that's an impossible task.

Julie Denny, now president of Resolutions, a mediation training and consulting firm in Amenia, New York, still shakes her head when she thinks about a boss she had at an old job years ago. "He would not give an inch," she says. "He loved to squash the other person. It didn't matter if the issue meant anything to him or not." This was a guy who wouldn't budge on anything — not even when it came to scheduling a lunch date. "Watching him upset my stomach," Julie recalls. Sometimes, after standing by while her boss hammered his opponent into the floor over some minor point, Julie would yell, "That didn't even matter to you!" "Yes, but I want to have some leverage," he'd say. In the short term, her nasty boss made some good deals. "But people grew to hate him," Julie says. The happy ending (at least from the good girl point of view) came a few years later, when he lost his authority and then quit his job.

Tough guys (and gals) who model their negotiating styles after Julie's boss-from-heck could learn a thing or two from women like Amy and Julie, and perhaps even you. All you need to do is cultivate some of your good girl personality gifts into secret weapons you can wield when you sit down to make a deal.

SECRET WEAPON NO. 1:
EMPATHIZING WITH THE OTHER SIDE

It's hard to imagine any mother who wouldn't get a little choked up at the vision of a disabled child left sitting on the sidelines. But Amy Barzach doesn't limit her empathy to cute kids who tug at her heartstrings. Her special gift is her ability to put herself in the place of everyone she encounters, even crusty corporate executives.

When Amy first envisioned that playground, she thought of it as "Jonathan's Dream." The idea caught on quickly; soon a core group of volunteers began donating their time to help with fund-raising and recruiting more workers. Local businesses offered supplies, food for volunteers, and landscaping services.

But when it came time to contact larger corporations for money, Amy stopped to figure out exactly what she wanted, and what the companies might ask in return. She imagined herself wheeling around a spacious office in a high-backed leather chair. If I were a corporate executive, she asked herself, why would I want to help pay for a playground? If I did agree to fork over some funds, what would I want in return?

The first question was pretty simple. Underneath their expensive suits, the executives were human beings. If she could just make them feel how important it is for handicapped children to play with their friends, the executives — like anyone else — would want to do whatever they could to help those kids have more fun. "We decided to personalize the story," she says, "focusing on a few of the children who would benefit from the playground."

The tougher question was what that executive would want in return. When a corporation gives a major donation, it often expects to get its money's worth in the form of public recognition. Most often, a big check comes attached to a firm request that the donor's name be written in big letters over the front gate. So Amy had to decide whether the playground's name was for sale. "I had wanted to name it Jonathan's Dream," Amy says, "but the playground was important to me. Maybe giving the name away was a worthy trade-off, in return for getting it off the ground." Then Amy imagined herself walking past the completed playground. What would it mean to her if the nameplate read something like, The Really Big

Corporation Community Playground? After pondering the question, she realized that she'd reached her own bottom line: creating a memorial for her son. "In my heart," she says, "I knew I wanted it to be called Jonathan's Dream." So she had to figure out another option that would still offer a win-win solution to her potential donors.

When she sat down with two senior executives from United Technologies, the community's biggest employer, the meeting went about as she expected. At first the atmosphere was very formal. Then, as she told the two men about some of the children the accessible playground would serve, and how much it would mean to those kids to play freely, the mood in the room shifted. One of the executives stopped her suddenly and said, "Amy, I'm a grandfather, too. I think this is an important thing to do." On the spot, he pledged $23,000, the amount needed to complete construction.

Then came the question Amy had anticipated: "How can we make our donation visible to the employees so they feel that they are part of it?" He didn't ask her directly to name the park after the company, but Amy knew it was one of the options on the table. She didn't want to give up "Jonathan's Dream," but she knew she had to acknowledge the company's generosity. So she asked for some time to come up with a proposal. "We left and regrouped," Amy says.

When she came back for the next meeting, she had a plan in hand. Somewhat hesitantly, she suggested giving the company's name to the park's central feature, a child-sized accessible wooden stage and surrounding benches. To Amy's great relief, the executive "loved" the idea of the United Technologies Children's Theater.

Baking a Bigger Pie

Amy and her volunteers had stumbled onto a classic negotiating technique: expanding the pie. To understand how it works, picture yourself at home on Thanksgiving Day. You're just about to cut the pumpkin pie into eight pieces, one for everybody at the table. Suddenly the doorbell rings. It's your sister and her family, making a surprise trip home. As everybody's kissing and hugging, you're thinking about dessert; if you try to cut that pie into twelve pieces, they're going to look pretty pitiful. Then you remember the gallon of ice cream in the freezer. "Who wants pie, and who wants a special Thanksgiving ice cream sundae?" you shout cheerily. Just as you expected, all the kids opt for ice cream, and everybody's happy.

If Amy had limited herself to two conflicting options, naming the whole playground after her son or giving all the credit to United Technologies, somebody would have left the table feeling awfully hungry. But by coming up with a whole new dessert — naming the children's theater — she satisfied both sides. And if another generous donor came along, she still had a nice plate of leftovers: The Extremely Large Corporation Swing Set and Slide.

The executive was so pleased by the proposal that he asked Amy to print up bright red T-shirts to hand out to United Technologies employees who volunteered at the playground. That way, even if workers from different offices didn't know each other, they could spot each other easily. Amy readily agreed.

His enthusiasm spread throughout the company. When United Technologies donated a tree for the playground's landscaping, a group of employees volunteered to plant it themselves. Amy was overcome when she read the poem they had written to mark the occasion; it was titled "Jonathan's Dream."

Empathizing with the Enemy

Of course, it's easy to empathize with people you like, who cherish the same values you do. But empathy can even help in acrimonious encounters. One example: Owens Corning general counsel Maura Abeln, a highly competitive corporate attorney whose successes were profiled by the *New York Times*. While she's careful to keep her client's agenda in mind, she has used her empathy to piece together a settlement with eighty plaintiff's law firms representing 200,000 asbestos claims. She tries to "see things from the plaintiffs' perspective," drawing on her own family experience. Her father was a foreman in a Pennsylvania copper tubing plant. "He'd come home with copper dust on his shoes," she remembers. That toxic dust may have contributed to his death from emphysema in 1986. Her sensitivity to the other side's viewpoint inspires their trust, even during contentious litigation. "I'm a big fan," admits Chicago lawyer John Cooney. "It's hard for a plaintiff's attorney to say that about a corporate attorney."

To influence the other side, it's not enough just to acknowledge that they see the world from a different standpoint. "If you want to influence them, you also need to understand empathetically the power of their point of view and to feel the emotional force with which they believe in it," negotiation gurus Fisher and Ury advise. "It is not enough to study them like beetles under a microscope; you need to know what it feels like to be a beetle."

Stanford professor Margaret Neale, coauthor of *Negotiating Rationally,* cites one disastrous example of what happened when a hive of corporate worker bees lacking in empathy tried to negotiate with some wary beetles. Some time ago, a group of American developers decided they wanted to construct a huge theme park in Europe. To convince local government officials that the park would be a great asset to their communities, the developers flew the officials to an enormous American theme park. It seemed like a brilliant idea; let these Europeans see the clean, well-manicured grounds, ride the thrilling roller coasters, smell the hamburgers sizzling on the grill, taste the hot buttered popcorn, and hear the delighted squeals of thousands of children having the time of their life.

Well, that was the plan. But what the Europeans experienced was a shock wave of American culture. Everywhere they looked, their senses were assaulted by something loud, garish, or gimmicky — in a word, something *American.* When the Europeans got home and shook the peanut shells off their shoes, they gave the developers their answer. No, thank you.

Perplexed, the American negotiators huddled together to find a way to sweeten the pot. They came up with a brilliant idea: Let's offer free trips to even *more* European officials *and* their families. So that's what they did — with exactly the same negative results. The officials came home immovably opposed to allowing the Americans to graft such a disfiguring edifice onto their quaint homeland.

What those clueless developers needed was an empathetic good girl with some cultural sensitivity. Instead of spending thousands to immerse the skittish Europeans in everything they most disliked about American culture, the developers should have invested their money in creating a beautifully crafted model showing how the park could be tailored to local tastes.

Swedish Synergy

Those developers needed to realize that a well-developed sense of empathy can create a bridge between continents. Gun Denhart, of Hanna Andersson, proved that in the mid-1980s, when a proposed quota on Swedish imports threatened her company.

Gun's entire business was based on marketing Eurostyled children's clothes crafted in Sweden from brightly colored Scandinavian fabrics. Her great taste, combined with the clothes' high quality, had made her business a smashing success. But she feared that with new import restrictions, she could run out of supplies.

After researching the congressional proposals, Gun found a loophole: Precut but unsewn fabric would be exempt. So she asked her primary Swedish supplier to set up a sewing shop in the United States, preferably near her company's Portland, Oregon, headquarters. Gun and her husband, Tom, had always had a good relationship with the supplier. But they knew they would have to persuade the owner to take a leap of faith and set up shop across the Atlantic.

Gun had no trouble putting herself in the supplier's place; she'd made the same transatlantic leap herself. A native of Lund, in southern Sweden, she was keenly aware of all the fears and concerns of an entrepreneur setting up business in a foreign country. One possible stumbling block was finding space, so she found a suitable location near her office. She even recruited another native Swede to serve as office manager and link to the Swedish headquarters.

As it turned out, no quotas were ever imposed. However, both sides have benefited from the supplier's American outpost, which provides Hanna Andersson with 25 percent of its merchandise. "It's been a win-win situation for both of us," Gun says. "They have a nice profitable business here. And because they are just a block away from us, we have shorter lead times. We also have greater flexibility because we can just go in and pick up what we need."

Take My House, Please: Selling Your House

Do you remember the day you moved into your house? While your husband hauled chairs into the dining room, you madly scrubbed the refrigerator and laid down fresh shelf paper. Finally, exhausted, you ordered a giant pizza and collapsed. Then your husband pulled out a wonderful surprise — a beautiful handpainted plaque reading: "The Smith-Jones Home, Est. 1993." When he nailed it beside your front door, you felt you were truly home.

Now, years later, you and your family are moving on to a new community and a new life. You're excited and scared at all the challenges ahead — starting with the sale of your beloved home. Nervously, you're trying to figure out how to find a buyer who will love this house as much as you do.

Well, here's our first piece of advice: Get rid of that darned plaque.

You see, that's the problem when good girls try to sell their houses. Everywhere we look, we see warm, happy memories. There on the kitchen wall are the marks of the kids' heights on their birthdays, while the bathroom door still sports that crayon portrait of your dog, created by a two-year-old artist. When you look at these things, you see a loving family home; a buyer sees a house in dire need of a new paint job.

When it comes time to sell your house, you've got to make a mental distinction between your house and your home. Your home, with all its memories, is priceless. But the house is a real estate investment, with a market price to be determined by one able and willing buyer. You need to get a handle on your emotions and get down to the business of selling your house.

First, call in Team Good Girl.

Ask your friends to walk through your house and candidly point out potential sales assets and drawbacks. (Once buyers start traipsing through, you'll be hearing downright rude comments about your taste and furnishings; it's better to get the straight story from your friends ahead of time.) Then ask them to suggest some good local real estate agents, and enlist their help in marketing your house to their friends and neighbors.

Depersonalize the house.

A buyer needs to imagine herself living in your house. That's much easier if she's not running into your family pictures and mementos at every turn. Strip the artwork off the refrigerator and box up the beer mug collection. Your goal is to make the house look like a professionally managed bed-and-breakfast — warm and cozy, but slightly impersonal. Get rid of all the clutter; every horizontal space should be clear of objects, except for a couple of artfully placed candlesticks or a vase of glowing daylilies.

Accentuate the positive, eliminate the negative.

Figure out each room's most attractive feature, then do something to underline it. If you've got big, beautiful windows in the master bedroom, strip off your heavy curtains and let the sun shine in. The buyers won't realize this means you have to protect your modesty by dressing in the closet; they'll just remember your bright, pretty bedroom.

Similarly, get rid of any immediate turnoffs. A few months ago, Beth looked at a big Victorian house that had been sitting on the market for months. The owners' information sheet, in ornate script, declared: "Main floor bathroom has a broken tub pipe." Beth couldn't believe it. "They're asking close to half a million dollars for this place," she said. "That repair would probably cost less than $500." Instead of fixing the pipe, the owners spotlighted the problem for every buyer who crossed their threshold.

(For detailed help on this step, take a look at *Dress Your House for Success: 5 Fast, Easy Steps to Selling Your House, Apartment, or Condo for the Highest Possible Price!* by Martha Webb.)

Pick the right real estate agent.

Choosing the right agent may determine whether this experience is a dream or a nightmare. Don't automatically hire the person who sold you the house. Interview four or five candidates, then make an informed decision.

Of course, you'll need to do your homework on this one, too. If you don't know the right questions to ask, you'll just wind up picking the broker who seems the nicest — or the one who promises to list the house at the highest price. (This is a ploy called "buying the listing." The agent dazzles you with a number beyond your wildest dreams. After your house sits on the market for a month with no nibbles, she crossly tells you your price is unrealistic, then knocks it down to the level everyone else suggested in the first place.)

The wrong real estate agent nearly cost our friend Darlene her home. Darlene's husband was transferred, and she needed to sell their suburban Chicago house quickly and get settled in Minneapolis before the school year began. In a hurry, she called up the one real estate agent she knew, a nice enthusiastic

Selling Your House (cont.)

lady. The agent assured her there'd be no problem. The house was gorgeous and they'd easily get $445,000.

So Darlene and her husband happily went house hunting in Minneapolis and snapped up a beautiful Tudor house for $497,000. Their real estate agent's enthusiasm convinced them their own house would sell within weeks, so they arranged for bridge financing — basically taking out a big, short-term, high-interest home-equity loan to give them the cash to cover the down payment, plus a few months of double mortgage payments.

Darlene dutifully followed all her agent's advice. When an early bid came in at $397,000, she turned it down flat. As summer faded into fall, her friends urged her to move up to Minnesota and get her daughters enrolled in their new school. But her broker said an empty house wouldn't be inviting to buyers. So she sat tight, staying in the Illinois house during the school week and shuttling her daughters up to see their dad on weekends.

Over the passing months, she grew increasingly desperate. The two mortgage payments, combined with airline tickets for those weekend commutes, were eating up huge chunks of their savings, and the deadline on the bridge loan was looming. She cut her asking price, first down to $435,000, then to $415,000. Finally she called in a new, no-nonsense agent. "I don't understand where you got this price," the agent said flatly. "It's a beautiful house, but nothing on this side of town has sold for over $400,000 in the past two years." When she heard that hard fact, Darlene immediately cut her asking price to $399,500 — and sold it for $385,000 within two weeks.

To protect yourself, shop around for the best agent you can find — then sign a short-term listing agreement. Sixty days should give your agent plenty of time to show what she can do.

Think like a buyer.

Remember how incredibly stressful it was to buy your first house? Many of your buyers may be in that position. Use your good girl empathy and do everything you can to ease their anxieties. Compile an annotated history of all your home improvements. This should include warranty certificates and instruction booklets, plus recent copies of your utility bills. If your house has a problem you're unable or unwilling to solve — say, that pesky tub pipe — ask the three best contractors in your area to give you estimates on the repair, then put their reports in the scrapbook, too. This shows buyers you're a thoughtful, well-organized, trustworthy homeowner.

Check out the competition.

Take a look at all the similarly priced houses on the market. What does your house have that they don't? If all the other sellers are brewing coffee with cinnamon to make their houses smell inviting, set yourself apart from the competition by shoving a loaf of frozen bread dough in your oven before your open house. Ask yourself what it would take to make someone choose your house over the one down the street. Consider installing closet shelving units, or putting an inexpensive freestanding island in the kitchen. It doesn't cost much to put out a couple of window boxes filled with petunias, or to brighten up the bathroom with a fresh, pretty shower curtain. Those touches may be all it takes to make your house stand out from the crowd.

Woo the other brokers.

You won't sell your house if you can't get potential buyers across your threshold. And most of those buyers will be escorted by real estate agents. So make your home as agent-friendly as you possibly can. When an agent shows up at your door, meet her with a big smile and a plate of brownies. Then leave. "If the homeowner is present, people don't feel free to convey their thoughts or concerns," says veteran real estate saleswoman Ginny Barbier, of Glenwood Springs, Colorado. "The agent doesn't want to hurt your feelings by saying, 'Imagine how it would look if you ripped out all this carpet and polished the floors.' So go for a walk, and let the agent perform her magic."

If a house isn't selling, Barbier often advises her clients to sweeten the deal by offering a $1,000 bonus to the agent who sells the house. That's a nice extra on top of the standard commission. But from the seller's standpoint, offering the bonus is much cheaper than cutting the house price by $10,000 — and it usually results in a swarm of new customers.

Be hospitable.

When you're trying to sell your house, it's easy to view prospective buyers as the enemy. They interrupt your meals, wake up your baby, and tramp all over your clean carpets. Beset by the space invaders, you set up elaborate defenses. At your open house, you allow only one couple inside at a time. You

Selling Your House (cont.)

post signs demanding that they remove their shoes before entering. Then you wonder why the buyers aren't lined up demanding to pay full price for your beautifully kept home.

Well, put yourself in their shoes (which you've insisted that they leave out on your front porch). You're asking these people to give you hundreds of thousands of dollars for the privilege of battling with your temperamental hot water heater. They're not professional crooks trying to case the joint. They're your clients, your customers. Make them feel at home.

Listen.

Thicken your skin and listen to what the buyers and agents are saying, and respond to their concerns. If your suburban property tax bill is scaring buyers from the city, put out information on your fabulous school system and park district; let them know what they'll get for their money. If your dynamic chartreuse walls make buyers reach for their sunglasses, tone down your color scheme with a couple of gallons of pale yellow paint. If a buyer grumbles that the kitchen is too small to accommodate her trusty butcher block table, that's a signal that she's mentally moving in. So instead of frostily showing her to the door, pull out your handy tape measure and try to find a likely spot. Or mention that you might be willing to leave your sleek little folding kitchen table in place — subject to negotiation, of course.

"Put something on paper and I'll think about it."

Embroider this phrase on a sampler and hang it over your desk. Whenever a prospective buyer asks, "Would you consider a lower price?" this is the only appropriate response (with a friendly smile, of course). Otherwise, they learn what you're willing to give up without making any disclosures or concessions in return. Don't negotiate against yourself.

Stay calm.

This can be a nerve-wracking time. But if you're working in good faith, using all your wonderful good girl skills, you can make this a more pleasant experience for all — and still get the best possible price for your home.

Anything You Can Do . . .

Now, we've told you that empathy is a good girl trait. But don't get all cocky just because you're missing that Y chromosome. And don't assume the guy across the table is a dolt just because he's wearing wingtips and a necktie. Daniel Goleman, writing in *Working with Emotional Intelligence,* reports that tests among thousands of men and women show that we, on average, are more aware of our emotions, show more empathy, and are more adept interpersonally. But he adds: "Some men are as empathetic as the most interpersonally sensitive women."

Years of scientific research have shown that no matter what psychological aptitude you measure, the sexes are more alike than they are different, Goleman reports. So it shouldn't be surprising to discover that men have the ability to empathize with finesse equal to women. If the men you know seem reluctant to walk a mile in your shoes, it's probably because our culture doesn't encourage them to take that trip. In Western cultures like ours, Goleman contends, "girls are raised to be more attuned to feelings and their nuances than are boys." It's like a man having to admit he's lost by asking for directions. Since our culture considers empathy a feminine trait, sharing someone else's perspective can mess with his self-image.

It's too bad, because lacking empathy puts you at a decided disadvantage at the bargaining table. " 'I want it because I want it' just doesn't work," warns Kellogg School of Management professor Leigh Thompson.

Former banker Rosemarie Greco learned her lesson on that score twenty-five years ago, when she was up for her first promotion. "I went in with incredible expectations," Greco recalls. "I figured I was worth $10,000; it would be my first five-figure salary."

The executive vice president called her in, congratulated her on her new position, and announced her new salary: $9,600. "I was crushed," she says. For a few awkward moments of silence, Rosemarie considered turning him down and walking away. Then she pulled herself together and asked him to raise that to $10,000. He told her he couldn't go a penny higher. She reluctantly accepted. But on her way out, she delivered this parting shot: "You will soon come to realize that I am worth $10,000, because I will give you more than $10,000 worth of work." Then she ran to the internal stairwell (she was afraid to run into someone on the elevator), sat down on a step, and shed a few tears.

Six months later, Rosemarie's paycheck included a raise. When she thanked her supervisor, he acknowledged her competence. "You were right," he said. "You are worth $10,000."

When Rosemarie looks back on that first encounter, she doesn't congratulate herself. Rather, she faults herself for pushing her own agenda without thinking about the big picture. "Ten thousand dollars was a marker only for me. It was entirely personal," she explains. "Women need to learn to ask 'Why?' or 'Why not?'" Rosemarie pushed for a higher salary without knowing her supervisor's own objectives or budget constraints. If she'd turned him down, she might well have lost the first in a string of raises and promotions that led her all the way to the bank president's office.

Detecting Hidden Interests

Does this mean you should always side with the other guy, in hopes of getting that pie in the sky by and by? Absolutely not. But you do have to balance what you want against what the other side might reasonably have to give. Remember, empathy is different from sympathy. Sympathy is defined as feeling pity and compassion for someone else, adopting their feelings as your own. Empathy "requires neither sympathy nor agreement," explains Robert Mnookin, former director of Harvard's Program on Negotiating, in *Negotiation Journal*. Empathy is "a journey in which we explore and describe another's perceptual world without commitment."

Taking that empathy journey can sometimes lead you to insights about your opponents that they don't have themselves. As CEO of a Nashville-based mergers and acquisitions firm, Whitney Johns Martin often finds that entrepreneurs who are selling their businesses want to stay involved after the sale. As the world's greatest experts on their own companies, they assume the new owners will be delighted to have them available for consultations. They don't understand that most new owners don't want the old boss hanging around, and that few are willing to buy a company if it comes with a former CEO attached. Those entrepreneurs also don't realize how painful it will be for them to relinquish control to the new owners.

Rather than giving the sellers a flat-out "no go," however, Whitney approaches the problem from their point of view. "I say things like, 'You may think you want to continue with the company now, but you will only get frustrated. You are used to running your own ship. You will lose interest.' By the time I'm done, they are ready to sell and move on to something else."

You don't always need empathy to figure out what someone else wants — as anyone who's ever negotiated bedtime with a toddler can tell you. But it's not uncommon for adult opponents, especially less experienced or less motivated ones, to need some prompting. Sometimes all it takes is a direct question. "I have often asked my opponent, 'What do you want from this negotiation? What do you expect? What would you like to accomplish?'" Gerard Nierenberg writes in *The Art of Negotiating*. However, it may take a few rounds back and forth, or even a side trip to someone else in the organization, before you can figure out what the other side really needs.

A Woman, a Dream, and a Really Big Sled

For Jeanne Ashcraft, negotiating her dream required empathy, persistence, and a dozen really big furry dogs. After working in Intel's sales and marketing department for less than three years, Jeanne decided to ask for forty days off — plus an extra $18,000.

Sound crazy? Keep reading. The fifty-two-year-old woman had decided to take on the Iditarod Challenge, the grueling 1,100-mile dogsled trek from Anchorage to Nome, Alaska. Jeanne's grandfather, a gold miner, had covered some of the same territory nearly a century before, and had left a diary that was now a family treasure. Jeanne hoped to retrace his steps.

The trip wouldn't be cheap. Hiring a sled and trained dogs would cost about $15,000. So Jeanne sent an e-mail message to Carlene Ellis, Intel's first woman vice president, asking for corporate support. "I didn't know her from a wall," Carlene recalls, "but I was pretty visible, and she knew I'd sponsored some controversial things in the past." After hearing her story, Carlene says, "I wanted Jeanne to be able to go because I admired what she was trying to do."

The two women realized they'd have to use some careful strategy to woo the company's bean counters. Why would Intel have any interest in financing her arctic dream? If the company manufactured skis instead of computer chips, it might have been a natural fit. But Intel had a policy against sponsoring any sporting events.

Then Carlene had a vision. "Hey, I can see this: A banner on the sled, a mobile laptop wrapped in a blanket so it won't freeze. It's so marvelous." With a Pentium chip–equipped laptop on the trip, Jeanne could send regular race updates back to the home office. (And she'd also be able to communicate easily with friends and family.)

So Jeanne whipped up a written proposal. At first it was hard sledding. "We got a little heat in the kitchen, a little resistance from, as I call it, narrow thinking," Carlene says. But the feisty vice president convinced her colleagues that in a world in which Everest climbers routinely pack their cell phones, the Iditarod could demonstrate how well Intel's product performed in the unforgiving Alaskan cold. "We could play with technology and get credit for it." Ultimately, Carlene's enthusiasm won out. Intel equipped Jeanne with a laptop and agreed to cover all her expenses. The company even gave her six weeks of paid leave, a much better deal than the unpaid vacation time she'd requested.

Once on the trail, Jeanne was a trouper, valiantly enduring temperatures of 45 below zero. "She tested out some stuff, talked to us by sending notes, told us when it worked and when it didn't, and she got a lot of press," Carlene says. And her dream of retracing her grandfather's steps came true. She carried her grandfather's diary along with her on the trip, visiting frostbitten villages he'd written about ninety-five years before. She even saw the ruins of an old wooden roadhouse where her grandfather had once spent the night.

When she came back, Jeanne felt she had tested more than the computer equipment. "I'm far more assertive about some things than before," says the voyager. "Knowing what you can really accomplish makes you see yourself a little differently."

Beyond the Numbers

Using empathy also worked for childcare advocate Faith Wohl, who took on Du Pont's childcare benefit policy back in 1984. Faith — now the director of the New York–based Child Care

Action Campaign — was working in the chemical manufacturer's public relations office.

Faith and a small group of women employees thought Du Pont's management should offer childcare assistance as part of its benefit package. In planning their strategy, they figured the science guys atop the company's corporate ladder might feel acutely uncomfortable if they were bombarded with sob stories of desperate young mothers unable to afford good childcare. Instead, they took a quintessentially Du Pont approach, using hard data to make their case. "Research has kept the company together for two hundred years; they prize it," Faith explains.

The women first polled the Du Pont workforce about their childcare needs, which were enormous. Then they compiled figures from the Bureau of Labor Statistics, showing that the Du Pont workers' needs were part of a national trend. "We put it together in a fact-filled report that we felt was very compelling," she recounts. "As it turned out, we were very naive."

Unfortunately, the report landed on the desk of a guy who apparently had spent his whole life living next door to Ozzie and Harriet. "He didn't believe our numbers because they didn't match his personal experience," Faith says. After he read the report, "he started mumbling to himself. He told us later what he was doing. He went from house to house on his block in his mind. Everyone in his family and everyone he knew fit the traditional family model," with Dad working at the office all day and Mom cheerfully staying home with the kids. To him, the women's data were obviously incorrect.

That encounter drove home a very important point, Faith says. "You cannot think that an argument, no matter how compelling, will convince someone. You are negotiating with a person who is reacting viscerally, and with their heart and their emotions," she says.

Patiently, Faith set out to convince the executive that most of the company's employees weren't living in a 1950s sitcom. That took an appeal to his emotions — the approach she'd originally rejected. She detailed just how hard it was for the company's women workers to find trustworthy childcare, and to hand over the enormous chunk of their paychecks each week. Finally, the executive got it — a breakthrough that turned out to be the crucial first step in making Du Pont a national leader in providing employee childcare.

The Empathetic Educator

Ava was a college president who adored her job. The school's board of trustees adored her right back. But their happy relationship headed toward the rocks when the board offered Ava a contract she found completely unacceptable. Could this marriage be saved? Yes, thanks to Ava's ability to think like a trustee.

The board's five-year contract offer actually looked pretty good. They offered Ava a six-figure annual salary, plus two large performance-based bonuses — the first after two years, the second after five. To most of us, that sounds pretty fair indeed. But Ava, in her mid-fifties, was looking down the road. If she left the school at the end of five years, she'd be a little too old to attract the best offers, and she didn't want to end her career on a disappointing note. "Each year, as I get older, my position in the marketplace will worsen," she says. The more she thought about it, the more she realized she and the board had overlapping interests. The trustees loved her performance, and she loved the institution. What she really wanted was a long-term contract that would take her to the end of her career.

First Ava attacked the money issue. She knew the trustees were careful with the school's money, so she wasn't asking for a larger piece of the financial pie. Instead, she wanted the performance bonuses cut in half. "I don't like to be incentivized," she says, "because I can't work any harder than I do." Instead, she asked for a slightly higher salary for the first five years of the contract. "I knew they wanted to be generous, so I did some research on the market rates and told them they could be a bit more generous."

Ava then asked the board to put the remaining bonus money toward a seven-year guaranteed teaching contract, with a salary equal to that of the highest-paid liberal arts professor. That would take effect in five years, when she would step down as president.

Before she presented her proposal, Ava tried to anticipate the board's objections. "I did my best to imagine all the issues that might lead them to say no," she says. "I wanted to show them that I understood all of the worries and then built in safeguards." Looking at her offer from the trustees' perspective, she realized she'd inadvertently included one completely untenable provision. If she went straight

Pay Dirt: How to Get the Salary You Deserve

When I was growing up, I dreamed of becoming a reporter for *Time* magazine. My mother had worked there as a researcher before I was born, and I always loved hearing her tell stories about her colorful coworkers and the glamorous people she interviewed. (She once interviewed Leopold Stokowski, the great — and highly temperamental — orchestra conductor. At the end of the interview, she asked the musician how old he was. This routine question so enraged the maestro that he hurled her notebook into the fireplace.)

You can imagine how thrilled I was when *Time* offered me a job as a reporter-researcher. I was so excited, I barely remembered to ask what (or if) they were going to pay me. To my youthful ears, the starting salary sounded more than fair. And I was sure that my enthusiastic performance would soon send me rocketing to the top of the pay scale.

I really loved that job. For six years, I covered business and media. I interviewed everybody from Australian media mogul Rupert Murdoch to ice cream barons Ben and Jerry. And sure enough, I got a nice little raise every year.

I can still remember the annual ritual of the salary review. My supervisor, Betty, would call me into her big, plush office and hand me a little square of colored paper. On it she had neatly written my previous salary, plus the standard increase negotiated by the union, the merit raise I had earned through my good girl job performance, and the grand total. Every year, I looked at the numbers, smiled sweetly, folded up the paper into a neat little rectangle, and said, "Thank you." I never wondered why the figures were all written in pencil — which is, as you know, quite easy to erase.

As I look back, it's hard to believe that I never even tried to negotiate a higher salary. I think I was afraid I might seem greedy or ungrateful. I also had no idea where I was on the pay scale. I assumed I was near the top, but I never took the time to do some discreet digging into the prevailing wage. (That's more than a little embarrassing, when you consider that I was a professional researcher at a major magazine.) But I also think my mother's stories had a lingering effect on my attitude. I must have listened to dozens of tales about her exciting adventures in the glamorous New York of the 1950s. But not once — not one single time — did we ever talk about how much she got paid.

How to Get the Salary You Deserve (cont.)

If you're like most good girls, you've probably got a few similar salary "negotiation" stories of your own. (When Beth got her first job, at her local newspaper, the managing editor announced the starting salary: $202.20. Beth nodded sagely. "Great, $202.20 a month," she repeated. "No, per week," replied the disconcerted editor. Dumbfounded, Beth collapsed in happy giggles. "See what the boys in the back room will have!" she cried.)

Of the two million—plus people who start new jobs each month, more than 50 percent won't even try to negotiate their starting salaries, says salary negotiation expert Robin Pinkley in her book *Get Paid What You're Worth.*

Don't despair just because you've flubbed salary negotiations in the past. Try thinking of your career as a work in progress. Up until now, you've been focusing on honing your skills and expanding your professional network. (That's career-speak for what good girls do on the job, which is work very, very hard and make lots of friends.) But now it's time to turn your attention to the bottom line, and to start getting the money you deserve.

What's Stopping You?

Ask a good girl why she's underpaid and she'll probably hand you a lot of lofty excuses: She's opted to work in a lower-paid but socially responsible field, or she's more focused on family than on career, or she's interested in creative expression, not material gain.

Sorry. We don't buy it. We've said all those things ourselves, at one time or another. But in our secret hearts, we were just scared.

We were afraid They wouldn't like us anymore. We thought They would tell us we were already paid far more than we were worth. We didn't ask for more because we didn't really believe we deserved more.

It's time to get over it. Right now. This is not about the value of your mind and soul. Your salary has nothing to do with your inner self. It's simply an expression of your professional worth in a capitalist marketplace based on supply and demand. And the supply of smart, honest, hardworking, dedicated workers like us is always limited.

Keep in mind that your perceived value goes up if you show your new employers you're prepared to negotiate. In a survey of corporate headhunters and placement officers, Pinkley asked whether they would be more impressed by applicants who (1) negotiated in a professional manner, (2) accepted an offer as made, or (3) laid down a list of salary demands. She found that 80 percent chose the applicant behind Door Number One. "If you didn't negotiate, that sends a signal about your worth," she says. So get ready to go on in there and ask for what you deserve.

Getting Ready

If you're like us, you get giant prehistoric dragonflies in your tummy every time you think about asking for more money. However, you can force those primordial insects into extinction (or at least reduce them to a more digestible size) by doing some homework.

When it comes to getting ready to negotiate your salary, a good girl's best friend is her computer. In the pre-Internet days, figuring out your worth in the marketplace was mostly guesswork, based on water cooler gossip and out-dated salary figures from the public library. But today you can find up-to-the-minute salary information by job category, region, and sometimes even specific employer, with just a few clicks of the keys. The Net abounds with numerous Web sites listing salary information that will help you figure out your target range. As a starting point, take a look at the terrific Web site affiliated with Richard Nelson Bolles's classic *What Color Is Your Parachute?*

Supplement your research with an emergency call to Team Good Girl, girlfriends in your field who can give you the real lowdown.

My friend Colleen tapped into her old girls' network when she decided to leave her government job and become a computer consultant. After sending out a few resumés, she got an offer from a Texas firm. The money looked good; she'd get a $5,000 raise immediately, with the possibility of bigger raises down the line. But before she jumped at the offer, she made a call to her old college and got the name of Lisa, a Texas-based alum with a similar job. Their conversation opened Colleen's eyes. While her salary wasn't bad, Lisa felt trapped in an electronic sweatshop, working ten- and twelve-hour days. "She helped me see it was a terrible offer," Colleen recalls.

Ask your friends and contacts what benefits are available, and what traps you should avoid. This is not the time to be demure: Ask for details on precisely what they got, and exactly how they got it.

Once you've got a clear picture of the marketplace, take a good, hard look at your own performance. Career counselor Jack Chapman, author of *Negotiating Your Salary: How to Make $1,000 a Minute,* tells about one of his clients, a female engineer in the gas industry who thought she had the best deal in the world. A talented troubleshooter, she was sent all over the country

---

How to Get the Salary You Deserve (cont.)

whenever a problem cropped up at one of the company's plants. Once she'd triumphed over the crisis in Seattle or New Orleans, her grateful employers usually allowed her an extra day for sightseeing before she had to come home. "She felt really good about it," says Chapman, who served as her career coach.

Then Coach Chapman told her to figure out how much actual cash her troubleshooting skills saved the company each year. By getting the plants back online in record time, she'd saved the company millions in lost sales. Suddenly that free bowl of gumbo didn't seem quite so satisfying. When it came time for her next performance review, she presented her calculations and asked for a whopping raise — $40,000 — and a promotion. She got both.

Make sure you think about the whole package, not just your salary figures. This one can be tricky; sometimes employers distract good girls with a few cheap benefits, in hopes that they won't notice how pitiful their salaries really are. At one memorable job interview, the department head told Beth that, while the salary was a little on the low side (a masterpiece of understatement), all "the girls in the office" got an extra day off in December to do their Christmas shopping. "With what? Wampum?" Beth replied.

Rehearse the Right Script

Once you've pulled all your research into a short, persuasive package, it's time to take that script and start rehearsing until you know it by heart.

This may sound dorky. And you'll probably feel incredibly silly as you look in the mirror and sternly repeat, "Ms. Brown, I've done some research on the prevailing wages in this industry, and I think a 12 percent raise would bring my compensation package into a competitive range." But you need to realize that you've been rehearsing this scene all your life — only you've been reading from the wrong script. Over and over, you've listened to those inner voices that tell you not to ask for too much, for fear you'll wind up with nothing. Sandra Pesmen, the "Dr. Job" columnist, says women tend to focus exclusively on the worst-case scenario, imagining horror-show job interviews or salary reviews that leave them feeling defeated before they start. "By the time you walk in, you've decided you're no good, they don't want you, and you're lucky if they just let you clean the presses," she sighs. So you need to practice out loud, in a strong, secure voice that will drown out those inner critics that have kept you from getting what you're worth all these years.

Elizabeth Gray put this advice to good use when she applied for a job as a business analyst at Dell Computer. Her husband already worked as a data architect at the company, so she knew — to the penny — what the salary range should be. Still, she felt funny about asking for the going rate. "At that level, I thought I would be grossly overpaid."

But Elizabeth was determined not to let her inner voices spoil her chance for equal pay. "During my research on pay scales, I kept reading that women underestimate their worth." So over and over, she practiced saying, "I'd like $62,000." When the time came, she asked for that "ridiculous" figure. She ended up with $60,000 — $13,000 more than she'd made at her old job as a city employee. "I was thrilled."

Elizabeth's experience illustrates a recent research finding by Professor Leigh Thompson, of Northwestern University. When women students were told explicitly that they weren't expected to do well at the bargaining table, Professor Thompson found, they actually improved their performance. Although she cautions that this is preliminary research, the professor theorizes that those reminders may encourage women to think, "I'm not going to fall into that stereotype."

Before you go in for that meeting, take a minute to recite a revised version of *The Little Engine that Could:* "They think I can't, they think I can't, they think I can't. Well, I can!" It couldn't hurt.

Just Say Nothing

Once you've decided what you want, the next step is incredibly difficult — and incredibly simple: Shut your mouth.

By the time you're finished researching and rehearsing, you'll probably feel so wound up that you'll burst out your salary demand at the slightest provocation — such as a waiter's innocent query: "What do you want?" But now is the time to button your lip and listen to what your employer (or future employer) has to say. Yes, you know exactly what you want. But don't share your bottom line until there's an offer on the table.

If you're looking for a new job, your first priority should be to find out whether this company is a good match for you. Don't bring up salary until the interviewer broaches the issue. Even then, be careful what you say. If the interviewer asks what salary you are looking for, don't commit to a figure. If your bid is less than they'd expected to pay, you're negotiating against yourself. If you aim too high, you may yank yourself out of consideration altogether.

It's usually unwise to reveal precisely what you are making currently, especially if you're underpaid. (If you are responding to a want ad that asks you to submit salary information, experts advise writing in "competitive.") If you're pressed to name a salary figure, some experts suggest offering a range and adding a remark like, "Considering my experience, I'm looking for something on the higher end." But personally, I think that if a prospective employer wants to play games and keep you in the dark about the financial landscape, you should seriously reconsider whether you want to work with him in the first place.

Once there's an offer on the table, try following Chapman's advice. Don't say yes or no; just repeat the figure and then be quiet. "If you had not repeated the figure or the top of the range, the silence would be awkward or dangerous," he writes. "The interviewer might think you were accepting or that you're too shy to talk about money. But when you repeat it, the interviewer knows that you heard it, and fears you're disappointed." This tactic is almost certain to lead to an awkward pause in the conversation — which most good girls avoid like the bubonic plague. But in those quiet seconds (or minutes, if you can stand it), the interviewer will be thinking about what will happen if you're so disappointed in the offer that you walk away from the company. Most likely, he'll jump into the silent void with an improved offer.

If the offer is too low, it's time to put your research to work. Explain what you think would be a fair wage, based on prevailing salaries and your own background and strengths. Ask him how he came up with that particular figure; his response may lead to a new, more frank discussion of how to put together a compensation package that can satisfy both sides' needs.

Bring Your BATNA

Never go into a salary negotiation without a good BATNA (which, all together now, stands for Best Alternative To a Negotiated Agreement). If you ask for a raise and don't get it, what are you going to do? Are you willing to start looking for another job? At the risk of tying your stomach into even tighter knots, you need to remember that it's never a good sign when a company can't (or won't) pay you what you deserve. It could mean your supervisor isn't happy with your work, or that budgets are getting so tight that there's no room to reward even the best workers. Either way, you need to start thinking about the future. (Now, don't panic. If you're modestly underpaid and otherwise pretty happy with your work situation, you've got a nice, easy BATNA — enjoy what you've got, and start planning now for next year's salary review.) You need to make a conscious, informed choice about what's best for you, today and ten years from now.

The best BATNA, of course, is a competing job offer. Even if you like your job, you'd be smart to follow the example of our friend Maureen. Although she's perfectly happy with her job editing an online magazine, she goes on two job interviews every year, as faithfully as she goes to the dentist. That way she keeps abreast of current pay rates and always has her options open when it's time for a raise. At the very least, put together a list of prospective employers you could contact if you decide to make a change; you'll feel better.

Sleep Your Way to a Raise, Good Girl–Style

Okay, you got the offer. You are so thrilled and relieved, you're ready to jump up and shout, "Fine! Great! Okay!" Sure, you didn't get quite the money you hoped for, or you're giving up a week of vacation. But you're tired of looking for a job, tired of worrying about money. Every fiber of your exhausted being is shouting, *"Take it! Take it!"*

Don't listen. Instead, smile brightly, say thank you, and then ask for a few days to think it over. Sit down with a trusted friend and review the offer with a clear head. Together you may come up with a strategy to boost your salary — or you may realize that the offer is better than it sounded initially.

My friend Katrina inadvertently used this maneuver to her benefit last year. She and her salesman husband were living in Los Angeles, but the high cost of living was devouring their combined salaries, and they hated bringing up their daughter so far from her grandparents. So Katrina started job hunting in her hometown of Des Moines. After long months of searching, she finally got a decent offer — not great, but acceptable. "I'll have to talk this over with my husband," she told the interviewer, quite truthfully. "He's on the road right now, so it may take a day or two for us to connect." Then she headed back to L.A., anxiously reviewing the offer all the way home. When she walked in the door, the message light was blinking on her answering machine. It was her prospective boss: "Would an extra $3,000 make this

How to Get the Salary You Deserve (cont.)

an easier decision?" It sure did, and she's now happily back in the cornfields once more.

Get It in Writing

When you finally put together the compensation package of your dreams, get it in writing. If you're offered an employment contract, take the time to read it carefully, and make sure it reflects your agreement. If your boss offered you another salary review in six months, don't assume she'll remember — or that she'll even be around. Learn from our friend Serena's experience. When she was four months pregnant, a friend recommended her for a copywriting job in a big advertising agency. Despite her protruding tummy, Serena decided to give it a shot. As it turned out, the supervisor was a truly wonderful guy. When he saw the samples of Serena's work, he looked her in the eye and asked, "What would we have to do to convince you to come work for us?" Startled, Serena named a midrange salary figure, combined with a flexible work schedule once the baby came. "No problem," the supervisor said. "Welcome aboard." They shook hands, and she started work the following Monday.

For a year, everything was great. Then the agency was sold, and Serena's saintly boss got the ax. A few weeks later, the new supervisor called Serena into her office. "You seem to be having a serious attendance problem," the woman said sternly. Stunned, Serena stammered out that she'd been working from home two days a week with her boss's full approval. "There's no record of any such agreement in your employment file," her new boss said crisply. "I'll expect you in here every day at 9 A.M., just like everybody else." Heartsick, Serena resigned on the spot.

The moral of the story: It's not an agreement until it's written and signed. Your deal memo doesn't have to be an imposing legal document. Just make sure all the major points are covered — and that your boss's signature is clearly written at the bottom.

from the president's office to the classroom, she'd still be on campus and in her successor's hair. So she added a provision stipulating that she would take a year's sabbatical leave after she stepped down.

The resolution: The trustees approved her counterproposal without any significant changes, and they all lived happily ever after.

The Danger: Oversympathizing

There's just one danger in being good at empathizing. If you're too nice a gal, you may lose sight of your own goals. It's that old Popsicle problem again. When you know how much the other guy loves chocolate, how can you refuse to trade your favorite Fudgsicle for a Creamsicle? "If you see an emotional quality that gets your sympathy, you need to go beyond sympathy, and into empathy," warns Joan Goldsmith, coauthor of *Resolving Conflicts at Work: A Complete Guide for Everyone on the Job.*

Amy Barzach had to guard against her own overactive empathy gland in dealing with one of the condominium owners who lived next door to the Jonathan's Dream playground. Worried about people peering in their windows from the playground, the neighbors had extracted a commitment from the playground's builders to block the view by planting sixty trees and shrubs. About a year after the playground was finished, Amy realized that even with the trees, one woman's home was still in full view. Feeling sorry for her, sympathetic Amy decided on the spot to raise an extra $1,500, the cost of five six-foot pine trees, to mask the view.

Then her Sympathy Control kicked in. Based on her past dealings with the condo owners, she realized that they'd expect her to take responsibility for any future problems with the trees. And now she had enough experience to know that newly planted trees don't always survive. So she moved her emotional dial past Sympathy and placed it securely on Empathy. To prevent the new tree donation from turning into "an ongoing saga," she decided to donate the $1,500 directly to the condominium association. That way, they'd be responsible for purchasing the trees — and for taking care of them once they were planted.

Sure enough, a year later her phone rang. It was a member of the condo board, reporting that two trees had died. She gently reminded him that the condo association owned the trees, and so they needed to follow up with the nursery on their own.

SECRET WEAPON NO. 2:
LISTENING TO YOUR OPPONENT

It's a rare book on negotiating that doesn't hammer its readers with the importance of listening. Many of the books written by men assume that hearing what others have to say is an arduous task. But those of us raised as good girls learned early how to hang on someone's every word. Our friend Sally, a southern belle, says she was taught to look directly into her beau's eyes and silently repeat the mantra "I think you're wonderful."

Okay, that one's a little extreme (although Sally insists it's quite effective in some limited circumstances). But it shows just how keenly many women have honed their listening skills.

When it's time to make a deal, listening means more than using your ears — or even batting your eyelashes attentively. Listening in a way that's useful in negotiating requires an open mind. In his 1958 classic, *The Art of Listening,* psychiatrist Dominick A. Barbara distinguishes between productive and unproductive listening. "Good listening demands active participation," Barbara writes. "It involves keeping one's mind in a state of relaxed alertness, open and flexible to all relevant changes in a given situation." That means that you keep your mind quiet and calm as you listen, giving the speaker a chance to present all the facts involved, without jumping to any premature conclusions. Ineffectual listeners, Barbara says, are like hyperactive defense attorneys, always interrupting to make objections or counterclaims. Effective listeners are more like jury members, quietly soaking up information until it's time to reach a decision.

Barbara contends that empathy and "good listening" go hand in hand. "It is the merging of one personality with another until some degree of identification is achieved," he says. You have to identify with a person before you can understand him. It's this temporary merger of personalities that makes conversation, in Alexander Pope's words, "the feast of reason and the flow of soul."

Even if you think you are a good listener, it might take some effort to bring you up to that flow-of-soul category. Studies find that most people take in only about half of what is said.

Getting Past *Nyet*

If you listen carefully at the bargaining table, it will enable you to pick up clues about your opponent that others might miss. Jeanette Wagner, vice chairman of Estée Lauder, credits her sharp ears and eyes with making her a successful negotiator. "If I'm good at this, and people seem to think I am, I'd say my ability to listen is probably most advantageous," Jeanette says.

Several years ago, Jeanette's listening skills helped to salvage a major deal that was heading toward Siberia. She was caught off guard when she flew into St. Petersburg to sign a contract with a Baltic shipping company. "I don't remember the precise figures, but it was about a $10 million deal, and I thought it was done," she says. "I was just supposed to fly in so we could sign the document and then congratulate each other and drink a glass of champagne."

When Jeanette walked in with two assistants, the vice president in charge of Estée Lauder's Soviet business and the attorney who had negotiated the deal, the Russian shippers greeted them warmly. But when it came time to sign all the paperwork, the Russians threw her a curve. "We're not going to sign it," they announced.

"What do you mean?" she gasped.

"We never sign contracts," they answered. "We don't need to."

Jeanette, completely nonplussed, took several deep breaths. She knew she couldn't base a multimillion-dollar contract on a handshake. With no signature, there was no deal. "Why?" she asked calmly.

They just didn't like contracts, the Russians replied.

Gingerly, Jeanette probed a bit further. "I don't understand that. Tell me more." She suspected they didn't understand the contract's language, but she felt it would only embarrass them to ask about this directly. She just hoped that if she could get them to talk, she would hear something that would give her an opening.

Jeanette listened attentively as they complained about the contract's excessive length. (It was only three or four pages, as she recalls, a miracle of brevity from an American corporate standpoint.) Then she heard six magic words: "If it were only a page."

From their tone, she sensed that they wanted to go ahead with the deal but felt intimidated by, the complexity of the contract. "Oh, I see," she said quickly. "Why don't you give me an hour and a room, and I'll see if I can't do that?"

Her assistants were aghast. "Our vice president was panicked at her deal collapsing," she says. "The lawyer was having a fit because it was the middle of the night on the weekend in New York and he couldn't reach lawyers from either of our offices for advice. But I knew if I left without a contract we'd never have a deal." So Jeanette herded the team into a room with a computer and went to work.

As a former editor-in-chief of the Hearst Corporation's international editions, Jeanette knew her way around a red pencil. "I crossed out all the boilerplate jargon. Then I narrowed the margins on the top and the bottom, and on the left and the right, and got what was left to fit on one piece of paper."

An hour later the Russians had their contract. "They signed it, and we never had any problem with them," she says with satisfaction.

Cut the Chat

The first step in listening effectively, of course, is learning when to shut up. Designer Charlotte Lyons, author of *Mothers and Daughters at Home,* has a big sign over her desk: "Listen." The sign "reminds me that I'm collecting information," she says. "I'm not rambling and saying things I shouldn't or showing too much enthusiasm. I'm just listening to what's being offered — and I take lots of notes."

As nice, friendly good girls, some of us tend toward the chatty side. (Beth admits that in her case that's an extraordinary understatement.) We hate those awkward pauses, so we just chatter madly away, keeping the conversation going by force, if necessary. But while a few pleasantries can break the ice, burbling nervously can prevent you from hearing some important information.

It's not enough to zip your lip. To really listen, you need to keep your mind silent, too. During a stressful bargaining session, you'll probably feel compelled to counter every point of disagreement.

But if your mind is whirring as you formulate a brilliant rebuttal to the other side's last point, you're going to miss their next one. As Ronald M. Shapiro and Mark Jankowski admonish in *The Power of Nice:* "Listening is not waiting to talk."

To listen quietly and effectively, here are some tips.

⇢ *Give your opponent's words your full attention.*

When somebody says something that upsets you, you may be bursting to break in with a "But, but, but . . ." That's natural, but it's not smart.

Before every tough negotiation, Jeanette Wagner puts together a crib sheet of the points she wants to make and the questions she needs to have answered (such as, "Does he really want $5 million?"). After each question, she leaves plenty of space to write down clues dropped by her opponent. If he says something unexpected, unclear, or just plain untrue, she simply makes a note of it. She waits until she's heard the whole story before she crafts her response.

⇢ *Don't interrupt.*

Period. It's rude, and it annoys the speaker no end. Interrupting is only justifiable in an emergency. If you're not shouting "Fire!" shut up. (If you need practice in polite listening, some negotiating books suggest practicing at home with your family. Set yourself a goal; see if you can let Dad go through the whole rambling story of how he found the violin in the attic without interrupting him once.)

⇢ *Give nonverbal cues that show you're really tuned in.*

Nod your head, smile, and look her in the eye. When you let the speaker know you're fully engaged in what she's saying, it encourages her to share her thinking with you. The more you understand her thoughts and motives, the more likely you'll be to propose a satisfactory agreement.

Letting someone know that you're listening attentively can also ease a confrontational mood. When you're angry or upset, the mere presence of a sympathetic listener can be tremendously soothing. As

William Ury observes in *Getting Past No,* when you're negotiating, giving your opponent your full attention may be the only concession you make that doesn't cost you anything — so be generous.

→ *Acknowledge your opponent's strong feelings.*

Remember that nice hospital billing supervisor, and the way she let you blow off steam? After you thundered for three full minutes about those repeated bills for a prostate exam that you quite clearly never underwent, she suddenly giggled. "Yeah, I can see why that one would be a little annoying," she said. All at once you felt so much better. Finally you'd found someone who understood.

It's amazing how effective it is to respond supportively to someone's emotional tone, even if you disagree with their view of the facts. Comments like "I can see why you felt that way," or "If it were me, I would feel that way, too," can go a long way toward cooling things down.

→ *Listen for clues.*

That extremely good girl Agatha Christie made a fortune from her ability to tantalize readers by hiding clues in plain sight. When it's time to negotiate, think of her deceptively astute detective Miss Marple, and listen keenly. Sometimes your opponent is trying to tell you something.

Supreme Court Justice Ruth Bader Ginsburg says she's surprised at the number of lawyers who don't listen when they're arguing before the high court. Often, a sympathetic justice will ask a pointed question, signaling a potentially fatal flaw in the argument. Smart lawyers follow those bread crumbs; less savvy ones keep their heads stuck in their briefs. "A counsel too intent on a prepared script may miss that kind of cue," Ginsburg cautions.

→ *Pay attention to the pauses between the words.*

It's just as important to listen to precisely what people don't say. "You really have to keep your ears open to pick up subtle clues," says Sheila Wellington, who was the first woman to hold the office of Secretary of Yale University before she took over the reins at

Catalyst. While at Yale, she led a series of tense negotiations with the city of New Haven over how much the school should pay for city services.

During one meeting, city officials were pressing for financial concessions. In response, Sheila quietly mentioned an issue that had been a bone of contention for at least a decade. Two city streets ran through the center of the campus; the university wanted them closed to traffic, but city officials had always vetoed the idea. This time it was a little different. After she glancingly mentioned that the university might pay handsomely to close the streets, she says, "I just watched and listened. And they didn't say 'No' quick enough. You could hear a pin drop. I thought to myself, 'My goodness.'"

From that point on, she says, the issue was "in the air, in play." She let some time pass, then raised the question again. When she did, city officials were willing to discuss it. "It turned out that keeping the streets open to traffic had less value to the city than the actual cash Yale was willing to put up," she says. "It was a real breakthrough, and this was a cornerstone of our agreement."

➜ *Listen to the spirit, not just the words.*

"I've had to learn how to listen," admits Internet entrepreneur Susan DeFife. She admits she once let a potential deal fall through because she allowed her ego to muffle her ears. At the time, she was discussing a possible partnership with a company not much bigger than her own. "We're willing to help you along," the CEO said. DeFife bristled at his words. To her it sounded like he was pulling rank, condescending to her without admitting how much her company could bring to the possible merger.

"I think we both need to feel like we're getting something out of this," she snapped back. Later she realized her curt retort had offended her potential partner. He subsequently backed off the deal, saying he thought she lacked the flexibility necessary to form a successful partnership.

"That was an eye-opener," she says. "In retrospect, I wish I had realized what was being said there." Instead of assuming it was an insult, she says, she wishes she'd come back with a more neutral response, like, "What is it that you want, and how can I help you?"

➜ *Listen for points of agreement.*

Make notes of every instance in which your interests overlap. You can open with these when it's your turn to speak.

➜ *If you're part of a team, assign one member to be chief listener.*

Everybody on the team should keep her ears open. But freeing one person from the task of responding ensures that at least one person is completely focused on taking in all the important information your opponent is trying to convey.

➜ *Listen for new ideas.*

Negotiating is most exciting when all sides create something new — a solution that none of you would have been able to see on your own. If you aren't open to ideas from the other side of the table, you may miss many a golden opportunity.

➜ *When they're done, bite your tongue for a few moments.*

Don't rush to speak the minute you hear a pause. Given a bit of unexpected silence, someone may add something he hadn't originally planned to say. These comments can be the least guarded and therefore the most revealing.

➜ *Clarify, then repeat key points back to your opponent.*

When it's finally your turn to speak, don't begin by challenging your opponent's point of view. Instead, start with questions designed to clarify what he had to say, questions that begin, "What did you mean when you said . . . ?" or "Did I hear you say that . . . ?"

The farther apart you are, the more important it is to assure him that he has been heard and understood. If you got it right, that's great. If you didn't, this is his chance to clarify and correct. Repeat the process as many times as necessary, until you can restate his views to his satisfaction.

Telephone Tips

Have you ever been surprised by a call from your sister-in-law and then heard yourself agreeing to baby-sit their St. Bernard puppy while they go on a two-week vacation? Intentionally or not, she was using a well-worn negotiating technique — ambushing the other side with an unexpected phone call. She was prepared. You weren't. And your new rug is about to become history.

Our dear friend Martha, a freelance writer in Portland, absolutely refuses to be lured into it. When someone calls to talk business, she always insists on calling back. "I say, 'I just stepped out of the shower,' or 'My dog just threw up on my shoe.' Then I pick a time to call back that's good for me, when I'm calm, collected, and know what I want to say."

If you know you're facing an overly aggressive opponent — whether it's your mean old boss or that perpetually sunny room parent who wants you to organize a pancake breakfast — make the first call yourself. Have note cards ready if you need them. Now you have the advantage.

Keep a notepad beside the phone, and write down everything that's said. When you reach an agreement, write up a memo and send a copy to your phone friend. (This is important even if it's not a business call. If you're worried that the temple's Hebrew School coordinator might try to railroad you into taking over a class, find a cute little friendship card and send it to her — along with a note saying how much you're looking forward to substituting for the next two weeks and how sorry you are you can't fill in for the rest of the year.)

Keep in mind that negotiating over the phone isn't as win-win—friendly as a face-to-face meeting. If you're bartering over the phone, you can't pick up on nonverbal cues, or use your own arsenal of sympathetic nods, encouraging smiles, and faint grimaces. You can interpret silences and tones of voice, but you can't look deep into your opponent's eyes.

On the other hand, if you have trouble saying no when a smiling friend asks for one favor too many, then the less personal telephone may be your best tool. If only we good girls could figure out how to use the ✳ or # keys to make those tough calls for us . . .

→ *Remember: Listening in is different from giving in.*

As Dominick Barbara writes, "The good listener must believe himself before he can expect belief from others. He must believe in the value of his own ideas and feelings and be honest with himself and others. He must also assume responsibility for his actions and admit to his own shortcomings. In so doing, he will listen with inner strength and conviction."

SECRET WEAPON NO. 3: INTERPRETING NONVERBAL CUES

Anne Pope, now commissioner of the Tennessee Department of Commerce and Insurance, once scored a huge coup by listening with her eyes as well as her ears. As a lawyer for a business owner trying to sell his company, she met with a potential buyer. "He said he didn't need to buy the company," Pope recalls. But as he spoke, she noticed he was gripping both arms of the chair so tightly that his hands were turning red.

"My partner didn't notice," she says, so Anne alerted him during a private caucus. Once her team understood just how hungry the buyer really was, they changed their whole strategy and told the seller to hang on and hold out for more money. He got it. "I'll never forget it," she says. "It's amazing what you can pick up by watching."

Experts in nonverbal communication contend that only 35 percent of what we're communicating is conveyed by our words. The rest of the message comes through in physical gestures, facial expressions, and tone of voice.

A number of studies suggest that women have an edge when it comes to "hearing" what people are silently saying. But the real experts in this field seem to be women of color. Because body language can reveal hidden prejudices, scientists say, both women and minorities are sharply attuned to it.

That's hardly news to Christine James-Brown, president of United Way of Southeastern Pennsylvania. Even after twenty years of working for United Way, she still occasionally finds herself in meetings with corporate leaders who won't look her in the eye.

"Sometimes I'll try humor," Christine says ruefully. "I'll say something like, 'Is there something in your eye?'"

At other times she's more direct. She recalls one meeting with a corporate executive, set up by one of her staffers, a white male. During the first few minutes of the meeting, the executive looked and spoke only to her subordinate. Christine decided it was time to set the exec straight on who was boss. "I understand that you two worked on this until now," she said crisply, "but here are the things you and I have to discuss."

Christine says she pays close attention to subtle cues during negotiations. If an opponent leans away from her, for instance, she takes it as a sign that something is amiss. If he crosses his arms, she assumes he feels uncomfortable and is putting up a barricade. When she sees those subtle signs, she immediately tries to figure out what's going wrong. In one case of corporate crossed arms, she discerned that the executive felt uneasy about a particular project because he had no expertise in that area. "Don't worry," she reassured him. "We'll provide all the information you'll need on that." The executive calmed down and the talks resumed.

When she's negotiating, California town manager Susan George says, she's always heartened by signals that the other side is ready to take a step in her direction. "You can always tell when it happens," she marvels. "Sometimes it will be verbal — they'll say they've got to caucus privately with their side. Or they'll just say, 'Hmmmm.'" But sometimes a physical cue is all she needs to know that her point is being made. Maybe a tense negotiator who's been huddled over the table will unexpectedly relax and sit back in his chair. "Then you know they've started to nibble."

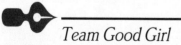

Team Good Girl

When you try to conjure up the image of a good girl, Bette Midler probably isn't the first person who pops into your mind. But when the Divine Miss M teamed up with some of New York City's most avid gardeners and conservationists, they wielded good girl power to save dozens of New York gardens from city bulldozers.

Team Good Girl (cont.)

Over the years, hundreds of tiny community gardens have sprung up in vacant lots throughout New York City. Community members see them as a source of solace and scenery in the cement wastes of the inner city. But Mayor Rudolph Giuliani thought New Yorkers would be better off if affordable housing were built on those empty sites. Bette, a New Yorker since 1994, has become deeply involved in improving the urban environment. Born and raised in the lush natural beauty of Hawaii, she found herself deeply distressed by the neglected state of many city parks and public spaces. So she set up her own organization, the New York Restoration Project, and also began working with other local environmental groups.

When the mayor announced a plan to auction off more than one hundred of the community gardens — some of them now beloved neighborhood landmarks more than twenty-five years old — Bette got steamed. But Mayor Giuliani turned a deaf ear.

So the garden lovers set out to win public sympathy for their plight. They held protests. Some protestors dressed up as tomatoes, sunflowers, and ladybugs to attract news cameras — and City Hall's grudging attention. With the auction deadline looming, Bette called the mayor's office and said, "All right, I'm tied to the railroad track and the train is coming. What do I have to do?"

The mayor's response was hardly encouraging. If Bette could come up with $4.2 million, the expected total from the auction, the city would be more than happy to sell the land to the conservationists.

The garden activists went to work. Bette secured a $1 million donation from the New York Restoration Project, and the Trust for Public Land pledged another $3 million. To meet the mayor's hefty price tag, Bette kicked in $250,000 of her own money. Their combined effort saved 112 of the gardens — and the glowing publicity given to their efforts may help to save hundreds more endangered gardens. (At this writing, a lawsuit filed to protect the gardens is still in court.)

Creativity in Numbers

Bette and the harried horticulturists proved that, in general, the more players you have on your side, the better. Research studies have found that teams of negotiators are more likely to find win-win solutions to complex problems. Even when you're flying solo, you're better off if there are extra bodies on the other side of the table; when there are more than two people involved, that generally results in better communication between the opposing sides, which raises your chances of finding a creative and satisfactory solution.

That certainly proved true for the garden rescuers, says Dave Lutz, executive director of the Neighborhood Open Space Coalition, a not-for-profit group dedicated to preserving, protecting, and educating about the city's public spaces. "There were many people operating independently, which gave the coalition flexibility, yet they could communicate with each other," Lutz says.

Joining together can also give you critical mass in tough situations. If you try to tackle a difficult problem on your own, your boss may show you the door. But if you raise a workplace issue with at least one other employee by your side, you're automatically protected by the federal National Labor Relations Act of 1935, notes Cindia Cameron, organizing director of 9to5, National Association of Working Women. If your superiors choose to retaliate rather than negotiate, they can be subject to an investigation by the National Labor Relations Board.

Team Tactics

While an army generally beats a single-combat warrior, keep some basics in mind to maintain a united front when you engage in group negotiating.

Communicate.

Dave Lutz says he believes a good communication strategy helped the New York activists to save the gardens. "We tried to see that as many people were talking to each other as possible. To keep all the various interested parties informed, the Neighborhood Open Space Coalition (NOSC) relied on its monthly online newsletter, *Urban Outdoors*. But as the deadline for the gardens' auction and destruction drew nearer, NOSC realized that community members who were offline needed to be in the loop. So they swiftly rounded up some donor support to create the *Community Garden Update*, a paper newsletter covering the crisis.

Communication is particularly important when the other side is attempting a divide and conquer strategy. It's very common for crafty negotiators to approach opponents separately and hand down this ultimatum: "Everybody else has signed. If you don't agree, you're out."

Use technology.

Equipping your team with the latest technology may translate into real power. When the National Association of Women Business Owners sent a

Team Good Girl (cont.)

delegation to the 1995 White House Conference on Small Business, entrepreneur Barbara Kasoff realized her company's interactive voicemail system could help tremendously. So she plugged everyone in the delegation into the system. That enabled the group's leaders to lasso its members onto the conference floor for critical votes, giving them influence far beyond their numbers, and helping them to shape the recommendations the conference eventually sent to Congress. NAWBO has continued to use electronic messaging to rally the troops before important votes in Congress, so members can call their representatives and lobby for their votes. "Our power now is phenomenal," Barbara claims. "No congressional committee holds hearings on our issues without calling us first. And when there is testimony, we are always invited to speak."

Don't fight in public.

It's likely that you'll have some differences with other members of your team. So get together before the negotiating session and decide what you want, what you need, and what you're willing to give away. As a negotiation goes on, you may find that you need to step back and reassess exactly what you all want. But take a break, so you can hash it out in private.

Play your part.

Figure out who's going to do what. Do you need a good cop and a bad cop? Someone to lead the negotiation? Another person to simply observe and take notes? "Be brutally honest as to people's strengths and weaknesses," advises Anne Pope, an attorney and experienced team negotiator. "Decide what each person's role is and absolutely stick to that."

Rehearse.

Run through your presentation before the actual bargaining session. If someone has trouble with his or her part, consider changing roles, or put together a fallback plan. Maybe the money expert on your team has trouble explaining things in clear, concise terms. If his presentation starts to dissolve into a complex matrix of numbers, wait until he takes a breath. Then say, "I agree with Michael" — and restate his position in plain English.

CHAPTER 4

●◆

PREP TIME

Be a good girl and do your homework."

We used to hear that every night after dinner, as the streetlights came on and the less conscientious kids lingered on the sidewalk for one last game of hopscotch. Back then, we sighed and pulled out our bookbags, knowing we'd rather miss a game or two than face that morning school bell nervous and unprepared.

Now that we're all grown up, however, we've developed an unfortunate tendency to skimp on our prep time, at least when that morning bell is calling us to the negotiating table. Yet if you don't do your homework, how do you expect to get an A?

Spare us the excuses. We know just how hard it can be to balance on that tightrope strung between office deadlines and family mealtimes, and just how easy it is to put your own agenda on hold as you madly try to meet everyone else's schedule demands. But your overcrowded calendar isn't the real reason that you're walking into job interviews and divorce mediation sessions unprepared. The real problem is the heavy stone of anxiety that drops into your stomach every time you think about facing down the opposition and advocating for yourself.

Certainly women aren't the only ones who close their eyes and whistle when it's time to prepare for a tough round of negotiating. I have an old college friend, now a physics professor at an Ivy League school, who cranks out dozens of academic publications each year and spends hours preparing his class lectures and conference presentations. Yet when it came time to prepare for his annual review, he devoted just a few moments between classes to thinking about his salary request. When his department head offered a small increase, he accepted it on the spot. Only later did he wonder whether he might have held out for a bit more.

But when it comes to coming in cold, nobody can beat a nice, sweet, completely unprepared good girl. Of course, good girls don't show up unprepared without a good excuse. "It made me so nervous, I couldn't think about it," is a great one. "I didn't know who to ask" is another favorite — although that usually means that we were too polite or too embarrassed to discuss such topics with our girlfriends. "Women talk about their sex lives, but it's taboo to talk about other things that are just as important to quality of life," observes former Colorado congresswoman Pat Schroeder. "We are going to have to get over that."

There's a cop-out for every stage of a good girl's life. "I don't want to hurt anybody's feelings," says the bride as she blithely signs up the first caterer she meets. "I don't know anybody in the field," says the college grad as she walks starry-eyed into her first salary talks. "I'm too exhausted," moans the young mother — although she always seems to find time to get those Halloween costumes finished. "I'm just lucky to have a job," says the mom returning to work when her kids hit kindergarten. "Once I get the title, the money will follow," says the manager on the eve of promotion. Then there's, "I don't want to rock the boat with my retirement just around the corner." If you go through life without doing your homework, you'll eventually end up paying too much for your coffin. (Don't laugh; Beth's grandmother did precisely that.)

Information is power. And at the bargaining table, power is money. Entering a negotiating session ill informed and unready is like being caught in a blackout without a flashlight; you'll find yourself groping in the dark, depending on dumb luck to avoid falling flat on your face.

"What's the thing we fail at most? We don't plan and prepare sufficiently," says Stanford business professor Margaret Neale. Naive souls walk in all spontaneous and unrehearsed, then assume they fell short because the other guy was just quicker on his feet. They don't realize how dramatically the odds of success drop when you're facing a better-informed opponent.

This is one area where all the experts agree. "There is no substitute for effective preparation," writes William Ury in *Getting Past*

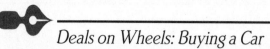

Deals on Wheels: Buying a Car

When it's time for Beth to buy a car, she goes through five predictable stages: denial, anger, bargaining, depression, and acceptance. But car buying doesn't have to be a near-death experience for good girls. With a little research (and a few hours spent on the Internet), you can find the right car at the right price — at the right dealership. Don't give your hard-earned money to a dealer who treats you with disrespect. If a car salesman makes you feel dumb or distressed, pick up your purse and leave.

Don't procrastinate.

If your car is stolen or totaled in an accident, you might need to buy a new one unexpectedly. But more often you get plenty of advance warning that your car is on its last set of tires. If you're shelling out $200 to $300 in car repairs every month or so, it's time to make the rounds of the auto dealerships. Don't put it off until the last minute. You can't make a calm, studied decision when you've just been told that the engine needs a $2,700 overhaul and you're planning to drive to your grandmother's eighty-fifth birthday party in Kentucky the day after tomorrow.

Do your homework.

You don't have to understand all of the gearhead gibberish they use to intimidate you at the dealership. Quite frankly, there are plenty of intelligent people (many of them male) who couldn't tell a MacPherson strut from an Electric Slide. Just ask your girlfriends what cars they drive, whether they like them, and why. If their transportation needs are similar to yours, they'll be an excellent resource. Use the Internet to look at cars in your preferred category — station wagons, compacts, minivans, whatever. Jot down the names and specs of the ones that take your fancy, then click on www.edmunds.com. This reader-friendly site offers detailed information from manufacturers, plus car magazine reviews and candid comments from people who bought the models you're considering. *Consumer Reports* magazine offers a fairly realistic idea of what you should spend on a basic model, and is a good resource for safety information. If you don't mind investing a few dollars, you can subscribe to Consumer Reports Online and save yourself a trip to the library.

Buying a Car (cont.)

Set your target price.

Don't venture onto the lot until you've set your target price. Be bold about asking for discounts; one research group claims the average car buyer pays 11.3 percent under sticker price. Start with www.autobytel.com or www.carpoint. msn.com. They'll usually connect you to dealers who will give you quotes via e-mail. (If a dealer insists that you come in to talk price, forget it.) Don't assume the e-mail price is the best you can do. One recent study found that online buyers actually pay above-average prices for their cars. Instead, shop around in your area and use that e-mail quote to negotiate a better price offline.

Don't buy the invoice ploy.

Overwhelmed by your negotiating skill, the salesman throws up his hands and offers you the car at invoice price. You smile, put out your hand, and clinch the deal. And the salesman goes back to his manager's office and turns cartwheels. That's because the invoice doesn't really reflect the dealer's cost. Thanks to manufacturers' rebates, allowances, and other incentive awards, the invoice price generally includes a hidden profit of 10 to 20 percent. So feel free to ask for a below-invoice price. If you've fallen in love with a hot new model, you may not be able to get much lower. But it's worth a try.

Find your own financing.

Call your bank or credit union to get prequalified for a loan before you shop. Be wary of car dealership financing. One recent investigation found that dealers industrywide were stacking hidden finance costs onto consumers' car loans. If you want to take advantage of a dealer's special financing package, take the paperwork home and read it carefully before you sign.

Don't let yourself be shamed into taking a bad deal just because you've had some credit problems in the past. And don't get steamrolled into buying credit insurance, to pay off the loan in case of death or disability. It's expensive and usually unnecessary. If you're worried, you're probably better off getting a regular life insurance policy.

Leave the kids at home.

For every dollar you spend on baby-sitting, you're likely to save $100. Most car dealerships are purposely set up to be kid-unfriendly. They know that if you've got two whiny kids tugging at your skirt, you'll sign anything to get a car and get out of there. Beth's friend Heather learned this lesson when she bought her minivan. As they were drawing up the final papers, her doctor-husband's beeper went off and he was called in to the hospital — leaving Heather stuck there with two toddlers and no car. She told the car salesman exactly what she did — and didn't — want, then hastily signed all the paperwork, rounded up the kids, took the new car, and went home. But a few weeks later, when she was filing the paperwork, she realized the salesman had taken advantage of her distraction to sneak in hundreds of dollars of extras — such as overpriced extended warranties — that she had specifically refused.

Hang on to your keys.

Unbelievable as it may seem, one hallowed car salesman ploy is to take your car keys (so the "guys in back" can check out its trade-in value), then "lose" them until you've signed the papers for the new vehicle. If this happens to you, don't mess around; demand your keys, then leave forever. And warn all your friends never to go near that dealership.

Take notes.

Bring a notebook to every dealership and write down the offered price for everything — not just the basic vehicle, but also the options and financing costs. Tell them up front that you're just shopping. Don't disclose your target price; make them tell you their price first. Watch what you say, and don't let them squeeze information out of you.

Take a nice, long test-drive.

I always feel kind of silly when I take a test-drive. I never know what I'm supposed to be testing, and the salesman is usually nattering away about stuff like racks and pinions — which, to me, sound like torture devices. So I usually circle around the block a couple of times, then head back to the dealership.

That's understandable, but it's not smart. If you take a long test-run, you'll often discover those little (and big) things that drive you nuts after you buy a car. So take it out on the road. Bring it up to expressway speed; do you have enough power to merge without terror? Take it home and pull into your driveway. Can you open the doors inside your garage? Ask some grown-up friends

Buying a Car (cont.)

to sit in the backseat. Roll down the windows. Go through a toll booth. Be sure this is a car you can live with.

Skip the service contract.

If you're replacing a sickly old car, a service contract may sound like a wonderful idea. Over the past year, you've poured thousands of unexpected dollars into your old clunker, and you never want to be in that spot again. But before you agree to the service contract, take it home, read it carefully, and think it over. Generally, the service contract doesn't give you much more coverage than the manufacturer's warranty. It also doesn't cover a lot of standard wear and tear, such as new brake shoes. You may also run into problems if you want to cancel or get a refund. (Similarly, rust-proofing and fabric protection increase your price without adding much long-term value to the car.)

Get your mechanic's approval.

Never buy a used car without having a trusted mechanic look it over first. Period. There are some red flags you can see for yourself, such as evidence of crash damage or severe rust. But you'll still need your mechanic's approval — and the $75 to $100 he'll charge could save you thousands.

Negotiate the trade-in separately.

Never allow a car salesman to put together a slick package of new car purchase, trade-in, and financing. I almost guarantee you there's at least $1,000 in extra charges hiding somewhere in there. Don't even mention a trade-in when you start negotiating. If the guy asks, tell him you think you might want to hang on to it, or give it to your sister, or something.

If you made a good deal on the purchase, expect a lowball on your trade-in. They know you're likely to accept it because you don't want to go through the hassle of selling the car yourself. To protect yourself, know the value of your old car before you walk in the dealership's door. (Look it up in *Consumer Reports,* or in the *Kelley Blue Book* or its Web site, www.kbb.com.) As another option, consider selling your old car to CarMax. After a thirty-minute appraisal, they'll give you a firm offer, whether or not you're buying the replacement from them.

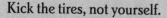

Kick the tires, not yourself.

Buying a car can be complicated. Despite your best efforts, you may not get the best possible deal your first time out. Don't despair; you'll learn and improve with every purchase. Just keep your head, stay calm and confident — and don't sign anything until you've taken it home to read it!

No. "The more difficult the negotiation, the more intensive your preparation needs to be."

That sounds pretty grim. But you don't have to turn the walk-up to every negotiation into exam week. Yes, you may have to make a few trips to the library. But you'll also be spending time fantasizing about what you want, grilling your better-informed friends, and exhibiting your hidden dramatic talents in role-playing sessions. You may even need to learn a song or two. Sylvia Rhone, CEO of Elektra Records, used her musical knowledge to beat out competitors Columbia and Epic in signing the hot music group Third Eye Blind. "She knew the lyrics to our songs," marvels lead singer Stephan Jenkins. Was she really a great fan of 3EB — or was she just a good girl who did her homework? Only Sylvia knows for sure.

To make your work easier, we've divided your prep school curriculum into three core subjects — the Other Guy, the Big Picture, and the Likely Options. Tackle them in that order, because the more you know about the other side and the larger context, the more effective you'll be at putting together your winning strategy.

THE OTHER GUY

When Beth was about ten years old, she got a wonderful Christmas present — that cool new board game Mystery Date. The object of the game, if she remembers right, was to go around the board collecting accessories for your dream date — maybe a swimsuit and towel for an afternoon on the beach, or a parka and skis for a day on the slopes. When you had all your appropriate paraphernalia in hand, you'd open the little door in the middle of the board. And there — if you were lucky — was revealed the date of your dreams. But if you weren't so favored, you'd be all set for a romantic swim, only to open the door to a Prom King. Or worse yet, you'd open the door and find the Dud, a bespectacled geek. (He probably went on to become a Silicon Valley millionaire, but that's another story.)

In a way, preparing to negotiate is like playing a round of Mystery Date. You have to make sure you've got the right cards in hand before you open the door and meet your perfect (or not-so-perfect) match. So, as the commercials crooned, "Girls, are *you* ready for your Mystery Date?" You'd better be. Just thank your lucky stars that in real life, you usually get to sneak a peek behind the door before you commit yourself to a date at the negotiating table.

"You can never know too much about the person with whom you will negotiate," advises Gerard Nierenberg in *The Art of Negotiating*. Sometimes that little bit of extra knowledge is all you need to set yourself apart from the competition. Beth stumbled onto this a few years ago, when she was up for a magazine job. Preoccupied with finding the right suit, she just didn't make the time to check out the editor who would be conducting the interview. Over lunch she babbled nervously about how much she'd always loved the magazine. "I still remember this one terrific piece that ran years ago," she said. "It was about hospital emergency rooms and the trauma care system." As it turned out, that candid remark was inspired by the angels who watch over good girls and fools. The editor's face changed, and he looked deeply into her eyes, to make sure she was sincere. "I wrote that piece," he said. "I think it's one of the best things I've ever done." Needless to say, she got the job.

Doing your homework doesn't just impress your opponent. It can also help you to figure out what the other side is looking for, and what they might be willing to give up to get it. Before Estée Lauder's Jeanette Wagner sits down to negotiate with someone, she says, "I call everyone I know who was ever involved with them or did a deal with them." (And remember — you probably don't have too many secrets from your adversaries. "If they are any good," warns Jeanette, "they'll have done the same thing about you.")

If you feel shy about interrogating strangers, think about those proverbial six degrees of separation. Most likely you know somebody who knows somebody who knows the person you're going to face. Once you've dropped the name of a mutual acquaintance, you'll be surprised at just how much people are willing to reveal. Beth once called an acquaintance to get some advance tips before negotiating a fee with a public relations executive. "Make sure you talk to him before noon," her source advised. "After lunch he's usually too drunk to remember what you agreed, and you'll have to iron out the deal all over again when he's sober."

Make a list of questions before you call. How does she typically operate? What does she care about? What is she willing to give away? What tactics have swayed her in the past? Does she have the authority to approve a final agreement? What tactics does she employ? Remember — style can be as important as substance.

"Some people throw out outrageous demands," says Scholastic Inc. executive vice president Deborah Forte, who oversees the deals that transform *The Magic School Bus* series and other popular children's titles into television fare. "If you know ahead of time that's characteristic, you won't be thrown off."

Master negotiators say no personal detail is insignificant. Harvey Mackay, author of the bestseller *Swim with the Sharks Without Being Eaten Alive,* keeps a sixty-six-point profile of every one of his customers, tracking everything from physical characteristics (including baldness and bad backs) to religion and basic personality traits. It may seem nosy. But you never know what detail will be significant. So check out everything you can. Where did she grow up? Where did she go to school? Where else has she worked? If she's an artist, where's her studio? If she's a philanthropist, what are her pet causes? What are her interests, her hobbies, her passions? A savvy attorney we know tries to schedule her appearances before one particular judge on Friday afternoons. "He raises show dogs, and he goes out to his farm every weekend," she says. "I know he likes to get an early start to beat the weekend traffic. So if I keep it short and sweet, I'm halfway to winning my case."

You may find that people who have struck out with your opponent are your best resources. "Frequently you will learn as much, or more, about people from their failures as from their successes," writes Gerard Nierenberg in *The Art of Negotiating.* "If you carefully analyze the reasons that a certain deal fell through or a negotiation failed, you will probably get a good understanding of how the opponent thinks, his method of operating, his psychological approach." (Just don't assume that every word you hear is gospel. Circumstances change, and not every source is reliable. My friend Linda was drooling over a house in her suburb that looked just perfect. Too shy to approach the owner directly, she asked a mutual friend whether it might be for sale. "Oh, she'll never sell that house," the friend said firmly. "I asked her about it once, and she said no way." Disappointed, Linda decided to look elsewhere — then kicked herself when she saw a moving van in front of her dream house six months later.)

Library Time

Don't despair if your best efforts fail to turn up an actual person who can give you the inside scoop. Spending an hour or so at the library or on the Internet may give you the information you need. Even the help wanted section can provide a clue or two: job descriptions, titles, salary ranges. (If an interesting job has been open twice before in the past year, that tells you something important, too; either this company promotes rapidly from inside, or the immediate supervisor is an unbearable horror. You'll definitely want to know more before you walk in the door.) Look for newspaper clippings and old magazine articles profiling your opponent. Trade publications are often full of information you're looking for.

Check out the company's annual report and familiarize yourself with the basics, things like corporate strategy, the organization's divisions, key executives, annual sales and revenues — and whether profits are going up or down. The annual reports are available by request from the company's investor relations department and are often posted on company Web sites. Other revealing sources are court records; they'll usually detail judgments against your opponent, and may provide a wealth of information about what was used as evidence. Ask the court records clerk for help, or find a legal librarian willing to walk you through a search of Lexis or Westlaw, the two electronic searching services for lawyers.

For general information online, we love www.hoovers.com, which gives capsule profiles of most major companies. For a fee you can also get Hoover's detailed report on the company you have in mind.

These days, most companies and nonprofit groups maintain their own Web sites full of useful items, such as press releases from the past year and short bios of top executives.

Don't focus solely on your target. Check out the competition, too. When New York–based writer and president of Mediabistro. com Laurel Touby decided to ask her dry cleaner for a discount, she first paid a visit to all the other cleaners within walking distance of her Greenwich Village apartment and asked for a list of their rates. Just as she suspected, her guy was charging more than most of his competitors. But since Laurel liked him, she decided to show him the results of her research and ask him to lower his fees. "I said, 'I'd love to stay with you, and I expect to spend a lot of money on dry cleaning in the next year. Is there any way you can give me a break, if not on all items, at least on some of them?'" she recounts. Her research paid off handsomely. "From then on, when I went in, I always got this special price" — about a dollar off on every garment, which adds up over a year's worth of wool suits and linen dresses.

Are you competing against other candidates for the same contract or job? In that case, any intelligence you can get on your own competitors also may be useful. Beth's friend Nell was desperately looking for a new job in Chicago. (Her mom's health was starting to fail, so she wanted to come back home.) Nell has years of experience in her field; she's also warm, friendly, and generally delightful. As a well-connected hometown girl, she had a small core of eager informants everywhere she interviewed who let her know what the hiring execs were looking for, and who the competition was. So when she walked into the interview, she could subtly highlight the skills she had that the other guys did not. Nell found the job of her dreams and even talked her new boss into a signing bonus.

If you stop and think a minute, you may not have to do all your own sleuthing. Try to think of someone whose job it might be to know precisely the information you want. If you're trying to buy a house and you're curious about how much the sellers originally paid for it, call the local tax assessor's office; that information is generally available in public records.

Is your parent group negotiating with your school principal to fund a program for gifted students? Call the board of education and ask about similar initiatives in your district. Ask your friend's sister at the teachers union for some background information; does the teachers' current contract hold any provisions that might help out your side? Contact the local education reporter. Maybe he can tell you how your principal has dealt with similar issues in the past.

Is your church's pastor balking at the idea of starting a nursery school? Trust me, as a minister's daughter, I can tell you there are probably several levels of hierarchy between him and God. Call your denomination's national headquarters. The church may have a policy calling for more outreach to working parents; there might even be some seed money available.

Make sure you don't overlook the information that may be lying right at your feet. Review your own office files for previous encounters with these same opponents.

No matter what you're trying to achieve, you can only benefit by considering the upcoming negotiation from your opponent's point of view. If you don't, you'll look stupid. And you might walk out empty-handed. When Beth was leading a negotiation seminar for writers a few years ago, she cringed at the story told by one hapless freelancer. For the past six or seven years, he'd been doing a small annual project for a local publishing company. Every year, the editor called him up, and every year the writer asked for a little raise. So when the editor called last year, he asked for his standard raise as a matter of routine. The editor's voice chilled. "I'll get back to you," he said. When the callback came, the news was bad. "We've decided to use someone else," the editor said. "It's been great working with you. Good luck." If only that writer had put in five minutes of research on his longtime customer, he would have found that the publisher's segment of the market had tanked and the company had just laid off dozens of employees — definitely the wrong time to ask for a raise. By his ill-timed and insensitive request, the writer revealed how out of the loop he really was.

Block Those Assumptions

Whatever you do, don't let a bunch of unfounded assumptions about your opponent lead you into making some fundamental mistakes. Most important, don't go in there underestimating the other side.

Never — ever — assume you're smarter than they are. "It's a mistake to go in thinking, 'Those jerks, I'm going to wipe the floor with them.' You've got to figure they're as smart and perceptive as you are," warns Catalyst's Sheila Wellington — and most times, they are.

Don't let a smart opponent scare you. If you're facing somebody sharp, consider yourself lucky. And if you're embarking on complex negotiations that involve many issues, you're extrafortunate if they are smarter than you. The smarter the team members are, the more likely they are to reach an agreement. Bruce Barry and Ray Friedman, professors at Vanderbilt University's Owen Graduate School of Management, proved that point in a study of hundreds of students. The students were put through a complex simulated negotiation between a shopping mall developer and a potential retail tenant, and were asked to hammer out an intricate agreement.

Experienced women negotiators know firsthand how dangerous it is to make false assumptions about the other side; they've been underestimated by their male opponents for years. "I'm frequently underestimated," smiles Sheila Wellington. "Maybe it's my age, or maybe it's because I'm polite. They think I'm one of those nice polite little old ladies."

Whitney Johns Martin still chuckles about the time she and her male business partner were meeting a Chicago investment banker at a Nashville restaurant. While Whitney was powdering her nose, the banker showed up, so the maitre d' showed him and Whitney's partner to their waiting table. Whitney returned, and followed.

"Why is she following us?" the investment banker asked her partner. "That's Whitney," he replied. The Chicagoan had assumed Whitney was a man, and thought someone was pulling his leg. He demanded that Whitney prove her identity by showing him her driver's license. When she produced her ID, "he turned so red I could have negotiated his pants off," she says.

THE BIG PICTURE

Don't limit your research to the opposing side. Find out everything you can that might affect your bargaining position. You'll find that knowing your subject inside and out makes you feel more confident and impresses the heck out of the other side.

Consider jewelry maker Dorn Cheske. When she's buying pearls, she makes the oyster her world. By cultivating a reputation as a dogged researcher, Dorn strikes fear into the hearts of pearl dealers around the world. A former Booz Allen & Hamilton management consultant, Dorn doesn't bid on pearls until she knows "exactly what millimeter I want, what grade, and what amount. I practically demand to know what oyster they came out of," she reports. "I get a fair price because they know I will always query about everything. I want the best. I don't want to fool around."

She does the same intensive research when she goes shopping for cars, first digging at the library, then visiting with the dealer's mechanics. "If I've read about a design flaw in the engine or the air conditioning system in *Consumer Reports,* for instance, I ask them to tell me about it. They either explain what the problem is or tell me that the magazine made a mistake. The salesmen don't like it, but it's a good way to find out more, and the mechanics are flattered. How often do they get someone back there to ask their opinion? I find they're honest and helpful," she says with a smile.

Even at the grocery store, Dorn never lets up. "When I buy produce, I want the best tomato," she admits. She may be high-maintenance, but the produce clerks know she means business. "It's gotten to the point that when they see me, they say, 'Oh God, here she comes again. Just give her the best ones.' "

Of course it's one thing to intimidate the grocery clerks with your exhaustive knowledge of the daikon radish. It's another thing to go eye-to-eye with a grocery chain. But once again, the information is out there. Sometimes all it takes is one telephone call to the right source. Cindia Cameron, of 9to5, National Association of Working Women, tells the story of a clerical worker who worked odd hours at a Michigan hospital. When she got pregnant, she was told she didn't qualify for maternity leave because she often worked fewer than twenty-five hours a week. Upset, she called 9to5 to ask for help. They told her to add up her hours over the last fifty weeks.

When she sat down with her pay stubs, she realized she'd worked 1,250 — or precisely twenty-five hours a week. That was the amount she needed to qualify for benefits under the federal Family Leave Act. Armed with that information, the clerk got her benefits. Then she shared what she'd learned with a pregnant friend in a similar job. Thanks to the two women's well-informed, effective advocacy, the hospital then corrected its policy, clarifying which part-time workers were covered.

It was 9to5 to the rescue again in the case of a Nashville accountant who hit the roof when she discovered that a male coworker with precisely the same job title was getting paid $2,000 more than she was. She thought that was wrong, even though he had a college degree and she didn't. When she called 9to5, they told her that federal law was on her side. So she got a copy of the Equal Pay Act and "put it down on the table," Cindia reports. "I don't think you want me to sue," she told her boss. She soon got a $2,000 raise.

What's It Worth?

Most of the time, the big issue you'll be researching is money: who's got it, who needs it, how much is out there, and what's a fair price. If you don't have that information before you go in, you've already lost. And if you're well informed about what the market will bear, you're halfway to getting what you want.

Lori Scott, the merchandise director for a mail-order catalog, says that knowing her manufacturers' costs and profit margins helps her to calculate win-win deals. "I pretty much know where my opposition stands, and how far I can push them," she says. "You need to be sure you get what you want out of a deal, but you also need to be realistic about how far you're going to be able to push that person. If my target is 35, and they start out at 40 and work back to 38, I'll take it." That's because she wants to make sure her vendors see her as a prized client and put her orders first. "You build relationships with manufacturers. You're not there to burn them at the stake. If you treat them good, they'll treat you good, and you'll get your product."

If you're selling something, advises business development coach Sue Yellin, get a reading on what your potential buyer is willing to pay before you set your price. "Don't shoot blind," she says. You'll be surprised at how often your opponent is willing to state a ballpark price. "What's the range? You need a frame of reference, so the number you plug in is realistic."

Syndicated columnist Sandra Pesmen lets her customers name their own price, at least to begin. "When price is the key factor, you're often guessing what they're willing to pay, and if you guess wrong, you lose the whole deal." So she often asks newspaper editors, "What do you pay other columnists? You name the figure, and I'll see if I can come down to it."

Of course your opponent may have heard that same piece of advice. You may have to rely on outside sources to figure out the appropriate price range. But make sure you're getting your information from knowledgeable sources, not just that circle of sweet, naive good girls who make up your social circle.

Consider the case of Jane, a nice Iowa woman who works as a commercial artist. At the request of a New York City–based art director, she was putting together a proposal to design a logo for a major new product. Before computing her fee, she called one of her friends, who had done similar work for local clients. With that input, she named her price: $3,000.

A few days after she faxed in her proposal, she got a call from the art director. "Let me tell you who else I've asked to bid, and what they've asked for," he said. Jane was shocked (and flattered) to learn that she was competing with two of the best-known artists in her field, one of them based in New York, the other in Los Angeles. The other two bids were roughly the same, the art director said. Both came in around $21,000. Jane almost dropped the phone. "I'm going to give you until morning to work up another bid," the helpful art director said. That night Jane put together a smarter bid: $14,000. Ultimately the company picked one of the other artists, but Jane remains grateful to the art director who took time to set her straight.

Sports agent Tom George was determined not to make the opposite mistake and overreach when he tried to secure Sheryl Swoopes's first endorsement contract. At the time, twenty-three-year-old Sheryl was working as a bank clerk, despite the NCAA championship Most Outstanding Player trophy she had sitting at home. The WNBA hadn't yet been founded, and the former college star had no place to play. But Sheryl was still a legend to young female players, and Tom wanted Wilson Sporting Goods to make a deal. He also knew that her previous agent hadn't been able to secure a deal, and he didn't want to throw another air ball.

So he calculated roughly what Wilson made on women's size basketballs each year, and decided to ask for a percentage of that. "Women's basketballs are a commodity, and the volume doesn't change much from year to year," Tom explained. "No matter how big the fish, it doesn't change the size of the pond." The result: a modest five-figure request.

"We can do a deal at that number," Tom's contact at Wilson replied swiftly. Normally such a quick yes would have put Tom immediately into the throes of "winner's curse," the torment that afflicts a negotiator who believes he demanded too little. But Tom knew his research had put him in the right ballpark (or, in this case, inside the three-point stripe). And Sheryl was thrilled. At that time in her career, says Tom, it was "a significant chunk of change."

Don't undervalue your worth in the marketplace, but don't be ridiculous. Asking for the moon without checking out the market is just plain foolish. My friend Kate, a self-employed Atlanta publicist, got a call a few years ago from a middle-sized New York company that wanted someone to oversee its corporate communications department.

After years of scrambling to find clients, Kate thought she was finally going to grab the brass ring. The first interviews went wonderfully. Within a week, they'd offered her the position and arranged to fly her out to talk about compensation.

She called me before she headed north, to rehearse her salary demands. I remember listening with a sinking heart as she detailed her demands: a six-figure salary, a housing allowance, a month of vacation time, and a company car. "That sounds like a bit much," I said hesitantly. "Have you done any research on this?"

"This is what the traffic will bear. You're just not thinking in New York terms." Maybe I wasn't — but neither were her prospective employers. They listened politely, then explained they couldn't possibly meet her terms and said farewell. If only she'd done some market research, she could have come in with a reality-based set of salary objectives. Then, once she'd dazzled them with her creativity and style, she could have started ratcheting up her pay.

Bettina Richards, thirty-four, a former executive for a major record company, says you need a sense of "where you are and what your leverage is." Bettina's label, Thrill Jockey Records, spends only a few thousand dollars to record each album. When she first started out, she accepted terms from Japanese and European record distributors that she'd laugh at today. "We were an unknown quantity, and we were happy to get records out there," she explains. "That was years ago. Now we have a sales history, so we have the leverage to ask for more."

Let's get this straight. We're absolutely not telling you to make modest requests to avoid getting turned down. But we are stressing how important it is to know your market before you start making demands. Think of Dr. Evil in the Austin Powers movies. A sixties-vintage villain, he's been cryogenically frozen for thirty years before thawing out in the nineties. In classic movie-villain style, he threatens to blow up the world unless he receives a princely ransom. Unfortunately, poor Dr. Evil makes a classic negotiating error. Without considering the current evil-villain market, he asks the world's leaders of the nineties for a staggering sum: $1 million. No problem, the chuckling world leaders immediately agree. It takes some coaching from Dr. Evil's savvier henchmen before he sets a more market-appropriate ransom figure of $100 billion.

After that experience, you'd think he'd learn his lesson. But when the sequel sends Dr. Evil back to the sixties, he asks the world leaders for $100 billion. Again they laugh; there isn't that much money in the world. It's sad to think that Dr. Evil will probably make the same mistake in *Austin Powers 3*.

Austin (Texas) Power

Minerva Martinez learned the value of research when her husband announced he was being transferred from El Paso to Austin, 550 miles away. It was a good move for him, but Minerva didn't want to leave her job as a probation officer in the West Texas Community Supervision and Corrections Department.

She saw one glimmer of hope. Four times each year, the department sent workers to Austin to check on prisoners who had been sentenced to drug treatment facilities. Each checkup required

The Check's in the Mail: Negotiating with Liars

Here's a reality check. As much as we hate to tell you this, honesty forces us to share this sad fact: people tell lies. And when they're negotiating, they may tell lots of them.

Lynda Obst learned this hard lesson when she became a Hollywood producer. In her book *Hello, He Lied, and Other Truths from the Hollywood Trenches,* she details just how wary a negotiator has to be, both in and out of Tinseltown.

"I think every negotiation is a poker game," Obst says. "You have to presume that everyone's lying, with the implicit understanding that 10 percent of their claims may be true."

At first Obst was horrified to realize that the guys across the table were telling whoppers. "It was terrifying when I first learned everyone was bluffing." She realized she was going up against men who spent their weekends playing high-stakes poker, while she'd grown up playing genteel games of gin rummy.

But over time, she learned how to get in the game — a transition made easier by a childhood spent playing sports with her two brothers. "That was really a great help," she says. She had watched them "psyching out" their opponents, and recognized that was precisely what was happening at the negotiating table. "I realized this was a good skill to bring to the table, and it's something most girls don't have. We don't think bluffing and boasting are so cool."

That doesn't mean that Obst has turned to the dark side and started piling it higher and deeper than her male counterparts. It means that she now approaches the table with more sophistication and much less girlish trust. "The goal is to take off those rose-colored glasses," she says. "You have to make the presumption that the other side is bluffing, and not go in with a naive posture which undercuts you when you're stunned to learn you've been hoodwinked."

The first task, she says, is to do your homework ahead of time. "Somebody may actually be holding a good hand. You need to do some intelligence gathering to find out." Make a few phone calls, and do a little background work. Are there really two other people up for this job, or are they just trying to make you feel insecure in hopes of reducing your price?

When real information isn't available, you have to put up your radar and try to figure out where reality lies. "If you can't get the proper intelligence factoids,

Negotiating with Liars (cont.)

you can sort of tap into the rhythm of the room," Obst says. "They can say they have 3,000 applications on file. If that's true, you'd better turn on the charm. But if they keep asking more and more questions, and they seem really interested in all your skills, it may be their goal to get you for the cheapest possible price. You have to use your women's intuition: Does he want me more than I want him?"

Once you've got information, Obst says bluntly, "you need to have some girls' balls. You need to have some courage. That comes from an inner confidence that you can walk away from a negotiation. You have to know your value in a situation, and define the boundaries of what you'll accept, and what you won't accept."

And if you're desperate, you need to put on a poker face and keep your cards close to your chest. "Never let your desperation be obvious. They have to believe you would walk away."

In addition to knowing how to bluff, Obst says, "you have to know when to fold. The important thing with girls is not to fold too early, and not to be so emotional that you never fold." Just don't play hard to get, she warns. "You can hold out for so long that they go away." (Obst admits that a poker face has never been her strongest suit. "I'm so passionate about my work that I always show my hand," she says. While her opponents can tell that she's wild about a particular script or director, they also know she's a smart businesswoman who isn't going to spend money foolishly. "For me to be a good producer, I have to know the top price I can pay for that script. In a way, that's just developing a head to match your heart.")

In dealing with a bluffer, Obst says, don't take it personally. It may be hard for a good girl to sit down across from a smiling guy who's lying through his teeth. But if he's got something you want, it's silly to get all huffy. Instead, be calm and businesslike, and don't let them play with your mind.

If you know that bluffing doesn't work for you, she says, "have someone help you negotiate — a partner, a lawyer, a best friend." If you can't call in reinforcements, then get off the playing field, fast, before you get your arm twisted into making a deal that's wrong for you. "I think you can be demure and say, 'This is very difficult for me; I have to think about it.'"

"Always, in these circumstances, be yourself," Obst says. "Know your own strength. You don't have to make a big play in the room. You can take power back by being gracious and demure. I don't think we have to mimic male behavior. We just have to find our best protective coloration so we can't be exploited, and we're not being dumb."

a couple of grueling days on the road. It occurred to Minerva that she might offer to do all those site visits after she moved to Austin. "It seemed like a perfect solution," she says.

Minerva's radical idea got the expected bureaucratic response: "You can't do that. That's not the way it's done."

Undeterred, Minerva did some research. She figured out the average bill for airfare, hotels, car rentals, and other expenses for each Austin trip and added in the extra revenues she could bring in by keeping tabs on El Paso prisoners who had been transferred to halfway houses in Austin. She realized her proposal could save her department "tens of thousands of dollars."

When she presented her plan, everybody agreed it made sense all the way around. The moral, according to Minerva: "Even if you work for the government, if you have a good idea and you know it, persistence and good research really pay off."

YOUR OPTIONS

Once you have a good idea of what to expect, it's time to plan your own strategy. Grab a pad of paper and let's go step by step.

➜ Step 1: Clarify your position.

First state your objective in one simple sentence, no more than fifteen words long. Some examples:

"I want to buy that house for $300,000."

"I want a promotion and a 5 percent raise within six months."

"I want my son to do his own laundry."

You'll be surprised at how many complex negotiations boil down to some very basic points. Even if you're facing a wide-ranging array of issues, you should have a short list of key goals.

Then look at your objective and imagine yourself coming out a winner. Okay, I can see you rolling your eyes. But if you can't see yourself scoring your point, there's no use trying. And if you let your imagination carry you away, you may think up some useful strategies on the trip.

Silent screen star Mary Pickford, whose trademark golden curls adorned an extremely sharp business head, started using this technique successfully when she was just fifteen, Eileen Whitfield writes in *Pickford: The Woman Who Made Hollywood*. The ambitious young actress was determined to meet Broadway producer David Belasco. In her daydreams, Pickford imagined herself slumping in a make-believe faint at Belasco's feet. Taken aback, the chivalrous producer would kneel at her side, trying desperately to rouse her back to consciousness. Then she would open her wide sparkling eyes and blushingly admit she'd been faking. Overwhelmed by the girl's incredible acting ability, Belasco would pull a contract out of his pocket and sign her up on the spot. The whole melodramatic scene depended on a key opening line: "My life depends on seeing Mr. Belasco!"

To transform her fantasy into reality, Mary wandered up and down Broadway, breathlessly repeating the line to everyone she met. Eventually Belasco heard about the single-minded teenager and became so curious he agreed to meet her. The fainting scene never took place. But a few months later, she had her first contract.

Salesman Harvey Mackay used a similar technique to sustain him through a seven-year effort to raise $75 million for a new baseball stadium in Minneapolis. When things seemed hopeless, he fantasized himself throwing out the first ball of the season under the new dome. "Not the mayor, not the governor, not Joe DiMaggio, but me," he revealed in *Swim with the Sharks*. And that's exactly what happened. "I came to realize that fantasizing, projecting yourself into successful situations, is one of the most powerful means there is to achieve personal goals."

Your vision may be more mundane: A Thanksgiving spent in your own dining room, or three extra personal days off each year.

But if you can see it in your mind's eye, you'll be inspired as you strive to get what you want.

→ Step 2: Uncover your interests.

Why do you want what you want? If you're clear on what's behind your objectives, you may be more flexible when it comes time to finding solutions.

If you're after a promotion, ask yourself why you want it. Are you looking for more money? More recognition? More windows in your office? "Know yourself," advises New York mediator Julie Denny. If you're trying to get established in your field, a fancy title on your resumé might be worth more in the long run than a $1,000 raise. If money is your issue, think about nonsalary options that might put a few dollars in your pocket. If there's no budget for the raise you deserve, a company car might save you several thousand dollars in auto expenses.

Beth used this style of thinking to renegotiate a contract with one of her favorite magazines. After several years of working on a freelance basis, she was offered a contract by a top editor. Instead of getting paid per story, Beth would agree to turn in a certain number of stories over the year. In return, they'd send her a monthly check.

The regular check proved to be a huge blessing for the family budget. But a year later, when it came time to renegotiate, she realized the contract was actually paying her less per story than she'd received before. She turned to a friend on staff for advice. He told her money was tight and a raise probably wasn't in the cards. So she put together a new proposal; the contract amount would stay the same but she'd write fewer stories. She also asked them to drop an exclusivity clause, so she could increase her income by writing for the competition. With her eye on the bottom line, the magazine editor immediately agreed. The story had an extremely happy ending a year later; Beth won a national award, and the magazine's editors were so delighted they gave her an enormous raise.

→ Step 3: Raise your expectations.

On her deathbed, Mary Pickford's mother gave her daughter an invaluable legacy. "Aim high," she whispered, "or not at all."

Are you aiming high enough? All the research suggests that higher expectations boost your chances for success. "People who expect more get more," contends Wharton School professor G. Richard Shell in *Inc.* magazine. "You focus on your bottom line and try to do just a little better than that," he writes. "And guess what? Your bottom line is exactly what you get."

Set challenging, highly specific goals. If you're in the mailroom but yearning for the boardroom, keep your sights high. You obviously won't make that leap in your first bargaining session, but at least you'll have your eyes on the prize. "Don't be afraid to be bold, to start off with very high expectations," says Scholastic's Deborah Forte. "Sometimes you just might get it."

Michele Hooper, now a seasoned corporate executive, learned that lesson from her husband, Lem Seabrook, twenty years ago, when they were looking for their first house. Although interest rates were at historic highs, they thought they might be able to afford a Queen Anne–style bungalow they'd found in Evanston, Illinois. It was hardly a move-in cream puff; the owners had moved to New York six months before, and the yard was a mass of overgrown weeds. The house itself seemed structurally sound, but it needed "extensive redecorating," Michele recalls.

Michele, who has an MBA from the University of Chicago, started running the numbers, trying to figure out whether they could afford the $150,000 price tag. Then her husband (also a University of Chicago MBA) intervened. He thought they had plenty of room to negotiate. Mortgage interest rates of 18 percent had knocked out all but the most determined home buyers, so Michele and Lem probably weren't facing much competition. They also had the cash to close the deal quickly, which would appeal to motivated sellers. "I realized that if I were in New York and somebody gave me a reasonable offer, I would consider it," Michele says.

Lem thought the home's dire need of redecorating should be reflected in their offer. Together, he and Michele calculated how much it would cost to bring the place to a "livable" but not extravagant condition. After deducting big chunks to account for the decorating, the sky-high interest rates, their own solid financial position, and the sellers' apparent desperation, they came up with a bid: $118,000. Attached to the bid was an explanation of how they'd arrived at that amount.

The sellers accepted it without a counteroffer. And when Michele and Lem realized they'd underestimated some decorating costs, they asked to subtract several hundred dollars more from their offer — with no resistance from the owners. "We got a fabulous deal," Michele says, thanks to Lem's willingness to ask for everything he wanted. "It was out-of-the-box thinking for me."

➜ Step 4: Determine your bottom line.

"Know what's sacred," advises Deborah Forte. "Before you go in, know what you can move on, and what you absolutely can't." Usually Forte finds only one point she's not willing to compromise. "Make it clear at the beginning, and constantly refer to it," she says. "Don't get yourself down a road that ultimately is frustrating."

Catalyst's Sheila Wellington says she's amazed by the number of people who enter negotiations without a bottom line. "I always know the point beyond which I won't move, and I won't move beyond it. Otherwise you can lose your shirt, and some people do."

➜ Step 5: Don't forget Plan B.

What will you do if you don't reach a settlement? As we told you back in chapter 2, you have to put on your BATNA helmet (which stands, you'll recall, for Best Alternative To a Negotiated Agreement). A good Plan B is a power booster. If you can take this deal and shove it, you're less likely to cave in to an unfair arrangement.

As you're getting ready to negotiate, review Plan B. Is there anything you can do to improve it? Suppose you're trying to get a promotion. If your boss refuses, Plan B is to look for a new job. So now's the time to get some resumés out there; having an actual offer in hand will make your position even stronger.

➜ Step 6: Develop your proposal.

If you're thinking of a negotiated settlement as a pie, spend some prep time going over your grocery list. You may be thinking in terms of a frozen piecrust and a can of strawberry pie filling. But just as in cooking, you'll find things generally turn out better if you bake from scratch. Break down each one of your requests into its component parts and see if that gives you any fresh ideas.

By reducing your issues to smaller points, you can be very specific about what's important to you. Imagine that your youngest son is having trouble in school, and you think he needs some extra attention. Well, that's a pretty vague request. Even if you break it down into "give more help with homework" and "provide consistent consequences," there's still a lot of room for misunderstanding. So try to calm down and figure out precisely what you want.

Maybe your son doesn't understand why he's getting D's on his math homework. Don't just request "more feedback"; that could be anything from a weekly note home to a happy-face sticker when he finally gets a B. Would it help to ask the teacher if your son could come in early to review his equations before he turns them in? Propose some specific alternatives.

When you're clear on exactly what you want, you avoid the misunderstandings that can ensue when the other person bends over backward to give you something you don't really need at all. Ask for piecrust and you may get a fancy pile of crushed graham crackers. If you want flour, butter, salt, and sugar, then say so.

Be just as focused on breaking things down to their basic ingredients when it comes to what you're willing to give away. There's no need to hand over your new blue bicycle if all they want is your little white basket.

Rebecca, a part-time paralegal, resolved one thorny situation by taking a second look at the ingredients on her boss's grocery list. For a year, Rebecca had been coming into the office on Wednesdays and Thursdays. But over time, it became clear that the office really needed her help on Fridays. When she came in and found a note asking her to shift her schedule, Rebecca thought she'd have to quit. At the beginning of the year, she'd set up a nursery school car pool, and all the other mothers had arranged their schedules accordingly. At this point, the 11 A.M. carpool pickup was set in stone.

Sadly, Rebecca went in to say good-bye to her boss, a sympathetic working mom. "We'll really miss you," she said. "And quite frankly, it will take forever to bring somebody else up to speed. Isn't there anything we can do to keep you?"

Rebecca promised to sleep on it. When she woke up in the morning, she realized the difficulty wasn't Friday; it was just that midmorning car pool run. So she presented her boss with a plan. Rebecca would come in an hour early on Fridays, then take a two-hour lunch at 10:30. That would give her time to pick up the car pool, have lunch with her little girl, and get back to the office.

Everybody won. By breaking the nonnegotiable Friday into some negotiable chunks, Rebecca kept a job she liked and needed, and her daughter got a weekly lunch date with Mom. Even better, Rebecca proved to herself, her boss, and everyone else in that office that it's possible for a smart woman to combine work and family without cheating either side. "I felt like a real role model for the younger women," she says proudly.

➜ Step 7: List their objections.

Even if you think your proposal is a masterpiece of win-win dealmaking, don't expect your opponent to swallow it whole. Make sure you're ready to field questions and respond to objections.

We're assuming you've already done enough research to make sure your proposal is workable. Obviously, if you're asking the bank to fund a daring new mixed-use land development plan, you'd better be sure it meets zoning restrictions. If there's any question, you'll need to cite some objective sources the bankers will trust. We know how reliable you are, but the bankers don't.

If you're asking your boss for a more flexible vacation schedule, you can pretty much figure that he'll counter with, "We've always done it this way." So spend some quality time with the company manual, or have a heart-to-heart chat with that nice guy down in human resources. Have they always done it this way because it's company policy, or is it just that nobody ever asked for anything else? And if your boss is the type who blows off every request with, "What if everybody wanted to do it this way?" you'll need to have a smart, thoughtful answer up your sleeve.

Get ready to do some fancy footwork if your plan will cost the other side major dollars. You'll need to prove that your ideas are worth more to them than their money.

"There's no room on my shelves." That's the objection Michele Hoskins, president of Michele Foods, a manufacturer of specialty breakfast syrups, frequently hears from buyers when she makes sales calls at grocery chains. But this former welfare recipient, who built a

$7 million business based on her grandmother's recipes, is prepared. She visits the stores of her prospective clients ahead of time and searches for a choice spot on the shelves. Faced with the lack-of-space objection, she'll point out exactly where her products should sit, or, if space is really tight, suggest that her product replace another brand that she regularly outsells. "If they tell me they have no space and I have to go back and look at the shelves after the meeting, by then it's too late," she says.

↪ Step 8: Put it in writing.

Go ahead — be spontaneous. Give someone a daisy. Kick up your heels. Break into song. Express your wonderful, bubbly, delightfully unpredictable self. Just don't do it when you're negotiating. After you've gone to all this trouble to prepare yourself, don't blow it by getting flustered and forgetting what you were going to say.

Martha Furst, a former investment banker who formed a gourmet mustard company with her sister, arms herself with a "term sheet" that lists her ten objectives, divided into "need to haves" and "nice to haves." When Martha sits down to negotiate, she keeps that sheet in front of her for easy reference. Some seasoned negotiators go so far as to write up a position paper and hand it out to their opponents. "I write out my case and give a copy to the other side," says Ava, the college president. "That solidifies it."

Make sure you list your objectives in the right order. Put your key points at the beginning and the end; you don't want to bury the important stuff in the middle, where it might be overlooked.

Underline the points that are attractive to the other side, and make sure you emphasize them. "Many people spend more time defending what's attractive to them[selves]," Professor Roy Lewicki observes in *Negotiation*. This is a classic good girl blunder, which can result in some incredibly unattractive whininess. We understand. From your perspective, simple justice demands that your landlord agree to let you sign a six-month extension of your lease; you're a finalist for a prestigious fellowship that would send you to the Sorbonne for a year, and you won't hear whether you got it for another two months. It would be horrible to have to find a temporary home, and it would be devastating to give up your cozy apartment and then end up missing out on the fellowship. But even the most sympathetic landlord doesn't really care about how much you've yearned to wander down the Champs Élysées. Instead, focus on what a perfect tenant you've always been, and point out that more renters will be looking for new digs in September. Write that down, now, so you don't get distracted by visions of yourself in a chic little beret when it's time to confront your landlord.

Once you've written down your strategy, compose an agenda. If you can pick the order in which you present your points, you'll have an enormous influence over the tone and pacing of the discussion. But don't spring your agenda on the other side unawares. Instead, circulate it ahead of time, and ask for input. You'll signal how flexible and well prepared you are. And if they agree to the agenda in advance, you'll have much more authority to enforce it if things get off track once you finally sit down at the table.

→ Step 9: Rehearse.

Imagine playing Juliet without a rehearsal. You'd probably fall right off your balcony.

Well, you can expect about the same level of performance if you walk into a negotiation without running through your lines a few times. Theresa Montaño, formerly of the United Teachers of Los Angeles (UTLA), was the designated union advocate for enhancing teacher training. In that job, she worked with school system officials and teachers to improve teachers' effectiveness in the classroom, an incredibly delicate task.

When Theresa faced particularly difficult discussions, she sometimes asked her husband, Terry, to help her with some role-playing. "I typed up different scenarios — what they say, what I say," Theresa explains. Then she asked him to help her run through her lines.

Her husband acted as both costar and critic. If he wasn't swayed by her argument, it made her stop and take a second look at her position. If he couldn't buy it, she probably wouldn't convince a less affectionate audience.

While husbands are handy for impromptu rehearsals, you might also benefit from running through your presentation with a friend who knows your field. "Try enlisting a mentor to guide you through your lines," advises Jeanette Wagner of Estée Lauder. No matter who your partner is, switching parts and taking on your opponent's role may give you additional insights into their reaction to what you plan to say.

➜ Step 10: Pull yourself together.

Okay. You've done your homework. You've planned your strategy. You've practiced your presentation. Now it's time to pull yourself together, so you'll be calm, cool, and collected when it's time to make your case.

Lay out your clothes the night before. That way you'll avoid one of those anxious morning scrambles searching for an intact pair of panty hose. You'll also have some time to think about the impression you want to make. Merchandising maven Lori Scott often relies on fashion to make her points nonverbally. "If I have a presentation to make, I always make sure I'm wearing an outfit that says something about business, and something about fashion. If I have a meeting with the board of directors, I wear a red suit, because red is a powerful color," she says. "On a day when I knew I was going to have to bust some balls, I'd put on a black suit. My staff would see it and go, 'Ooh, someone's in trouble.'"

As you're planning what to wear, think about how that outfit makes you feel. I don't care if all the books tell you to wear a navy blue suit to a job interview. If you think that blue suit makes you look washed out, wear something else. Don't let your appearance distract you from your goals. Beth still shivers when she remembers one excruciating job interview. Anxious to look her best, she scheduled a makeover at an expensive downtown beauty salon the day before. The stylist talked her into a perm; when they pulled out the curlers, there was a bald spot the size of a half-dollar gleaming on the top of her head. We wish we could tell you a happy ending. What really happened is that Beth walked into the interview feeling like a beluga whale with an exposed blowhole and proceeded to make a complete fool of herself.

If you don't particularly care about clothes, fine. Wear whatever you like. But if feeling you look your best improves your attitude, know that in advance, and play that card. I know a young agent in Los Angeles who takes strength from donning a power suit for her negotiations, even though they are all conducted over the telephone. If something works for you, go with it. Wear your lucky red shoes. (As U.S. energy secretary, Bill Richardson kept his aging lucky blue blazer in his closet, handy for international troubleshooting assignments.) Put on your most expensive lingerie. When Theresa's negotiating, she always wears a medallion her mother gave her. She says it reminds her to be strong.

Take time to center yourself. Take a long bath. Meditate.

Finally, when everything's ready, and you've finished all your prep work, put your papers carefully in your briefcase, turn out the lights, and get a good night's sleep.

CHAPTER 5

◆

TABLE MANNERS

Grandmother Vivian was setting the table, carefully laying out her delicate china cups on a lacy antique cloth, and precisely situating her shining silver teapot on its big, elaborate tray. The afternoon's menu was simple: tea, cookies — and a negotiation that could change the lives of her children and grandchildren.

The situation was delicate. In her mid-seventies, Vivian was the coowner of a small family-owned chain of stores. When her husband had died twelve years before, Vivian decided to leave the day-to-day management of the company in the hands of her husband's business partner, Frank. But now Vivian's daughter, Jill, and granddaughter, Sandra, wanted to take over the reins themselves. Legally, as majority stockholders, they were entitled to assume control. But Frank was both part-owner and a major supplier to their chain. If he wanted, he could throw a huge monkey wrench into their business plan.

So Vivian decided it was time for a heart-to-heart talk. She called Frank and invited him to tea. The invitation seemed innocent enough; what could be less threatening than afternoon tea with a little old lady? But Vivian's friendly overture was a carefully considered move. She knew she'd feel strongest on her own turf, and she wanted to schedule the meeting at the time of day when she usually felt sharpest and most alert.

When Frank showed up promptly at 3 P.M., Vivian greeted him graciously, with the warmth an old family friend should expect. She offered him some home-baked cookies and poured out a steaming cup of tea. Then Grandmother went to work. In a soft but assured tone, she informed Frank that she and the girls were ready to take over running the company. "I think you're making a mistake," Frank retorted quickly. Calmly, and without notes, Vivian ran through the four or five key points that supported her position. She noted, for instance, that her granddaughter now had enough experience to step into the company's top job and that having decisions made on-site was more efficient than waiting for approval from Frank's company, miles away. A half hour (and four cookies) later, Frank was convinced. He agreed to relinquish control without a fight. Together they worked out the details of a new partnership agreement that has now lasted for more than fifteen years.

Would Frank have agreed to the same proposal if he'd been enthroned in his fancy downtown office? Would Vivian have felt equally assured if she'd met Frank in the "neutral territory" of some high-priced restaurant? Maybe. But maybe not. What counts is that she carefully thought about what she wanted to say, and how, when, and where she wanted to say it.

Think about how much thought and effort you put into planning a big dinner party. If you're like us, you obsess about the guest list, the menu, and the seating arrangement. When you think about it, you're going to an enormous amount of trouble just to provide your guests with about 1,000 calories and roughly half their minimum daily requirement of vitamins and minerals. You could accomplish the same goal with a Double Whopper with cheese, a glass of skim milk, and a One-A-Day vitamin.

But if you're the kind of person who pores over the *Silver Palate Cookbook* to find an impeccable salad to complement a crown roast of lamb, and sorts through a foot-high stack of CDs to choose the perfect mood music, why on earth would you walk into a car dealership at 7 P.M. after a long, taxing day at the office? You know how important it is to create the right atmosphere for a successful dinner party. It's just as critical to set the proper mood for a negotiation.

THE GUEST LIST

When you plan a dinner party, you start out with your guest list. And your first objective is putting together a group of people who generally get along with each other. Even if you and your guests enjoy a lively debate, the last thing you want at a dinner party is a food fight. The best way to avoid an ugly confrontation is to select guests who already know and like each other, or those who can be expected to relish each other's company.

The same principle applies to a negotiation. Obviously you sometimes have to sit down and strike an agreement with a complete stranger. But whenever possible, it's a good idea to introduce yourself before you make a deal.

Sisters Martha and Susan Furst have made their midwestern friendliness part of their business plan. Martha, a former investment banker, and Susan, a chef with four-star credentials, decided three years ago to join forces and start their own business. Drawing on Susan's culinary expertise, they developed their own brand of gourmet mustards, Terrapin Ridge. The mustards themselves have won a string of awards for their innovative flavors, such as wasabi lime and brown sugar pecan. But the Furst sisters have put just as much thought into the ingredients that flavor their relationships with their business partners. Before they even start to talk business with potential partners, the women invite them to dinner at one of their favorite restaurants. "We like to get to know people socially," Martha says. "Assuming you respond well to each other, this experience gives you a foundation of understanding, which will be useful when difficulties arise. And there are always bumps." A shared dish of olives today can blossom into an olive branch next year. And if somebody doesn't measure up as a dinner partner, it's a good idea to think twice before inviting him to be your business partner.

The Fursts' friendly strategy is particularly effective for us good girls. With our warm, winning personalities, we're great company. People like us. They want us to like them. And that's often an advantage in a negotiating situation. Wendy Sarasohn, a real estate broker specializing in luxurious Manhattan homes, says people generally prefer dealing with nice people, whatever their income bracket. "Personality can play as much a role as money," she says. "Very often, people want to know that they are selling their homes to someone they like." She's actually had clients take lower offers from buyers they preferred.

Believe it or not, niceness can work on lawyers, too. Marcia Sterling, Autodesk's senior vice president and general counsel, says she finds that others will cut her a little slack when she turns on her southern charm, even in the cutthroat world of Silicon Valley. "I grew up in Fayetteville, Arkansas," she says. "As a girl, I was taught how to help other people feel comfortable, and I've found it works in the outside world," she says. "I exude warmth when I deal with people. And it's just as effective at a pretrial hearing in the judge's chambers as at the mall. People who can't do those things have a strike against them. At its heart, negotiating is communication. If [your opponents] like you, you're going to do better."

By no means are we suggesting that you relapse into that good girl "I'll do anything to be liked" mode. Your ultimate goal in any negotiation is to be respected, not just liked. But that doesn't mean you should throw your social skills out the window. When you let your good girl warmth shine through, you're being neither weak nor insincere. You're simply using a real, God-given asset in an intelligent way.

Patricia Eanet is a good example. When she was assistant counsel for negotiations for the National Treasury Employees Union, Patti made a point of being friendly when she sat down to negotiate with government managers. "Some people say they don't want to be friends with the other side," she says. "But I talk to them like they're people. I develop my relationships." She just can't help it. Patti is compulsively outgoing, to the point that male colleagues tease her about it. "They say that by the end of a plane trip I know everything about all the other passengers," she says, smiling.

Because Patti once worked as a senior attorney in the office of the chief counsel for the Treasury Department, she had long-standing relationships with many of the people who sat on the other side of the table. For some unreconstructed good girls, that situation might create intense inner conflicts: "Oh, no! My friends versus my employer!" But Patti handled the situation with grace and a wry sense of humor. At one negotiation, a former colleague and old friend walked into the room. Patti hesitated, then planted a big kiss on his cheek. Amused and alarmed, another member of his bargaining team blurted, "You're not going to kiss me, are you?"

"Not on your life!" Patti retorted with a smile.

Make no mistake. Patti, whose newest job has put her back at the Treasury Department, was a passionate union rep who got incredibly steamed up when managers "did ridiculous things" to their employees. Still, she welcomed the opportunity to sit down with them in a "pre-decisional mode" before they locked horns. "I don't waive the right to bargain," she explains. "But at this point we meet as equal partners, and develop ideas together." Even when the negotiations become intense, she says, "I don't do fist pounding, because I see us as doing this together. You actually get a much better product that way."

Don't get the idea that you can develop a warm working relationship over a single cup of coffee. Remember that wonderful quote from painter Georgia O'Keeffe: "Nobody sees a flower, really — It is so small — We haven't time, and to see takes time, like to have a friend takes time."

That's especially true when you're sitting down with someone who sees the world in a very different way. To understand the needs of the mostly male drivers in her union, Bhairavi Desai, organizer for the New York Taxi Workers Alliance, has spent fifty hours a week just sitting down and talking with them. "I wanted them to know I was taking this job seriously and was not afraid of entering a male space. I'm learning from the driver leadership and trying to understand the complexities as a younger, single woman. Sometimes I have arguments with drivers, but I try to convey honesty and a sense of confidence."

When you make a sincere effort to create those relationships, when you take the time to find out just who it is you're working with and what they really need, it can pay off tremendously. Frankly, many businesses offer roughly similar products at roughly similar prices. So customers often choose "vendors, consultants, clients, and partners based on whom they like to be with," says entrepreneur Sarah Hoit. "You don't need to be a confrontational power player to do business. If you're having fun being here, it's infectious." With a hundred customers in seven states, it can be a challenge for Sarah to maintain those fun, friendly relationships. So whenever she happens to be in a client's area code, she stops in, even if she doesn't have any pressing business to discuss. "I'll call and we'll go out for a coffee or a beer," she says. It works because it's real; she really enjoys her client's company, and it shows.

You don't have to be a frequent flyer to nurture those relationships. Consider Beth, whose editors are mostly based in New York and Washington. "I have a friend who tells me I should visit all my New York editors at least once a year," she says. "That's easy for him

Love Is a Miracle, Marriage Is a Contract: Prenuptial Agreements

For good girls, a guide to the ultimate prenuptial agreement can be found in Elaine May's wickedly funny movie *A New Leaf*. It's the story of a self-absorbed playboy who spends all his money, then goes hunting for an heiress he can marry — and murder. His hapless victim is Henrietta, a sweet, dowdy, unworldly botanist.

When the happy couple announce their upcoming wedding, her lawyer calls the couple into his office to discuss a prenup. Henrietta says she's given the matter a lot of thought — and has decided to sign over everything she owns to her fiancé. "This way," she explains with wide-eyed sincerity, "he'll already have all my money, so that no one can possibly think that he's marrying me for it." It's no wonder that her fortune-hunting lover tells her, "You're a good girl, Henrietta."

For most good girls, the whole idea of a prenup is tremendously distasteful. If he's the one with the larger fortune, your first instinct is to sign away all your rights in a big, grand gesture. After all, you're in love with him, not his money. And if you've got a pile of assets, you'd rather cut out your tongue than ask your beloved to sign a paper stating, in legal terms, that you really don't trust him.

Well, that's romantic, idealistic — and just plain silly.

Do you know what marriage really is? For some people it's a sacrament; for others, it's a public statement of love. But in the eyes of the law, it's a contract. And there's nothing wrong with spending some of those deep, heart-felt late-night discussions talking about the terms of your own individual contract with each other. "This acute romantic phase, when you still think it's cute when your partner leaves his underwear on the floor, is the perfect time to start talking about these issues," says Jacqueline Rickard, author of *Complete Premarital Contracting: Loving Communication for Today's Couples.* "The communication ends up being more important than the document you create."

Quite frankly, anybody who thinks it's "too unromantic" to talk about money, property, children, and death isn't grown-up enough to get married. If you can't tackle these tough subjects now, when are you planning to start? Right now, you and your beloved are creating the patterns of communication and negotiation that will shape your entire marriage. So let's talk about some real-life issues that could perplex you and your Prince Charming.

Prenuptial Agreements (cont.)

Real-Life Issues

He's rich (or his family is) and you're not.

This is a classic prenup situation. Some incredibly wealthy guy (let's call him Ronald Frump) comes in and sweeps you off your feet with his dashing ways and dazzling gifts. When he can see the stars in your eyes, he pops the question: "Will you sign a prenup?" "Anything, Ronald," you reply. So off you go to his lawyer's office, where you cheerfully put your Jane Hancock on a document stating that, in the unlikely event of your divorce, your beloved will hand you a check for $500,000 and give you a good-bye peck on the cheek. Why not? You're not marrying him for his millions; you're smitten with the shape of his passionate mouth. You're never going to divorce him, so it's all moot anyway. And the truth of the matter is, half a million dollars is more money than you can imagine.

If you sign without a second thought, you're making a mistake. This is a document with enormous implications for you, your children, even your grandchildren. So don't sign and smile. Tell the lawyer you'll need time to run it past your own attorney. Then use your good girl skills to find out what's going on in your fiancé's mind. Ask him why he wants a prenup. Did a previous marriage end in a nasty divorce? Does he worry that no woman could love him for himself and not his billions? Ask how he came up with that $500,000 figure. To be legal, a prenup must be accompanied by a complete financial disclosure statement. Does he really think it would be fair to throw you out with 1 percent of your combined net worth after eight years of faithful marriage?

A lot can happen in the course of a marriage, even when you love each other dearly. A failing parent, a child with a chronic illness, a collapse in the stock market — these are just a few of the variables that can strain a relationship. If you sign that paper, you're giving him permission to walk away when the going gets tough. If that's not what you want, say so.

You're a dot-com millionaire and he's your gardener.

Or, if that's a bit extreme, you and your best friend run a secondhand bookstore and he's a graduate student in French poetry. Whatever the details, you've got more assets than he does. But you feel funny about asking him to sign a prenup — even though your business partner, a battle-scarred marital veteran, is hysterical at the thought of your getting married without one.

A prenup may be the best way to get this cluster of relationships off on the right foot. Sit down separately with your friend and with your lover, and talk about how they envision all of this working out over the next ten years. What happens if your fiancé finishes his Ph.D. and then is offered a job at a college in Seattle? Could you expand the business out there, or would your partner have to buy out your share? If a disgruntled customer trips over a bookshelf and breaks a leg, could you and your new husband end up losing your house in the resulting lawsuit? You need to talk out all these scenarios and come up with some livable solutions. "If you have something you really want to protect, the best way is to be open about it," Rickard affirms. "You need to let your fiancé know where you're coming from, and what you want."

You have children from a previous relationship.

Your husband-to-be may have "Great New Dad" written all over him. But you still owe it to your children to look after their interests, especially if you have a house or other assets from your previous marriage. You also need to figure out at what point in your marriage the house becomes "our home" and the children become "our kids."

This can be a tricky situation, as Rickard knows from experience. After a tough divorce, she says, "I was very frightened of getting married a second time, and I wanted to protect my children and their inheritance." At first, her husband-to-be was taken aback. "But once I explained that it would be considering his children as well, that put it into a different perspective."

Your prenup should reflect your own individual situation. If your children are very young and their dad is out of the picture, how will they be treated in your husband's estate planning? Right now it may make perfect sense for you to split your assets cleanly according to bloodlines. But if this man takes them to their Little League games, applauds at their high school graduations, and walks them down the aisle, will your children feel harshly disinherited if they're not mentioned in his will?

There's no single right answer to this one. Just make sure you and your fiancé are in agreement before embarking on the difficult task of blending families.

Don't Sign If . . .
. . . You feel your fiancé views this as a test of your love.

It's difficult to harden your heart against a lovable man who has been wounded by painful relationships, either with his family or another woman.

Prenuptial Agreements (cont.)

But "that's a big trap," Rickard warns. "A lot of women believe that, through their love and caring, they're going to change their spouses. That's not how it works. Needy people just stay needy. If someone has a real fear that is deeply ingrained, he has to heal it on his own." Signing an unfair agreement just to reassure a fearful lover sends the message that his anxieties outrank your security. And if his fears never subside, and his unhealed emotional wounds eventually undermine your marriage, you'll wind up getting punished for your warm, unselfish heart.

. . . *You don't have your own attorney.*

You need to run any agreement past a lawyer with substantial experience in prenups and family law. You also should talk to a certified financial planner, to make sure you're considering all the financial ramifications before you sign.

. . . *Your fiancé hands you a prenup the morning of the wedding.*

This actually happened to one of my best friends. Just before she flounced off to get her hair styled and her veil arranged, her fiancé's father told her to sign a prenup or the wedding was off. Stunned, all she could think about was how much the wedding had cost her parents, and how much all her friends and family had spent on traveling to share this day with her. So — without telling a soul — she signed. I spent the whole day at her side, helping her to get ready, and I'd never seen such an upset, angry bride. Only years later, when the marriage collapsed, did she confess what had happened.

In general the courts will not uphold any prenuptial contract signed under duress — and threatening to cancel the wedding when the church is already full of flowers and candles should count as duress by anybody's definition. But even so, you still shouldn't sign that paper, Rickard believes.

Instead, she says, "you and your fiancé need to find a quiet corner and talk." Instead of getting hysterical and giving in, or getting hysterical and storming out, you need to open your ears and find out what's turned your beloved into this ultimatum-brandishing stranger. "Close the door," Rickard says. "Let the caterer wait. It's an emotional shock that someone whom you loved and trusted, and who you thought loved and trusted you, would do this to you." Maybe he's got a bad case of premarital cold feet, or his idiot best man took him out to a strip club and poured stories of coldhearted gold diggers into his ear all night long. Whatever it is, you need to work it out before he puts that beautiful ring on your finger. I'm sorry — if you let him steamroll you into signing that paper, this will not be the last special day this man will ruin for you. If he insists, you owe it to yourself to gather up your long white dress and run.

to say; he's a man with no kids. Frankly, it's easier for a mastodon to escape the La Brea tar pits than it is for me to get out of town." Instead, Beth relies on phone calls, notes, e-mails, and the occasional bouquet of flowers to keep those connections alive. "It's funny; I don't really think of keeping in touch as a business skill," she says. "Even though I've never met some of my editors face-to-face, I still consider them real friends. It feels very natural to send them birthday cards and baby gifts. But when it's time to renegotiate a contract, I feel very comfortable presenting my case to someone who values me as a person, as well as a writer."

GETTING THE RIGHT PEOPLE IN THE ROOM

You can't negotiate effectively if you're facing the wrong person — even if it's someone you really like and who really likes you. So ask yourself: Does this person have the authority to make a deal, or is there a higher power who must be consulted? And if there is, is there any way to get the real decision-maker to the table?

Any hostess knows that you can sometimes nail down a skittish guest by inviting someone that person wants to meet. Who's going to turn down an invitation that begins, "Steven Spielberg is coming for dinner on Thursday, and he says he'd love to meet you"? Alas, most of us don't socialize with the Hollywood A-list. But you can use the same principle to reel in an otherwise unenthusiastic negotiating partner. Minerva Martinez applied it to excellent advantage when her boss absolutely refused to consider moving her job from El Paso to Austin. She simply sent out a couple more negotiation invitations — to his boss, and to his boss's boss. When her supervisor realized they were willing to sit down and discuss Minerva's plan, he knew he could either join the talks or be left out of the loop. So he wisely helped to move the discussions along by providing Minerva with some key pieces of information.

In the best of all possible worlds, you'd love to invite only the people you like to your negotiation party. But when you're planning your guest list, be a big girl and make sure you include everybody, even those unpleasant folks who nevertheless can serve as dealbreakers. Bonnie learned this the hard way, when she was planning her wedding. In her defense, we should mention that Bonnie was only twenty-one, and her fiancé, Roger, was just twenty-four. She was finishing her senior year in college, while Roger was completing law school, so most of the prewedding negotiations were conducted via long distance.

In hindsight, Bonnie realizes she should have expected trouble. She and her fiancé were both eldest children, and neither family had gone through a wedding before. Bonnie's mother, a small-town Baptist, envisioned a wedding like those she'd attended as a child — a sweet little cake-and-punch reception in the church hall, followed by champagne at her home for their closest friends. Roger's mom, who grew up in an ethnic city neighborhood, was thinking more in terms of a rented hall, an open bar, and huge plates full of Italian beef and mostaccioli. Bonnie and Roger weren't sure exactly what they wanted, although the phrase "elegant little hors d'oeuvres" became Bonnie's mantra.

Well, the situation quickly went from bad to worse. Over the phone, Bonnie and her mother would sketch out a plan, which Bonnie then submitted for Roger's approval. He'd give his okay, then head to the phone to share the plan with his mother — who would promptly throw a fit. "It was so awful," Bonnie remembers. "She objected to the church, to the minister, to the wedding party, to everything — especially the reception." Ever the obedient son, Roger would relay his mother's latest tantrum to Bonnie, who then dutifully repeated it to her mother. "It got to the point that I was so angry I didn't even want to be in the same room with my future mother-in-law." By the time the wedding day rolled around, negotiations had broken down so completely that Roger's mother actually held her own competing reception at a hotel a mile from

No More Tears: How to Keep from Crying

Big girls don't cry.

Yes, we know you're emotional and softhearted. That's what we like about you. We think it's cute that you cry at sentimental movies and kindergarten pageants. But when it's time to negotiate, you need to put your hanky away. "There's no crying in a negotiation," says film producer Lynda Obst.

At work, tears can make you look childish or hysterical. "People stop taking you seriously," comments Elaine, a New York editor. Even at home, crying can make you seem manipulative and unstable. And when you're dealing with children, your sobs can be tremendously upsetting.

Some women freely admit using tears to get their way in intimate negotiations. And it's true that some men don't pay attention until you melt down. But the tears-as-tools approach is dangerous and ultimately self-destructive. These outbursts aren't good for your physical or mental health. Expressing your emotions is a good thing; tearing yourself to pieces is not. And you'll find that the stakes keep rising. The guy who couldn't bear to see a single teardrop shining in your eyes five years ago now just rolls his eyes when he sees you sobbing into the sofa pillow. If you want to make a serious point, solid negotiating skills will beat mascara tracks on your cheeks any day.

So what's an overstressed good girl to do? Consider these hints.

Look up.

When you raise your eyes, it squeezes the tear ducts and holds the tears back. But remember, this is only a temporary solution; if you spend a whole meeting gazing expectantly at the ceiling, you're likely to spark rumors of an impending alien invasion.

Schedule your battles carefully.

As much as possible, avoid confrontational negotiations when you're in a fragile state. Suppose you've been pulling all-nighters to meet a pressing work deadline — only to hear your boss take credit for all your hard labor. Don't storm into his office, sleep-deprived and emotionally drained, to demand fair treatment. You'll just collapse into a large, quivering bowl of Jell-O. Instead, try to take a weekend away, to rest and clear your mind. Then write down your position in a clear, calm memo and ask to schedule a meeting at a time when you're feeling stronger.

How to Keep from Crying (cont.)

Ask for an adjournment.

If you're in a tense meeting and feel the waterworks threatening, ask for a break. Excuse yourself to go get a glass of water or make a quick phone call. If possible, take charge; say, "Let's do this later," and walk away until you feel better. (A sneaky option is a self-operated beeper. If things get too intense, push the button to set it off, then take a few quiet minutes to respond to your "urgent call.") One caution: If you're the tearful type, either give up mascara or always carry a spare tube with you. Emerging from the ladies' room with newly scrubbed eyelashes is a dead giveaway.

Create a diversion.

If you're trapped in an unpleasant meeting and you can't hold back the tears, drop your briefcase. Knock over a glass of water. Pop out your contact lens. (This one works even if you don't wear contacts — but not if you're wearing glasses.) Do something to divert their attention (and yours) away from your emotional distress.

Explain what's happening.

Sometimes your tears have nothing to do with the subject at hand. Beth's friend Mary Ellen went through a horrible siege last year, when her father was gravely ill. Every day brought a new medical crisis, to the point that poor Mary Ellen started bursting into tears whenever the phone rang. You can imagine how this affected her work relationships. In client meetings, almost without warning, she'd find herself with a lump in her throat and tears pouring down her cheeks. "I just got used to carrying Kleenex with me all the time," she says. "Instead of saying, 'I'm very upset,' I'd say, 'This is an upsetting time for me.' Then I'd just ignore it and keep going." She made a point of keeping her explanations as brief and unemotional as possible, to avoid making a cheap bid for sympathy. "I made it very clear that this had nothing to do with work."

Talk now, cry later.

Sometimes, of course, a good cry is exactly what you need. And knowing that you've got a five-hanky session coming up on Friday night may be all you need to get through your workweek without a breakdown. So schedule in some crying time. Go to the video store and rent *Now, Voyager.* Stash a pint of Ben & Jerry's Cherry Garcia frozen yogurt in the freezer. Invest in a big box of extrasoft, oversized, lotion-enhanced facial tissue. Turn off the lights. Unplug the phone. Just let go.

Bonnie's family's reception. "Needless to say," Bonnie remarks, "our marriage got off to a rocky start."

In retrospect, Bonnie realizes that playing telephone was no way to plan a wedding. "We should have called a mandatory meeting of the mothers," she says. "If I had it to do over again, I'd insist on everyone sitting down together in neutral territory. I'd arm myself with a yellow pad, and write down everything we agreed to. I'd have everybody at the table sign off — literally. Then when they changed their minds, I'd just show them the signed document and tell them to shut up."

PATIENCE, DEAR

Getting some people to the bargaining table isn't as simple as issuing an invitation. You can't force them into it by shoving a dining room chair under their bottoms. In negotiating as in entertaining, you have to wait until your guests are hungry.

Sometimes it's easy. Retired rear admiral Marsha Johnson Evans, now the national executive director of Girl Scouts of the U.S.A., headed Navy recruiting after the Tailhook scandal. A more timid woman might have been hesitant to push female recruiting in the wake of the sexual harassment investigation. But Marty realized that Tailhook could raise the top brass's consciousness that women in the Navy deserved to be pilots, not party favors. "The military has not always embraced the idea of employing women to the fullest extent, and I was interested in how we could break down the barriers," she said later. "I was passionate about developing opportunities for women." After Tailhook, she says, "people on Capitol Hill were speaking out. Sometimes the climate is right."

It can be hard to wait for the right moment. But rushing toward an agreement is like biting into an unripe apple; you can end up with a sour taste in your mouth. In *Nation's Business,* communications consultant Kare Anderson observes that "Americans are very impulsive, because we're trying to get more done faster. As a result, we get into conflict sooner. And we end up making agreements that don't stick." Former congresswoman Pat Schroeder agrees. "The culture fans an attitude that is too impatient to negotiate," she says. "We have to win totally, and win right now."

Luckily, we good girls are brought up to be patient and wait our turn. That can be an advantage when it comes to wooing an unwilling partner. Irma Elder, now seventy-one, has proof that patience can pay off. Irma became president of Troy Ford, in Troy, Michigan, after her husband's death in 1983. At that point, she says, "I was a very shy homemaker," so unsure of herself that "if I bumped into the furniture, I'd apologize to it." Now, despite plenty of mistakes, she's built Troy Ford into one of the most successful car dealerships in America — thanks in part to her patience.

When Irma took over the business, it was a single dealership. But Irma had her eye on Mary Falvey Motors, the Detroit area's only Jaguar franchise. Obviously, as female executives of traditionally male-owned businesses, Mary and Irma had a great deal in common, and they got to know each other over years of luncheon dates. Irma was too smart, and too sensitive, to try to pressure Mary into a deal. But through the years, she gently repeated: "If you ever want to sell, call me first."

So when Mary was ready, she dialed Irma, even though she had three or four other potential buyers in the wings. "We negotiated for many months over lunch, over dinner, quietly, one-on-one," Irma says. Eventually, one of those meals ended with a deal.

A sense of timing also paid off for Jan Yeomans, a graphic designer for the Jewish Community Center in Seattle. While she loved her part-time job, she realized that her $20,000 paycheck was way below local market rates. But she felt uneasy about asking for a raise. "I was thinking about the possibility of rejection," she says. "I love where I am, so I was just grumbling to myself." Because Jan has multiple sclerosis, she also wanted to postpone any stressful negotiations until she felt healthy and strong.

Then came two incidents that boosted her determination to ask for the raise she deserved. First, a new employee in her department was brought in at a higher salary than hers. Then her supervisor resigned, leaving her to organize a golf tournament for 128 players, followed by dinner for 200. "I did it all," she says, "with the help of many volunteers and a great staff." The event was a huge success, raising $95,000 for the center.

Despite the frenzy of planning, Jan felt great. Physically and professionally, she was at the top of her game. So a few days later, while the office was still flying high from the event's success, Jan decided to make her case to the center's executive director. She dressed up in her favorite pantsuit and put on her pearly earrings and matching bracelet.

Then she knocked on the director's door. "I was steady. I smiled. My voice didn't shake," she remembers. After a few minutes of small talk, "I said, 'I want a $10,000 raise.' I was real strong and forward." The director sat there, silently. " 'So we're agreed?' I continued. Then he said he needed some time to think it over."

The next day, the director offered Jan an $8,000 raise; she took it. "I felt great," she says. She's already planning for next year's salary discussion. And she intends to be just as strong and confident in the next round of talks. "I always waited for somebody else to go to battle for me, which never happened," she says. "This time, I really have a plan."

Sandra Pesmen (Dr. Job) says appropriate scheduling is imperative when you're negotiating. She cites a banker friend who teaches a tough but important lesson to her employees. "Every year, people come into my office at the end of the year for review," the banker told Sandy. "They'll say, 'I did very well, and now I want a raise.' We always say to them, 'I would love to give you more, but next year's budget is already planned. I'm sorry.' The dumb ones say, 'Okay,' go back to their desks, get discouraged, and eventually quit. But the smart ones will go back and find out when we make up the budgets, and put in their requests then."

If you're the one facing a deadline, keep it to yourself. You're likely to get a better deal if you don't tell the car salesman that your old station wagon has less than six weeks to live. Whenever possible, do your shopping ahead of time, so you don't feel pressured to accept a bad deal.

Think about timing whenever you plan a bargaining session. Consider your internal rhythms. Are you a night owl who's groggy in the morning, or do you wake up perky and run down by 8 P.M.? Look at your calendar. If you have to pick up the car pool at 4 P.M. sharp, don't agree to a 3 o'clock salary review meeting. Take a look at your own hormonal calendar, too. While we believe that PMS is far more common in stand-up comedy than in reality, some women do feel a little tearful at that time of the month. Follow the example of one of our friends, an accountant, who was taking fertility drugs that left her, in her words, "a basket case." When it was time to renegotiate her biggest client contract, she scheduled a month-long drug "holiday" to make sure she'd feel strong and stable. (P.S. She kept the client, and she's now the mother of a beautiful baby girl.)

Never, ever allow some crafty adversary to schedule a meeting when you're clearly not going to be at your best. You're asking for trouble if you agree to a breakfast meeting with your London client just two hours after your overnight flight to Heathrow. Insist on postponing the meeting until after you've had a chance to catch up on your sleep.

Don't try to play those schedule sabotage games with the other side either. It's a cheap, cheesy trick. And from a practical standpoint, the more synapses your opponent has firing, the better able she'll be to come up with win-win solutions. Even if she's not interested in a win-win deal, an opponent who starts out tired is likely to be more cranky than compliant. (Of course, don't be ashamed if you win concessions because you have more energy and outlast her at the end.)

LET'S BAKE A DEAL

Once you've got a guest list and a date, it's time to plan the menu. There's nothing like breaking bread together to build a relationship. Even if you haven't established rapport before you go in, the simple gesture of offering your opponents an urn of coffee and a box of doughnuts can promote goodwill. Think of all those TV dramas that show hostage negotiators bravely carrying in pepperoni pizzas to the desperate bank robbers. Eating together reinforces the notion that, whatever our differences, we all share basic survival needs — even if it's just our cravings for junk food and caffeine.

Bobbe Lyon, a comedian and motivational speaker, served up the unexpected one afternoon as she led a communication session for a group of male executives. She realized the arrogant execs couldn't even manage a few minutes of small talk, much less a productive business conversation. So Bobbe ordered in a lunch of hot dogs and ice cream sundaes in little plastic cups. The men, normally accustomed to snubbing each other over steak and wine, were enchanted by the fun, simple meal. "It broke the ice," Bobbe says. "They started talking about their childhoods. They let their guard down, and that helped them to be a little more productive."

Then again, the negotiating process is sometimes best served by a brief bout of fasting. Or, as some savvy old wife probably put it, "Feed a conversation, starve an impasse." After one long day of stalled talks, attorney Anne Pope decided it was time to cut to the chase. By the end of the next day, she wanted a final deal. So she and her partner moved the talks to a stark, windowless room. "After lunch, we served no food, no nothing, except water — and you had to go in the hall for that," she says. "By dinnertime they were hungry and cranky. We had a deal by 8 P.M." Pat Schroeder offers an even tougher strategy to wrap up bargaining sessions: "Sometimes I cut off bathroom privileges."

It's unfortunate that some people misinterpret a woman's gracious offer of refreshments, assuming it means she's willing to accept a subservient role. That's why some women refuse to go near the office coffeepot, especially when they're negotiating opposite a team of male chauvinist pigs. However, Chicago attorney Laurel Bellows says she advises women to do what feels right when it comes to food service. If you think passing around the milk and sugar will undermine your authority, don't do it; set up a self-service tray instead. But Laurel — a clever negotiator who specializes in employment law — says she occasionally makes strategic use of the coffeepot. A smiling offer of a steaming cup can keep her opponents off balance. "Sometimes I pour the coffee right before I say the meanest thing I plan to say all day," she reveals.

YOUR PLACE? OR HIS?

Normally, a well-brought-up good girl would never invite herself to someone else's home. But when you're negotiating, it's considered perfectly proper to suggest that the other side play host. The best venue — whether your place, theirs, or some mutually agreeable neutral spot — is the one that you consider most likely to yield a pleasant and fruitful discussion.

Estée Lauder vice chairman Jeanette Wagner usually prefers to go to "his place," because it makes her opponents more comfortable. But she tries to do some location scouting before the actual talks begin. "I learn more about them by seeing them in their surroundings. You can get a sense of the other side's group relations. Is one guy bowing to the other? Is there a gray eminence someplace? These are all very helpful clues to help me understand the process I will have to go through."

She learned just how valuable those site visits can be when Estée Lauder reached an impasse with a European entrepreneur. The problem, a common one for big multinational corporations, was a trademark dispute. Estée Lauder wanted to introduce a new product in the market, but the entrepreneur's little company had already trademarked the brand name in several countries. So Estée Lauder either had to change its product's name for these markets (an expensive move that could confuse European consumers) or persuade the company to sell the rights to the brand name.

When Estée Lauder's lawyer asked the CEO to sign off on the trademark, he named his price: 3 million — dollars, not deutsche marks. That figure was out of the question, but the market was too valuable to give up without a fight. So Jeanette wrote a personal letter directly to the CEO. "I'd be glad to come meet you, wherever you are," she offered. Intrigued, he agreed to a meeting.

When Jeanette got off the plane in a small European town, she was greeted by the CEO, his son, and his lawyer. The CEO was flabbergasted to see the American corporate hotshot alone and carrying her own tote bag. " 'Where are your bodyguards?' he asked. Where are your lawyers?' He thought I would emerge from the plane as a big gorilla," she remembers. "I told him, 'I thought I was just coming to chat with you. If I was going to bring anyone else, I would have told you.' "

Disarmed, the CEO proceeded to give Jeanette a guided tour of his life and work. "I met his wife and his daughter, and I began to get a picture of this self-made man and his family business. I began to see that money was not the key issue." Instead, he was worried that giving up his trademark would cripple his business, leaving him unable to fulfill his dream of handing down a successful business to his children and grandchildren. "By this time, we were drinking beer and eating sausage," she says. "Sure, he would have been happy to take $3 million if anyone would have paid it to him, but that wasn't the real issue. This talented, hardworking man wanted an association with a big company. He really wanted help from us, our expertise. That would cost us something — but not as much." They struck "a reasonable deal," in which Estée Lauder agreed to pay a fair sum, help recruit expert marketing staff, and act as matchmaker between the little company and several mass distributors. And on the way back to the airport, the CEO took Jeanette to his favorite bakery to buy a bagful of jelly doughnuts. As the CEO might say, it was all *gemütlich*.

On the other hand, if you are trying to educate your opponent about your own situation, hold the meeting on your turf. Josie Ippolito, the president of La Canasta Mexican Food Products Inc., makes a point of inviting suppliers to her factory in Phoenix when it's time to renegotiate prices. When the visitor comes to Josie's office, she makes sure his seat gives him a clear view out her office window, overlooking her bustling production floor. "I lay out some projections, to give them an idea of our growth." When a supplier hears that she's planning to increase her order by 60 percent — and sees that she has the production capability to back up those projections — he's much more likely to make a deal.

When Loida Lewis negotiates, she says, she likes the "home court advantage." For several years after the untimely death of her husband, Reginald Lewis, in 1993, she used that advantage to benefit TLC Beatrice International Holdings. Reginald's billion-dollar leveraged buyout of Beatrice in 1987 made the food megamarketer the largest minority-owned enterprise in America. But when Loida took over, a year after her husband's death, the company was mired in debt. So she sharpened her pencil and went to work, shutting down or selling off unprofitable operations.

Loida set up shop in the company's headquarters overlooking

New York's Central Park, and asked interested buyers to meet with her there. She figured the expense and inconvenience of an out-of-town business trip would spur prospective buyers to sign on the dotted line as swiftly as possible. Her quick work recharged Beatrice and kept the company afloat. (She also sold the company's private jet, got rid of the limos, and moved into smaller offices — economical moves that won her the respect of Wall Street.)

However, if you're expecting emotions to run high, try to meet in neutral territory. Couples in the midst of a divorce do better when they meet in a mediator's office or some other neutral site, says Sam Margulies, author of *Getting Divorced Without Ruining Your Life*. Finding a place that holds no emotional memories for either of you "creates a little formality in order to screen out some of the distractions that arise from your intimate, but damaged, relationship."

A neutral spot can also serve your purposes if you're trying to blow a little smoke in your opponents' face. Beth used neutral ground to good effect when she was negotiating with a Swedish publisher about setting up a partnership. Olle was a well-to-do, middle-aged European businessman; Beth was a middle-class mid-western wife with a new baby and a house in midrenovation. When Olle called from Sweden to set up his brief Chicago visit, Beth looked around her living room. There was the old sofa her Labrador retriever, Benchley, had once attacked in a fit of puppy rage. In front of it were the two battered end tables she'd inherited from her grand-aunt Geneva, renowned throughout the family for her habit of leaving lit cigarettes burning on her furniture. On the other side of the room, surrounded by gracious bay windows, was a large empty space waiting — and waiting — for a grand piano. It was a sunny, cozy room for a lively young family. But Beth knew Olle would take one look and decide she was too small a fish for his net. So she made a gracious counteroffer. "You know, it's really out of your way to come to my house," she said. "Why don't we meet at the airline club at the airport?" Olle was thrilled to avoid an excursion into the suburbs. When his flight landed, there was Beth, cleverly costumed as an affluent young executive. She whisked him off to a quiet room in the glossy airport club, and the meeting went beautifully.

No matter where you decide to meet, it's a smart idea to check out the lighting and noise level ahead of time. You want to be sure all participants can see and hear one another without distractions. You should also make certain there's plenty of light for reading. (But make sure there isn't too much light; if you're in a west-facing room in the late afternoon, you'll need adequate curtains to keep from being blinded by the sun.) In short, make a quick advance trip so you won't be uncomfortably surprised.

In the summer of 1999, Josie Ippolito got word that President Clinton was planning to visit her tortilla factory, to spotlight his economic programs for depressed areas. Once she recovered from her shock, she immediately started lobbying the White House about seating arrangements. Josie wanted to sit at the president's right hand during the televised roundtable in her factory. The president's panel was to include a roster of local heavy hitters, including her congressman and a bank president. "Who am I?" she said. "I'm nobody, just a tortilla maker." She figured the guys wouldn't let her get a word in edgewise — so at least she wanted to sit beside the president. After multiple "diplomatic" phone calls, she got the seat of her dreams.

The telecast itself was a bit of a fiasco. A huge storm struck during the taping session, and the roundtable participants couldn't hear each other over the rain hammering the roof. The only person who could hear Josie's remarks about the importance of giving federal aid to established firms like hers, as well as struggling start-ups, was the guy seated just to her left: the Leader of the Free World.

Many male-oriented negotiating books advise scoping out the seating plan to figure out the power position — then scurrying across the room to get there first. If there's a long conference table, always nab the end away from the door, so you can give your opponents the evil eye as they walk in. If you're facing a round table, take a tip from King Arthur's quarrelsome knights and try to score the seat nearest the king — represented in the modern world by the audiovisual screen, the cynosure of all eyes. And whenever possible, they say, grab the tallest chair.

However, most women in search of win-win solutions reject such obvious power plays. For instance, entrepreneur Sarah Hoit furnishes her office with a couch and two comfortable chairs. And although Hanna Andersson CEO Gun Denhart does operate out of the corner office (on the fourth floor of a converted bicycle factory), it's set up to charm, not impress, with pale walls splashed with pink. Her long, rectangular desk sprouts a round bud at one end, surrounded by a set of identical chairs. "Whenever I meet someone in my office, I go and sit at that round table, so we're all on an equal level," she says. "I'm a consensus builder. I'm very sensitive to how people sit in a room. It's physically painful to me if someone sits way to one side. I ask them to move closer, to make sure we are all on equal footing."

If you're tuned in to the emotional Feng Shui of the room, you can use it to your advantage. In *The Art of Negotiating,* Gerard Nierenberg offers a neat strategy for disarming your opponents: Sit on their side of the table, and agree with them on minor points. You'll start to seem like a member of their team — a real plus when you tackle points of disagreement.

When she expects the discussion to be particularly acrimonious, former teachers union staffer Theresa Montaño asks each team to split up and sit side by side with their opponents. "It breaks up the us–versus–them feeling and makes it so much more cordial," she says.

Personally, my favorite seating arrangement is side by side on a couch or love seat. That physical closeness almost forces you to search for something you have in common.

Finally, just as if you were planning a dinner party, you need to consider the little touches that provide the ambience of the room. Should there be flowers on the table? Quiet music in the background? Or, if the talks are likely to be unpleasant, should you rent a few doves to fly around with olive branches in their beaks? Such strategically placed "context cues" can't guarantee a win–win outcome, but they can't hurt. "Some research shows people are affected by what seem to be irrelevant factors," acknowledges Leigh Thompson.

During the secret Middle East peace talks in Oslo in 1993, Marianne Heiberg, wife of Norway's then–foreign minister, wielded her own secret weapon. To keep the high-level talks confidential, the negotiators often met in Marianne's roomy country house outside Oslo. Heiberg's hospitality and home-cooked meals set the tone of the discussions. "It was important to bring in the humanity of normal life, the life of a private home," Heiberg later told an interviewer from *The Jewish Week.* "So we stayed together, ate together, lived together. You need social contact to negotiate; you need to learn how to interpret each other."

Throughout the often emotional talks, Marianne noticed that the Arabs and Israelis always halted their heated arguments whenever her four-year-old son, Edvard, entered the room. Sometimes they even stopped to sit on the floor and play with the boy. So she made a point of bringing Edvard in frequently, believing that his presence reminded the negotiators that what was at stake was nothing less than the safety of their own children and grandchildren, and all children whose futures would be shaped by their agreement.

Medical Maneuvers: Negotiating with Your Doctor

When you were little, your mother may have told you to be a good girl and take your medicine. But now that you're all grown up, it's time to realize that you deserve a voice in deciding which medicine you take, and why.

Again and again, studies have shown that educated patients who ask questions and get thoughtful answers do better over the long haul. It's sad to think how many women have been taught to nod passively whenever the doctor speaks — and how their passivity may have harmed their long-term health.

But it is possible for doctors and patients to work together to create manageable treatment plans, insists Zeev Neuwirth, M.D., a medical educator at Lenox Hill Hospital in New York City. As a doctor — and as a patient — Neuwirth believes that almost everything in medicine is (or should be) negotiable. The trouble is, most patients don't have the knowledge, or the emotional resources, to negotiate effectively. As a result, a sick person and her family can end up feeling as though they've jumped on a runaway train of medical care.

Neuwirth got a taste of life on the other side of the white coat recently when he went to see a new doctor for a routine checkup. The doctor poked Neuwirth's abdomen a bit, then pointed to a lump in his navel and diagnosed a possible cancer. Neuwirth vainly protested that he'd always had a bumpy belly button. It didn't matter. The doctor (who didn't realize his protesting patient was a physician) picked up the phone and scheduled an appointment with a surgical oncologist. "He sent the clear message that a discussion or negotiation was not going to be part of his game plan," Neuwirth says. And that gave Neuwirth the clear signal that it was time to find another doctor.

Negotiating with Your Doctor (cont.)

Neuwirth, an internist who teaches patient relations to physicians and medical students, says he thinks it's important to find a doctor who views you as a partner, not a pawn. And a growing body of research supports that belief. For example, one study, published in the *Annals of Internal Medicine,* found that diabetics who learned to communicate and negotiate with their doctors actually improved their blood sugar levels significantly.

If that sounds overly magical, just think about it. Suppose you're a diabetic and you're having trouble keeping your blood sugar stable. When you come in for your checkup, your doctor looks at your test results, shakes his head, puts his hand on the doorknob, and pronounces, "Make sure you eat your meals on a regular schedule." Then he walks out. Not much help, right?

Now imagine this: You sit down in your doctor's office — fully clothed, of course — and he looks at your test results and says, "What's the problem here?" Then you explain that your daughter has started taking skating lessons from an Olympic coach forty miles away. She's flying like a bird on the ice — but her practice schedule means you're constantly on the road during normal mealtimes. Your doctor nods understandingly (his son was a swimmer in high school), and together you work out a plan of portable snacks and diabetic-friendly fast food options that will keep you healthy while your daughter's pursuing that gold medal.

Of course, it's one thing to read about the benefits of negotiating with your doctor. It's quite another to sit there in a drafty paper gown and start grilling your doctor about treatment alternatives. As Neuwirth acknowledges, "This is not easy. You're not feeling well, you're scared, you're in pain, you may be embarrassed or ashamed — there's years of feelings tied into these issues."

So how do you handle these scary situations? Well, your good girl empathy can serve you well. Your doctor is probably overstressed and overscheduled. If you've got a ton of questions, write them down ahead of time — and make sure you mention the list to the office manager when you make your appointment, so your doctor expects an unusually long visit.

Remember that it's *your* health, so you set the agenda. Nancy Ainsworth-Vaughn, a professor of sociology and anthropology at Michigan State University, has found that patients who take control of the conversation — asking questions, changing the subject, and sharing personal information — are more likely to feel satisfied with their medical care. You don't have to be obnoxious. In her book, *Claiming Power in Doctor-Patient Talk,* Ainsworth-Vaughn notes that women often use verbal strategies, such as rhetorical questions and anecdotes, to communicate with doctors in a nonthreatening way. One patient broached a possible treatment option with the phrase, "My kid was wondering . . ." Another joked with her doctor, gently reminding him that she was a longtime patient and deserved respect. While it's not always necessary to use such roundabout methods, they may work better with doctors who become defensive when confronted more directly.

Don't be afraid to ask questions. If your internist grabs the phone to set up a biopsy, say, "Excuse me. Before we schedule this, I want to know exactly what's going on, and what I should expect." Being sick is frightening enough; going into a hospital unprepared is like walking through a Halloween haunted house, never knowing when someone is going to jump out of the darkness and wave a rubber knife in your face. And in a hospital, the knives are real.

Be open about your thoughts and feelings. "The more you can tell the doctor about why you're feeling a certain way, the more he's likely to understand and work with that," Neuwirth says. "Doctors are human." He tells of one patient who needed a potentially lifesaving test but repeatedly failed to show up at the hospital. "I called him and said, 'Could you tell me a little bit about yourself?' In a matter of minutes, it became so clear this person had a tremendous needle phobia. That was something I could understand and help."

If you still feel a little shaky about taking on an authority figure in a white coat, bring in some reinforcements. "Family members often remember things that patients, because of illness or nervousness, do not," Neuwirth says. "They can also keep track of what was said more easily than the patient." Having your husband, sister, or best friend standing by also reminds your doctor that you're "a social being, being cared for and loved by other people, and not just another disease to be treated or a broken bone to be mended," he adds.

Sometimes all you need is a little time — a day, a week — to pull yourself together. That's a legitimate need, and a good doctor will honor it whenever possible. "You have to feel comfortable with whatever you're doing," Neuwirth says. "In terms of scheduling, in terms of what you choose to have done, and who does it — all that has to be negotiable."

Don't be afraid that your assertive attitude will offend your doctor. A good physician knows, as Neuwirth says, that "the most powerful tools a physician can possess are a patient's trust and sense of collaboration." Caring doctors get frustrated when patients listen silently, nod passively, then go home and

Negotiating with Your Doctor (cont.)

completely ignore their advice. "The most satisfactory situation is when a patient comes in with an open mind and a willingness to discuss and negotiate and the physician has that attitude, too."

For those of us who grew up back when the doctor was God, it can be a little disconcerting to find that she's human — and fallible. When you sit down to have an honest, open conversation with your doctor, be prepared to find out there's a lot she doesn't know. "You need to let your doctors know that they're not just white coats to you," Neuwirth says. "They're people, and you respect and honor that." If your doctor is willing to listen to your questions, you have to be willing to hear her say she doesn't have all the answers.

Don't underestimate how tough it can be to create a new style of doctor-patient interactions, Neuwirth adds. "The health care system has traditionally been controlling and dehumanizing for caregivers as well as for patients. It's up to patients, at least in part, to make it more respectful, collaborative, and understanding of the needs of people and their families."

CHAPTER 6

●◆

THE NEGOTIATION DANCE

Close your eyes for a second and imagine yourself at a dance.

Maybe you're a debutante in a flowing white dress, nervously fingering the orchid in your corsage as a handsome young escort moves purposefully in your direction. Maybe you're a wallflower so abashed that you don't notice the equally shy guy in jeans and sneakers hovering nearby, gathering his courage as the band strikes up a slow, romantic ballad. Or maybe you're a nice middle-aged mom chaperoning the prom, suddenly astonished to find that rather good-looking physics teacher asking for the next waltz (or at least, the next garage-band version of "Stairway to Heaven").

Ready or not, it's time to dance.

Okay, okay. First we were setting the dinner table. Now we're off somewhere dancing to imaginary music. What is this — advice on negotiating or an evening at the country club?

The point here is that negotiating isn't something completely foreign and complicated. The skills that you use so effortlessly in the other spheres of your life are equally effective when you sit down to make a deal. And we find it easier to think in terms that relate to our everyday lives — not swimming with sharks, or matching wits with renaissance princes, but simply dancing with a partner.

In many ways the negotiation dance is much like all those other circuits you've made around crepe paper–strewn gymnasiums and parquet wedding reception dance floors. When the music starts, it's time to dance. You may be secure in the arms of a familiar partner, or you may be pulled onto the floor by some stranger who's making up the choreography as he goes along. Maybe this will be the beginning of a lifelong partnership, or maybe you're just hoping you'll reach the end of the song without breaking your ankle. Who knows? Perhaps someone more appealing may cut in and offer you a better deal. Once the music starts, anything can happen.

DANCING IN YOUR UNDERWEAR

Judy Rasmussen once found herself on the dance floor in her underwear. Judy, a nurse, lives with her Danish-born husband and their two young children in a modest house on the coast of Maine. She does all her shopping in local stores, with one colorful exception: She imports her family's stockings from Scandinavia.

Her sock fixation dates back to her first trip to Denmark, when she fell in love with the local legwear: colorful floral prints and tights with iridescent stripes. So she swore off boring panty hose and ho-hum knee-highs forever.

When her friends and neighbors noticed Judy's glorious gams, they asked her to pick up a few extra pairs on her next trip to Denmark. Strangers stopped her on the street to ask where she got her socks. Pretty soon she realized there was an untapped American market for European legwear. She ran the idea past a good friend, Laurel McEwen, who had a degree in marketing. Laurel loved the idea, and agreed to be her partner. So the fledgling entrepreneurs wrote to the Norwegian, Finnish, Danish, Swedish, and German embassies in Washington, D.C., asking for the names of likely suppliers. Then the two women mailed off letters to the European manufacturers, asking them to dance.

"At first I was scared to death," Judy remembers. "But I told myself, 'It can't be that magical. I should give it a try, because I have absolutely nothing to lose.' The worst anybody could say to me was no. The best was yes."

Her first yes came one busy morning a few weeks after those first letters went out. "It was 8 A.M. and I was up to my elbows in cereal," Judy remembers. She and the kids were sitting out on their secluded back deck, eating breakfast — and Judy was still in her underwear. Then the phone rang. It was a legwear manufacturer from Sweden, calling to say he was definitely interested in hearing more about her new venture. "I was dumbfounded," she remembers.

So, standing outside in her underwear, with her children crunching their Cheerios, Judy opened negotiations. As it turned out, she didn't have the capital to meet his required minimum order. But, she says, "it felt great that somebody was willing to talk to us."

As is usually the case, Judy didn't end up with the first guy who asked her to dance. Instead, she made a better match with a German manufacturer; she's now his exclusive U.S. distributor, through her new company Tights-On-Line (www.tights-on-line.com).

ON CONFIDENCE

When it's time to step onto the dance floor, the best advice can still be found in *Emily Post's Etiquette,* first published in 1922. In "What Makes A Young Girl A Ballroom Success," Mrs. Post wrote that the most important thing is "to be unafraid, and to look as though she were having a good time." That's equally wise counsel for today's woman venturing out on the negotiating floor. If you're confident (or at least, if you appear confident), you're well on your way.

Estée Lauder's Jeanette Wagner has a little mantra that gives her an extra jolt of self-assurance when she heads into a new negotiation. "I always start out thinking, 'I know I'll find a way.' I don't know what that way is, but if I listen, do my homework, and be sensitive, I'll find a way." She believes she inherited her "the glass is half full" outlook from her father, an Armenian who escaped from Turkey and settled in Chicago, where he opened a grocery store. For her dad, Jeanette says, "things were always possible." That doesn't mean every deal works out exactly as she hopes. But she always believes there's a possibility the dance will have a happy ending.

Self-confidence does more than straighten your spine and settle your stomach. It's also a critical ingredient in successful negotiating, because it helps you to keep your head when your dance partner starts whispering sweet nothings in your ear. In their classic study *The Psychology of Sex Differences,* psychologists Eleanor Emmons Maccoby and Carol Nagy Jacklin found that women weren't necessarily more open to persuasion than men. Instead, they concluded that people with less self-confidence, male or female, were more likely to fall victim to smooth talkers. "People who *believe* they are poorly informed about an issue will change their minds readily, whether or not they actually are less well-informed than others," they note.

Just think about that for a minute. Think about all those times you've allowed yourself to be talked into something against your better judgment, simply because you couldn't withstand an onslaught from somebody with more confidence (but less good sense). Our friend Kim still remembers one particularly painful encounter with a couple of human steamrollers. At that time, about ten years ago, she was the novice board president of a not-for-profit group working with the homeless. The board was putting together its major fund-raiser, and one of the board members had brought in two new recruits to help with the plan. One of the newcomers, a man, was a hotshot young attorney at a high-powered firm. The other, a woman, was a corporate exec on her way up the ladder. Both were decked out in designer suits and expensive haircuts — rather intimidating to Kim in her carpool couture.

When the fund-raiser came up for discussion, Mr. and Ms. Dressed for Success took over the floor. What the group needed, they said, was something glittering, something glamorous, something really top-drawer. What could be more dazzling than a Christmas party? The lawyer's firm was the anchor tenant of an extremely fancy skyscraper; they could hold the party in the penthouse suite absolutely free. For next to nothing — maybe 40 bucks a ticket — they could have a fabulous little event.

Despite the duo's overwhelming self-assurance, Kim was worried. Christmas was just a few months away, and $40 a ticket seemed a bit steep. "Nonsense," laughed the expensive suits. "Why, you spend $100 a couple anytime you walk out the door." To Kim, a big night meant pizza *and* a video, but she figured this impressive pair must have dozens of well-heeled friends. Despite Kim's feeble protests, the board voted for the party in the penthouse.

Ever the good girl, Kim set to work on this dream event, which rapidly evolved into a nightmare. True, the penthouse was theirs for the asking. But the building's contract with the chichi restaurant on the first floor gave them a monopoly on all catering, and the restaurant manager had no intention of trimming her profit margin to help a good cause. Poor Kim ended up asking her cash-strapped friends to spend $80 of their Christmas club money for a sumptuous dinner of roast beef sandwiches and potato salad. "It was horrible," she recalls. "I ended up selling ten tickets — and I bought five of those myself, which put a real crimp in the Christmas budget. Most of my friends simply couldn't afford to come."

The party was most notable for the empty spaces on the dance floor. The event earned a minimal profit, and on the following Monday Kim got called on the carpet by the agency's irate executive director. Infuriated at spending so much effort with so little result, the director dismissed the entire board. "If only I had spoken up louder at that first planning meeting," Kim says ruefully. "But they sure sounded like they knew what they were talking about."

DANCING BACKWARD IN HIGH HEELS

Just remember the difference between self-confidence and mulishness. If you insist on leading every step of the way because you only know how to samba, you may never learn to waltz. If you can appear "friendly and reasonable from the start," your partner is likely to mirror that approach, experts Roy Lewicki and Joseph Litterer advise in *Negotiation*. In fact, research shows that negotiators who start out assuming their opponents will fight them at every turn usually wind up fulfilling that unpleasant prophecy, even though there may have been plenty of common ground. In analyzing dozens of studies involving more than 5,000 people, Northwestern professor Leigh Thompson found that about half the time, negotiators failed to realize they actually had some compatible goals.

Does this mean you should check your skepticism at the door? Absolutely not. You shouldn't meekly follow your partner in a tango when the band is clearly playing a turkey trot. But it does mean you should be willing to let the other person lead from time to time. Professor Lewicki has a wonderful insight on this. Instead of simply trusting the other side blindly, you should realize that trust and distrust can exist within a relationship.

Ann McMillan, mediation program manager for the Center for Creative Justice in Ames, Iowa, describes a common scene: "The father is stuck on wanting primary custody and he's not going to give it up." After some gentle probing from Ann, he finally reveals his true concern. "I just want to see my kids," he blurts out. "I'm afraid if I don't get primary custody, I won't get to see my kids."

His wife is stunned by his outburst. "I never had any intention of keeping the children from you," she says. "I think you're a good parent."

Then they look each other in the face and realize they both want the same thing for their children — a strong relationship with both parents. At that point, Ann says, they can usually stop fighting, put aside their distrust for a few minutes, and put together a mutually agreeable custody plan.

Even in less highly charged discussions, you may still need to listen extra hard to hear what the band is really playing. One artful way to find the tune is to ask your opponent a series of what-if questions: What if we did it this way? What if we did it that way? It may take several rounds; you may be on the verge of asking, "What if I kicked you right in the shins?" But stay calm and keep dancing. "If you had to choose, which way would you prefer?" Ferreting out what will work, and what won't, will point you toward an eventual solution.

Remember, you don't have to stop dancing just because the music ends. Some of the most productive sessions take place out in the hallway, or during chance encounters between formal negotiating sessions. Former union negotiator Theresa Montaño often makes headway by posing her what-ifs away from the table. "I call them up and say something like, 'During our talks, I heard you say such and such. Well, what about this idea?'"

DANCE FLOOR DEPORTMENT

It probably goes without saying that most good girls are hopeless romantics at heart. We love to stay up late at night and watch chick flicks, with a big bowl of popcorn and a big box of Kleenex close at hand. My friend Lydia particularly likes those old costume dramas, where the plucky heroine goes prancing about in big, ruffled hoop skirts. In those overdressed weepers, there's usually a scene where the heroine is horribly insulted on the dance floor. So she gathers up

A Fair Split: Negotiating Your Divorce

Love stinks.

Okay, that's not a particularly good girl sentiment. But when you're facing the end of a romance that started out filled with hope and promise, it's natural to feel bitter and vindictive.

We understand, and we deeply sympathize. But we firmly believe that good girls who go berserk often end up with the short end of the stick in divorce settlements. Now is the time to keep your head — and your temper. Although you may be feeling like you've wasted your sweetness on a no-good ungrateful louse, you can use your classic good girl strengths to negotiate your way to a more satisfactory divorce. Whether you're the one who's ending the marriage or the one who's being left behind, you can still rely on your diligence, creativity, empathy, and listening skills to help you toward a win-win settlement.

Despite what many women think, divorce negotiations are not the time to exact revenge. "Work at being as reasonable as you can possibly be," advises Lynn Jacob, an Illinois-based divorce mediator and family therapist. "This is not about killing your husband, or even making sure he can't eat again," agrees former congresswoman Pat Schroeder, who practiced family law. "It's about getting a fair settlement so you can go on with your life."

Although it may be fun to fantasize about your ex huddling in a meager furnished room while you head to Acapulco with your alimony check, that's not realistic. What you really want is an equitable agreement you can both accept. Otherwise, you might spend the next ten years squabbling through the courts, trying to get your husband to cough up a child support check, while he's spending the children's college fund on lawyer's fees in a vain attempt to revise the settlement.

No matter how long you've been married or how righteous you feel, the prospect of negotiating with your husband can make your knees shake and your stomach hurt. But many of the lessons you've already learned about negotiating will help you make the best possible deal, for yourself and for your kids.

It's still possible to take a win-win approach to this time of loss. Remember that listening carefully to your husband's requests and creating a thoughtful, comprehensive divorce settlement is in your best interest. Sure, you can go to court and let a judge sort it all out. But judges typically rely on formulas and assumptions that don't fit the nuances of your situation.

Negotiating Your Divorce (cont.)

You can get through this. Before each bargaining session, take a few minutes to steady yourself. Take a deep breath. Let it out. Again. Good.

To further boost your confidence, here are some more tips.

Read up.

When your Girl Scout leader told you to be prepared, she probably wasn't thinking about your future divorce. But just as in any other bargaining session, you'll do better if you've done your homework. Before you make any sudden moves, make a research run. There are numerous helpful books and Web sites, including *The Complete Idiot's Guide to Surviving Divorce* (Alpha Books, 1999), *The Divorce Mediation Answer Book* (Kodansha America, 1999), and www.divorcecentral.com. These can give you a basic introduction to key legal and economic issues, such as alimony, dividing up marital property and marital debt, and child custody. You'll need to understand your state's laws on no-fault divorce and community property. It's also important to know whether a spouse's affair (or your own) might affect a property settlement or custody dispute.

Hire a pro.

Run, don't walk, to a good lawyer. You're going to need a divorce attorney to advise you through this process, and the sooner you get started, the better off you'll be. Try to get recommendations from other women who were satisfied with their divorce attorneys. Interview several lawyers in person, and take some time to make a thoughtful decision. (Ask them up front if they charge for an initial interview, so you'll know what to expect.) While you don't need a new best friend, your attorney will be a key support during some rough times ahead. Select someone you can respect, and who makes you feel better, not worse.

You need to realize that your lawyer is going to tell you some things you don't want to hear. This transition time is going to be tough, and you're likely to face a serious reduction in your standard of living. If you're expecting to keep the house and be a stay-at-home mom until your youngest child finishes college, you're probably going to be disappointed. Don't blame the attorney for giving you the straight story.

My friend Tina learned this the hard way when her husband of fifteen years walked out, leaving her with a twelve-year-old son and a broken heart. Tina has always been a full-time homemaker, and she had a real gift for stretching her husband's modest paycheck. When her husband left, I referred her to a divorce lawyer — a big, warm, red-haired Texan who's a real straight shooter. At their first interview, Tina explained that she'd need at least 85 percent of her husband's income to stay afloat. "Honey, that's not possible," the attorney said gently. "You're going to have to go out and get a job." Tina, overwrought, flew into a rage and walked out. Later, of course, the judge told her precisely the same thing. It might have been better if she'd accepted reality a little sooner, and started planning her job search.

One warning: If your husband has already hired a lawyer, run that name past your prospective attorney. Two lawyers with an acrimonious history can make the settlement process more drawn out and thorny than necessary. And whatever you do, never, never, never agree to share your husband's attorney. That's a one-way ticket to financial disaster.

Do some financial detective work.

One of my friends used to teach her children: "Murder before divorce. There's less paperwork." While we don't endorse that advice, it's true that a divorce requires a daunting inventory of the family finances. You need to know your husband's income, your own, and the value of your home and other marital property (both at the time they were purchased and now). You also need an accounting of investments and retirement accounts, as well as a list of all your debts and monthly bills.

Remember that divorces can turn formerly decent people into demons. If you're planning to ask for a divorce, or you suspect your husband is getting ready to leave, take steps to protect yourself. Ask your lawyer if it is appropriate to withdraw half of the money in your joint accounts. Cancel your jointly held credit cards, and safeguard your prized personal possessions. (Consider renting a safe deposit box for your beloved keepsakes. When our friend Lisa asked her husband for a divorce, he responded by pulling a precious photograph of her dead mother out of its frame and ripping it apart before her eyes.)

Pull yourself together.

You may not realize it, but you've negotiated every day of your marriage, as you've run your household, raised your children, and handled your job. Even if your husband has an impressive job title and hefty income, you need to remember that you're his equal. "Rarely is there a total imbalance," insists Nancy Chausow Shafer, a mediator in Highland Park, Illinois. "Even in relationships where the husband may appear to have more power."

Think about the ways you've managed to advocate for yourself during the course of your marriage. Talk to your lawyer about how to use some of those strategies to meet your goals in the divorce, too. Don't let your emotions cloud your judgment. During face-to-face bargaining sessions, try to picture yourself and your spouse calmly dividing a leftover piece of pie, or the proceeds from a garage sale. "If the case is to be resolved on the emotional level, the parties must move from an intimate, family pattern to a business-type interaction," says Connecticut mediator Carol Widing. If your husband tries to goad you, don't take the bait. "Be on your absolute best behavior," urges Lynn Jacob. "Don't respond to anything in an emotional way."

If he suddenly asks for custody of the kids, for example, don't blow up, or haul out your laundry list of all the school plays and Little League games he failed to attend. Instead, ask for a time-out. Huddle with your lawyer and try to come up with a custody plan that will give him adequate time with the children. We understand that dissolving an unhappy marriage may send you on a roller coaster of grief, fury, depression, and relief. Just don't vent your wounded feelings at the settlement table. Instead, find a good therapist who will listen to your pain and help you to figure out how to keep your emotions in check when you're in the lawyer's office.

Consider mediation.

Do you and your husband both want the divorce? Can you speak civilly to each other? If so, you might be good candidates for mediation, in which you negotiate directly with each other with the help of a neutral mediator. (However, you'll still need your own attorney to review the settlement agreement and draw up court documents.) Mediation can be cheaper and quicker than the usual sparring. In four sessions over several months, Darryl Brock and Eden Lustig dissolved their marriage of fifteen years with the help of Nevada-based mediator Charlotte Kiffer. The mediator, who has a master's degree in counseling and educational psychology, gave them a neutral place to meet and an outline of the topics they'd need to resolve to craft an agreement that would satisfy the court. She also acted as referee, blowing the whistle whenever the two started verbal sparring. "She prevented us from yelling at each other and helped us work toward a common end," says Darryl.

Sometimes mediators can help couples craft more creative, win-win deals than attorneys or judges might devise. That was certainly the case when Sam and Janet split up after two decades of marriage. Janet, who had tended the home front all those years, wanted to enter the workforce, but she knew she'd need some financial support from her husband until she could complete her education. She estimated it would take two years to finish the course work that would qualify her for a decent entry-level job.

Neither party wished to take their case to court, so they struck a deal. Sam would provide Janet and their two kids with a whopping 80 percent of his net income for the first two years after the divorce, permitting her to return to school full-time. Then the alimony payments would stop, and she'd be on her own (with child support). "The husband bit the bullet and gave far more than a court would require during that crucial time period," says Beverly Clark, a Detroit-based attorney and mediator who cites this case from a mediation training class she attended. "When a couple has their own concept of fairness, they are happy with an agreement like this, and they keep it."

Mediation doesn't work for everybody. If your husband is abusive, domineering, or intimidating, you should think twice before finding a mediator. This is the wrong time to start practicing how to stand your ground against a mean, overbearing jerk. It's also not a good option if you think your husband is going to lie about his financial assets. Unlike judges, mediators don't have the legal power to compel a spouse to release financial documents.

If you opt for mediation, look for a mediator who is a lawyer or licensed mental health professional with at least sixty hours of mediation training. To find mediators in your area, call the Academy of Family Mediators at 781-674-2663.

Never negotiate on your own.

While it's okay to talk over the settlement with your husband one-on-one, never, ever make any final commitments until you've consulted your attorney. "Clients come in and say they 'settled' certain issues in their case," laments Charlotte Adelman, a retired divorce attorney. "Well, they may think it's wonderful they got half of something — but I know they were really entitled to 70 percent."

Too often, husbands use those private conversations to apply pressure tactics they could never get away with in open court. "I see so many women

Negotiating Your Divorce (cont.)

clients in a long-term marriage who tell me what their husband has proposed, and it's not fair," says Carol Ann Wilson, a financial planner who specializes in divorce. When she asks why the women agreed to such unfair deals, they reply, "He told me if I don't go along with it, he'll fight for custody of the kids." You can protect yourself from this type of intimidation if you simply keep repeating: "I can't agree to anything until I've cleared it with my lawyer."

Be brave.

Don't go into negotiations with a chip on your shoulder. But remember — you no longer have to placate this guy. Walk in ready to ask for everything you need — and a bit more, to give yourself some bargaining room. Make sure you've got a clear priority list, so you can decide what you really need and what you're willing to bargain away. "Figure out what's worth fighting for," says mediator Jacob. "Then think about where you can compromise." If you're so upset that you can't bear to give up a single coffee mug, call up a wise, level-headed friend and talk it through until you're feeling more rational.

You don't have to worry about whether your opening request will upset him. "You don't want to provoke anger, but you shouldn't be afraid of it either," says Jacob. His feelings are no longer your problem. So don't back away from conflict. Stay calm, but be firm.

Think ahead.

In the heat of a divorce, it's hard to think about the future. But you need to make sure your settlement will work for you five, ten, and twenty years down the line. You'll need to think of as many contingencies as possible and build them into the final agreement. A financial planner can help you project your income and expenses, and can also help you consider the financial implications of various settlement offers.

For instance, will your settlement agreement change if one of you remarries? What if your daughter drops out of college for a year — will your ex-husband still contribute to her tuition bills after she turns twenty-two? If you're paying alimony or child support, what will happen if you lose your job? What if your ex-husband wins the Nobel Prize for work he did while you were married? (Don't laugh; a 1995 Nobel laureate had to share half of his $1 million prize with his ex-wife, under a divorce agreement signed seven years before.)

Don't stay married to the house.

We know how much that house means to you. Maybe your newlywed husband carried you over the threshold. Maybe when you were nine months pregnant, you climbed up on a ladder to stencil bunnies and ducklings on the nursery ceiling — finishing just in time to get to the hospital. Maybe you sat on the back porch with a sleepy son on your lap, counting the fireflies sparkling in the dark. Maybe you watched with misty eyes as your daughter floated down the staircase in a beautiful prom dress.

Those are precious, priceless memories. But they're all in the past now, and you need to start thinking about what makes sense in your future life.

"A lot of women say, 'I need the house,' and negotiate everything around the marital residence," notes mediator Carolyn Laredo. "This is a really big pitfall." You need to be realistic about the cost of maintaining that house. Even in a small house, a new roof can cost as much as a year's tuition at a state college; a big tile or slate roof can represent a full year at Harvard.

A house is not a home. No matter where you live, you'll be able to create a warm, pleasant home for yourself and your family. Don't commit yourself to a mortgage and maintenance expense you can't afford, just for the sake of sentiment and stability. Sure, it will be an adjustment to move somewhere else. But in the long run, you'll thank yourself for making a smart, unemotional move.

Be a wise and loving mother.

It's so difficult to be a good parent in the middle of a divorce. You want to protect your children's young lives from disruption, and you may want to punish the father you blame for breaking up their home.

Well, those feelings run directly contrary to what's best for a child in this situation. You need to make life decisions based on what makes sense for your long-term welfare — not what you imagine will make your children happier over the next few difficult months. You also need to respect and foster their ties to your ex-husband.

Laura, a dear friend of mine, is struggling with this right now. A few years ago, her husband, James, decided to pull up stakes in Minneapolis and move to a small Idaho town. Now James has announced that he feels unhappy and unloved and wants to start a brand-new life — without Laura. Devastated, Laura is returning to Minnesota. To ease the transition for their eleven-year-old son, Josh, she's planning to move back to their old expensive suburban

Negotiating Your Divorce (cont.)

neighborhood, where Josh believes all his old kindergarten pals are eagerly awaiting his return.

However, most of Laura's old friends live in a city neighborhood with plenty of nice apartments and excellent schools, and they're encouraging her to put down roots near them. They all know and love Josh, and are quite willing to provide plenty of free baby-sitting while Laura settles into her new routine. But Laura won't hear of it — even though she's appalled at how much she'll have to pay to live near their old house, and how much time she'll have to spend commuting.

Lately, after a few frustrating house-hunting trips back to Minnesota, Laura has been overflowing with venom toward her self-centered husband. Her fury toward James is visible to anyone within their zip code, and it's painfully obvious to her sad and confused son.

We completely sympathize with Laura, and we hope that James gets gored by a runaway elk. But we think she's taking exactly the wrong approach to helping her son get through this painful time. Instead of making decisions based on her son's short-term interest, while venting her rage at his father for putting her into this situation, she needs to look at the big picture. There's no way she can re-create Josh's happy preschool years for him; the best decision would be to find an affordable apartment close to her work, so she'll be able to spend as much time with her son as possible.

In the meantime, Laura needs to button her lip. While James is behaving like a rat, he's the only father Josh has. It's not right to try to poison a child's love for a parent — even a parent who isn't acting like one. Your son or daughter needs to feel a continuing bond with both parents. (And, pragmatically, you'll find it's easier to collect child support from a dad who still has a warm ongoing relationship with his child.)

Divorce is painful enough for a child. Don't add to the trauma by giving your son or daughter a starring role in your personal domestic drama.

her skirts and flounces right out of the ballroom, her composure shaken but her virtue intact.

Well, don't do that. Ever. There is to be no flouncing, no weeping, no storming, no pouting, no shrieking, no wailing, and no whining. Especially no whining. Because you're not Joan Fontaine. You're a grown-up woman in a grown-up situation. Behave yourself.

That can be tough. We good girls are an emotional bunch. We wear our custard-filled hearts on our sleeves. (Beth actually tears up at telephone company commercials.) But while your touching attempts to smile bravely through your tears may have convinced your dad to let you borrow his car, such dramatic tactics are generally a bad idea. When you lose your composure, you usually lose.

Whitney Johns Martin got a memorable lesson on this bit of dance floor deportment from a couple of grizzly bears. At the time, Whitney was having some conflicts with her original partner in Capital Across America, a venture capital fund that specializes in investing in women-owned companies. They were hoping to attract more investors, so they scheduled a formal meeting to discuss the future of their joint venture.

Whitney spent the weekend before the big meeting at her home in Montana, just outside Yellowstone Park. Her twenty-year-old nephew was visiting, so the two went for a hike in the woods. Unfortunately, a pair of grizzlies had the same idea. The two couples' paths crossed. Whitney's nephew (suddenly bearish on his own future prospects) hissed: "What do we do now, run?"

"I told him, 'Travis, you can't outrun a bear.'" Whitney stayed calm and kept walking, while the two furry giants looked on. "That day, bears could have eaten us," she admits. "But we were lucky."

By Monday morning, Whitney's partner suddenly looked much less threatening. He might be a bit unpleasant, but he weighed substantially less than 1,000 pounds. When he started the discussion by attacking her competence, Whitney stayed cool. "I thought to myself, 'This is not a life-or-death experience. He is not a grizzly bear. He can't kill you. All he can do is say mean things.'" So she sat back and listened impassively as her emotional partner kept escalating his demands. "It felt like it was coming down to him or me. There was no way I was leaving. I was full of faith and confidence." The result: exit partner, and enter Madame CEO. Which is not to say that you have to approach every negotiation as though you were a polar bear (which, as you may know, lacks facial expressions). It's just that you need to keep your emotions under control.

Ingrid, a twenty-five-year-old editor, still cringes when she remembers her first job negotiation. "I ended up in tears," she says. "I didn't know how to handle the situation."

At the time, Ingrid was twenty-two years old, just out of college, and working part-time as an editorial assistant at a small magazine. She was hoping to break into a job as an editor. When one of the junior editors left, it looked like her big chance. So she screwed up her courage, walked into the editor's office, and asked for a promotion. Her boss simply refused. And Ingrid started sobbing.

"Oh my gosh, it was so painful," she says. "My boss was amazingly comforting about it. She shut the door and said, 'It's okay, I know you're upset because this means so much to you.' She handled it so marvelously well, and I couldn't stop crying because I was so humiliated that I was crying. I finally got myself under control and trudged back to my desk, thinking, 'I just made the biggest fool of myself. I just asked for respect, and now I'm definitely not going to get any.' I was so emotionally invested; I hadn't learned you have to step back and be a little more objective."

Realizing that her boss wasn't likely to promote a crybaby, Ingrid quietly started looking for a new job outside the company — and she admits she got a big kick out of seeing the look of surprise on her boss's face when she calmly handed in her resignation.

If you find yourself on the verge of a torrent of tears (or a string of profanities), or if you think your opponent is heading off an emotional cliff, don't let it fester. Be straightforward and disarm the situation. "You can say something like, 'I'm feeling a little tense, do you feel tense?'" says management consultant Joan Goldsmith, coauthor of *Learning to Lead*. If you speak directly to the emotions that are floating in a dark cloud over the table, she says, "you can often crack the conflict right there."

ARTHUR MURRAY VERSUS THE MOSH PIT

You may be old enough to remember those old-fashioned dance studios where you learned the steps by following the footsteps painted on the floor. Or you may be of the generation that jettisoned all those rigid moves in favor of individualistic stylized jiggling. Whichever, you've probably attended a big family wedding where Lilith Fair met *Strictly Ballroom,* resulting in a trauma unit's worth of squashed toes and sprained ankles. Around the negotiating table, however, both types can coexist fairly peaceably. You just have to figure out whether your partner likes to dance by the numbers, or whether he's the type who lets it all hang out.

Autodesk attorney Marcia Sterling doesn't go for a lot of fancy footwork. "I decide in my own mind where I ought to be, and then I put all the cards on the table right out front," she says. "I say, 'If I were you, I'd worry about these things.'" Then she lists all the options she won't even consider. "I tend to get to my position pretty fast."

Lucinda Duncalfe Holt, CEO of Destiny WebSolutions, is also a fan of the direct approach. When she was barely out of school and managing the Philadelphia office of a start-up technology firm in Silicon Valley, her boss asked her to transfer to the New York office. She carefully calculated how much more money she'd need to replicate her quality of life in the Big Apple. Then she presented her boss with her salary demand: $48,000, precisely twice what she was making. When her boss countered with an offer of $40,000, she stuck with her original number. "I really meant that," she told him. When he realized she was serious, he met her demand. "It was a terrific watershed event."

Lucinda's straight-from-the-shoulder strategy is based on her training in martial arts. "If you punch someone with 90 percent of your strength, you may not get what you want," she says. "You need to use it all, or else you lose." She thinks stating her position directly is the most efficient way to do business. "I believe in being honest, and I don't have enough time in the day for posturing," she says. "I figure out what's fair, make my case, and hold to it." She's found that being disarmingly direct has a strategic advantage. Because candor is often unexpected, she says, "it tends to be unbalancing for the other party." That doesn't mean she's deaf to a thoughtful counteroffer. "If you don't agree," she says, "explain it to me." That's the point at which she hopes she and her opponent will start working together toward a mutually satisfactory solution.

Barbara Grogan, founder of a booming Denver-based firm,

Western Industrial Contractors, developed her no-nonsense approach for a very simple reason: She had no choice. In 1982 she was a thirty-five-year-old housewife with two kids and, after a divorce, a pile of debts. So she bought a $500 pickup truck, rented a small office across the street from the junkyard, and went into the business of helping companies relocate their plants, equipment, and people. While starting her own business sounds like a gutsy move, Barbara says she really didn't see any alternative. "I didn't believe anyone would hire me. The only entries on my resumé were 'housewife' and 'mother.' I was catapulted out of the nest, and it was fly or else."

She flew, and she made a point of flying straight. When she's bidding a new job, she says, "we tell our clients what it's going to cost — and then we work ourselves to the bone to make sure that's what it's going to cost by assisting them in avoiding any problems on the job. Unlike some contractors, we don't wait for the client to make a mistake and then charge a lot to correct it. We put together a bid that's fair and equitable, that allows us to make money and offer them tremendous value. We're very honest about what that's going to cost — and sometimes they don't like hearing that." If a prospective client doesn't like hearing the truth, she turns down the job. "I'm wise enough to know I don't have the time to try to push a noodle up a wall."

She has even less time for the back-and-forth bargaining usually involved in buying a car or a house. "I think women don't like these types of negotiations because making deals that way is dumb," she says. When she buys a car, she sends an employee to haggle on her behalf. "He calls me and says, 'It's all ready, you just have to go in and sign the check.'" When she bought a vacation home, she simply gave her real estate broker her offer and told her to call back only if the buyers accepted her price.

(But don't confuse straight shooting with strong-arming. These forthright women are making good-faith offers to people who have plenty of choices. That's far different from "boulwarism" — a take-it-or-leave-it approach named for Lemuel Boulware, longtime head of labor relations for General Electric. Boulware is famous — or infamous — for his "truthful offers," which were in truth ultimatums designed to bring the unions to their knees. After a number of years, Boulware's strategy backfired. The workers finally decided they'd had enough and called a strike in 1969 that shut down America's fourth-largest corporation for more than three months. The strikers won out, and the National Labor Relations Board eventually found that GE had been operating in bad faith.)

On the other hand, there's something to be said for taking a few carefully choreographed turns around the dance floor before you strike a deal. "For the no-nonsense types, your first offer can be relatively close to the final offer," says Catalyst president Sheila Wellington. "But with others you'll want to shoot for the moon."

Or the stars. Just ask Abbie Strassler, general manager for Iron Mountain Productions, a New York–based production company that has mounted numerous Broadway shows, including *The Iceman Cometh* and *Sideshow.* When she's trying to snag a star for a show, she always gives herself plenty of room to maneuver. She knows she's dealing with celebrities and agents who won't feel good unless they think they've wrung a few concessions from the producers. "I'll say, 'We won't pay for the dressing room.' We will. Or, 'Since we're paying so much, the actor can get himself to and from the theater himself.'" She knows perfectly well that she'll end up footing the bill for a car and driver. The agent knows it, too. What Abbie is really doing is allowing the agent, and herself, a few easy ways to trade concessions as they both work toward a yes.

Designer Charlotte Lyons says her husband, a project manager for a real estate developer, has taught her to ask for more than she expects to get. "He makes deals and negotiates all day long," she says. "He always asks for the moon and the stars in his own deals, and he's tried to teach me how to do this. He believes I'm worth the moon and the stars, so I always start from there."

But when you start making concessions, make sure you and the person across the table are giving up items of equal value. Don't trade Betelgeuse (the brightest star in the Orion cluster) for some crummy little second-rate moon.

To avoid giving too much away, let the other side present its entire proposal before you respond. "Wait until you've heard all of it," advises Linda Chaplik Harris, an attorney with Sonnenschein Nath & Rosenthal. "Say there are twenty issues. You may eventually agree to give in on ten, if that does the deal. But if you go one by one without knowing the whole landscape, you'll probably end up giving up more than that. You won't get the bang for your buck."

STRATEGIC SECRETS

Amy Louise, an old Texas friend of mine, had a grandmother who was a Houston lady of the old school. Although she and her grandmother loved each other dearly, her granny used to shake her head in despair whenever she saw Amy Louise walk in the room. You see, Amy Louise is the type of person who always has a lock of hair falling into her eyes and a half-inch of lacy slip showing under her skirt, while her grandmother was invariably immaculate. "My dear child," her granny used to say, as she tucked one of Amy Louise's straying bra straps out of sight, "a real lady never lets a gentleman know she has anything on under her dress."

That bit of grandmotherly advice holds true for negotiators, too. It's just like wearing a low-cut evening dress; you need to be very clear about what you want to reveal and what you need to conceal.

In general, it's a good idea not to be too cagey. "The important question is not *whether* to provide information, but *what* information to reveal," Professor Thompson writes in her book *The Mind and Heart of the Negotiator.* She points to research showing that negotiators who share their priorities with their opponents are much more likely to reach optimal agreements. So don't worry about making yourself vulnerable by letting the other side know what you want. It's usually smart to make your priority list public, and to ask your opponent to do the same. If he doesn't have a list, ask him to think about it and help you write one up on the spot.

Sometimes it's a good strategy to reveal confidential information — a tactic that one of Jeanette Wagner's male colleagues calls "tough truth." If the Lauder company needs to improve profits at a retail store and the owner won't budge, he'll pull out Esteé Lauder's profit and loss sheet for that store — which is normally confidential information. "He'll say, 'This is what we make at the bottom line, and so you can see that we need you to help us make money,'" Jeanette explains. "That breaks the impasse and opens up another dialogue."

But there are two things you generally should keep to yourself. First of all, never share your reservation point, the technical term for the point at which the deal stops making sense for you. If you're a buyer and the seller knows the highest price you will pay, he'll obviously try to hold out for that price. A pressing deadline is also best kept to yourself. If your opponent knows the clock is running out, he'll try to extract more concessions.

My neighbor Patty used this one to her advantage when she was shopping for a new house in a better school district. After months of looking, she had nearly given up hope. Until she found a darling little Cape Cod that seemed just right. Unfortunately, the asking price of $225,000 was about $30,000 above her price range. Dejected, she was about to walk away. Then her best friend got hold of a hot piece of information at a church supper. The sellers — members of the friend's church — were complaining loudly that they'd had no good offers, and the house was about to go to a relocation company for a quick sale. The friend immediately called Patty to tell her that if she waited for just one week, she'd be dealing with the relo people, not the owners. And relocation companies often accept the first reasonable offer they get. So Patty sat tight until the relo folks were in charge. Then she offered $185,000 — and got the house of her dreams.

WHO MAKES THE FIRST MOVE?

Back when young girls made their social debuts at glittering formal cotillions, a gentleman asked a lady to dance by walking across the ballroom and grandly offering her a party favor made of sparkling tinsel-threaded satin. In those days, there was no question of a lady's asking a gentleman to dance; such a sight would have been enough to send the matronly chaperones into apoplexy.

Today's emancipated young women would do well to follow those demure girls' example — at least when they're at the negotiating table. Whenever possible, you should let your opponent make the first offer. That way she has to throw out the first "anchor" (the starting point for discussions). That's especially important when your opponent has access to some classified information that you don't have. For instance, a prospective employer knows the general salary range she has in mind; if you throw out a number off the top of your head, you might price yourself out of a job — or lock yourself into a salary much lower than she is prepared to pay.

However, you should also remember that those blushing debutantes were careful not to accept the first invitations of every hopeful swain who came their way. Keep in mind that we warm, friendly extroverts are, in general, too easily swayed by an opponent's first offer. Bruce Barry and Ray Friedman, professors at Vanderbilt University, published a study on the relationship between personality type and negotiating strategies in the *Journal of Personality and Social Psychology*. They've found that "sociable, talkative, and excitable" types (which sounds to us like your basic friendly, chatty good girls) are often overinfluenced by the other side's first "anchor." If the salesman claimed the going price for widgets was $40 a dozen, people who were more "generous, cooperative, and flexible" gave that initial figure undue consideration. So they ended up paying more and getting less. In other words, nice gals finished last.

It's just amazing how often this tactic works, especially on good girls like us. It plays into all of our core issues: We don't trust our own judgment. We want to make new friends. We try to avoid conflict. So when some smooth talker comes in with an offer that's nowhere near the ballpark, we flutter our eyelashes, shrug our shoulders, and figure we must have misjudged the market.

Beth got a great tutorial in this tactic from an old friend of hers who has an astonishing track record at buying houses at far below their market value. "I always make a lowball first offer," he says. "You'd be surprised how often somebody will accept it." She remembered that bit of information when she put her first house on the market. Her asking price was $165,000, barely enough to break even on their investment. The house was in a marginal neighborhood, and she was desperate to move. But after several months, there were no takers. Then an offer came in — at $105,000. For a brief second, she didn't think it was worth taking seriously. Then she remembered her old friend Mr. Lowball and realized the prospective buyer was trying to set the "anchor" far below sea level. So she chuckled and told her agent: "Fine, counter at $163,000." They finally settled on $155,000. Unbelievably, at the closing, the buyer buttonholed Beth and announced in a huffy tone: "We were

Hiring a Pro

In most of your everyday negotiations, a big girl should be able to advocate for herself. (For those of you who haven't been paying attention, that's the whole point of this book.)

But when the Huns are storming the castle gates, a smart damsel goes straight to her princess phone and dials 1-800-GALAHAD. Then she sits back and lets her knight in shining armor do her battling for her, while she watches keenly from her bower in the tower.

In some situations, just about everybody brings in a hired gun to handle the person-to-person negotiating. Movie stars and football players hire agents. CEOs call in attorneys. Even your average home buyers and sellers usually prefer to let their brokers do the talking. But while the phrase "Call my agent" can make you feel like a Hollywood starlet, you've got to remember that you're still the one in charge. Letting your lawyer or real estate agent take the gloves off for some hand-to-hand combat can be highly effective. But you need to keep a shrewd eye on your own bottom line, and make sure your proxy is following your orders. You're the one who's going to have to live with this deal. Hire the best person you can find. Listen attentively to her suggestions. Then make those tough decisions yourself.

"Clients should stay in control of their lawyers," says attorney Linda Chaplik Harris, of Sonnenschein Nath & Rosenthal. "As a general rule, it's really a mistake to let lawyers do the deal without your input. You should assert control over the process, and not be intimidated by your own professionals." Take the time to interview a few candidates and hire a lawyer who seems willing to listen. While we hate to be cynical, we need to remind you that some lawyers, agents, and other hired guns get paid only when a deal is signed. Your real estate agent, for example, gets a commission only on closing. So she's taking money out of her own pocket if she advises you to walk away.

On the other hand, don't assume that every agent or lawyer is out to make a fortune at your expense. They do this stuff all day, every day. If you're represented by someone honest, smart, skilled, and experienced, you may end up with a better deal than you ever imagined. Consider the lucky athlete represented by sports agent Sue Rodin, who came up with this clever incentive for a footwear deal. Whenever a national publication shows Sue's client wearing the shoes, the athlete gets additional money. "That encourages the athlete to

Hiring a Pro (cont.)

wear the clothing, and it benefits the company even more," Sue says. So when that client flies across a page of *Sports Illustrated,* "we send a copy of the clip and an invoice." The sponsor gets national exposure, the athlete gets a check, Sue gets her commission, and everybody's happy.

So by all means, hire your knight in shining armor. Just check under the visor every so often, and make sure his trusty steed is pointed in the right direction.

---

very insulted by your first counteroffer." Beth just rolled her eyes and cashed the check.

It was fairly easy for Beth to hold the line in that negotiation. She had no choice, since that lowball offer wouldn't even have paid off her mortgage. But it can be very hard to stay firm in the face of an opening offer that's way out of line.

As always, preparation and confidence are key. (We've discussed this before, young lady. You simply have to do your homework. No exceptions.) If all your best sleuthing skills aren't enough to give you a clear picture of what the market will really bear, then you need to be confident, set high goals, and stick with them. It really works. "People with high aspirations seem to pay more attention to the dynamics of the situation and bargain more aggressively," Professors Barry and Friedman say.

And when it's your turn to throw out the first anchor, don't be shy. Friedman and Barry stress how effective an extreme offer can be, so long as it's not insulting or unrealistic. Beth managed to keep that in mind when she bought her current house. The seller had originally put it on the market for $262,500, but had dropped the price to $245,000 — still a bit too high, in Beth's opinion. So she came in with a low offer of $200,000. After bidding back and forth, they wound up at $218,000, well under the $225,000 Beth had expected to pay. That first anchor was worth about $7,000 — enough to buy a whole boat.

LOOKING AT A DEAL THROUGH ROSE-COLORED GLASSES

As your mother always told you, beauty is in the eye of the beholder. That's especially true in negotiating. The trick is to help the beholder on the other side see the beauty of your offer.

Let's say you're negotiating with your day care provider. She's been taking care of your daughter since the baby was just eight months old, and she's a beloved part of your little girl's life. When your daughter turned three last year, your baby-sitter offered to drive her to and from nursery school. In gratitude you gave her a 10 percent raise. But this year, as you're going over your household budget, you can only manage a 5 percent raise. From your baby-sitter's perspective, that's not nearly as good as last year. So you need to reframe your offer to showcase its benefits. Instead of presenting it as half of last year's raise, stress that 5 percent is still double the increase in the cost of living over the last twelve months. You could also point out how much her weekly take-home pay has risen over the last eighteen months. And, in an example of "tough truth," you might compare her raise with the 2.5 percent hike your husband is getting this year. (Then you might hand your husband a copy of this book; he obviously needs it.)

AND THE CROWD GOES WILD

At the end of those wonderful Ginger Rogers and Fred Astaire movies, there's usually a scene of the two of them whirling together around the dance floor while an admiring crowd watches, enraptured. Somehow the dancers seem to gain added grace and glamour from their sophisticated audience.

You may find that your dance around the negotiating table is equally enhanced by an attentive audience, particularly if your partner is stepping on your foot.

When Faith Wohl worked at Du Pont, she used audience participation to her benefit when she took on the task of convincing the company to improve its work-family policies. "We took our research on the changing role of men and the increasing interest in work-family solutions to the outside world," she says. "We released new ideas about our own workforce to the media, which influenced people inside. It was a useful strategy."

The tactic started a powerful feedback loop. National papers, including the *New York Times* and the *Wall Street Journal,* wrote stories heralding the forward-thinking family policies at Du Pont. All those glowing feature stories showcasing Du Pont as a family-friendly employer put pressure on the company to continue improving its childcare options and other work-family programs. "It increased pressure in a positive way, because the company sounded very good," Wohl says. "We could hold their feet to the fire." In 1992 the company was ranked on *Working Mother* magazine's list of the hundred best companies for working mothers. "Even though it didn't deserve it, in my opinion," Wohl says, "it was a standard Du Pont had to live up to."

You don't always need a national audience. Sometimes just knowing that your best friend will want to hear the full details can be enough to stiffen your resolve. "People negotiate more assertively when other people are watching them," comments G. Richard Shell, a professor at the Wharton School of Business, in *Inc.* magazine. "That is why labor negotiators are so tough — they know the union rank and file are watching their every move." So when you're getting ready to start the negotiation, tell someone about it. Explain your strategy and your goals. Then promise to report your results.

FOUR ON THE FLOOR

Of course, there's more to dancing than memorizing the steps. To really understand, you need to see dancers in action. Here are four profiles of women who had the courage to face the music.

Barbara Sells Out — Twice

In 1997 Barbara Kasoff and her husband were in a comfortable groove running the Michigan franchise of Voice-Tel, a voicemail service. Barbara and her husband had "mortgaged everything" to come up with the $200,000 needed to start up the franchise in 1988. But after years of seventy-hour workweeks, they had annual revenues over $2 million and profits in the high six figures.

Then — ironically enough — the phone rang. It was an emergency call, telling her that a big new high-tech corporation, Premiere Technologies, was buying out the parent company, and they wanted to acquire the franchise system, too.

"It was quite a big shock," Barbara recalls. "We, along with 120 other franchise owners, had to fly overnight to Atlanta to meet the buyer." The meeting with the president and board of directors went smoothly. "They were very friendly," she says. "They told us it was a great opportunity for all of us to work together and take advantage of the new technology, and we nodded our heads."

The honeymoon didn't last long. Negotiations quickly turned adversarial when the franchisees found themselves seated across the table from legions of highly paid lawyers and investment bankers. "It was a different league," Barbara sighs. She says the buyer tried to use a divide-and-conquer strategy, telling each reluctant franchisee that the others had agreed to the corporation's terms.

But Barbara and the other franchise owners didn't fall for it. They'd been attending meetings together for years, so they had developed very close working relationships. They also had unlimited access to their nationwide messaging service, which allowed them to stay in constant touch with one another. "We talked to each other. In addition to consulting with our own attorneys, we decided to hire one large firm to represent us, so the deals would be consistent," she says. "It was a great strategy."

Barbara and her husband found that putting the deal together became their full-time job for about three months. The whole process was incredibly stressful. At first, the buyers tried talking to Barbara and her husband separately, trying to coax concessions out of them. "Very quickly that stopped," she says. "We told them they could only have conversations with both of us."

Then Premiere's reps came to examine the franchise's books. Based on their recent earnings, the company made an offer. But Barbara and her husband thought their business was worth substantially more. So they declined. "We held out, and it was scary," she says. "We said, 'We will not move on this price,' and they said, 'Okay. Fine. Forget it. We'll move ahead without you.'"

For two nerve-wracking weeks, they didn't hear another word. Legally they were entitled to hold on to their franchise and keep operating independently. But practically they knew that hanging on after everyone else had sold would make them the odd franchise out, and Barbara didn't want to be the only petunia in an onion patch. To reassure herself, she stayed in touch with the other franchisees, who let her know where they were in their own negotiations. "Information is power," she comments. So they sat tight. "It seemed like forever." Finally the buyers came back, sweetening the offer substantially. "It was pretty close, so we took it," she says.

While the price was right, the terms were troublesome. Instead of cash, the buyers offered only stock in their corporation — not a particularly attractive option, given the roller-coaster-like track record of many high-tech companies' stock prices.

As it turned out, Premiere's stock soared after the sale closed. However, franchisees were required to hold on to their stock for a year. So twelve months later, Barbara sold her holdings — just before the stock plummeted from $30-plus a share to less than $8. "We were fortunate," says Barbara. "We got out before then."

And she had another ace up her sleeve — a second company, Voice Response Corporation, which she had founded in 1994. When her relationship with Voice-Tel ended, she turned her focus to her second business. Not three years after the Voice-Tel deal, Barbara found herself with two suitors trying to buy Voice Response.

This time Barbara was in the driver's seat. Both companies offered "very good deals," so she decided to work with the one that offered the best fit, LDMI, a Michigan-based telecommunications company. "We had a price, they came back with a counteroffer, and then together we established what both sides thought was the true and fair value," she says. "It was very amicable."

The second deal was a textbook example of win-win negotiating. They met in both sides' offices (to avoid turf issues), and spent a great deal of time discussing each side's needs and aspirations. In addition to a fair price, Barbara and her husband wanted a good transition for their employees. They also wanted to participate in the transition process. But because they're both in their fifties, "we didn't want a long commitment," she says. So Barbara and her husband signed a two-year contract to manage the business, which became an operating unit of the larger company.

Her experience with Premiere helped Barbara structure a much better deal the second time around. For one thing, she insisted on a cash payment. "I'll never do stock again. Are you crazy?" She also learned the value of "matching expertise with expertise. Don't get into a situation in which you are negotiating with a pro when you are an amateur," she warns. Even though her dealings with LDMI were "very clean," Barbara hired a strong legal team.

"Be very clear about your objectives," she adds. She and her husband spent hours discussing what they wanted their life to be like after the sale. "We learned you have to ask yourself: What do you want to come out with? Work it out ahead of time."

Alice: A Doormat Meets Mount Vesuvius

After years of happy marriage to Dr. Jekyll, Alice suddenly found herself living with Mr. Hyde. "He started to make fun of me, belittle me, and treat me like a servant," she recalls. While she's not sure exactly what triggered his midlife rage, "his behavior got worse over time."

As the couple's children got older, they all learned to tiptoe around their father, a professor at a prominent university. "He always had to have his way," Alice remembers. "If he didn't, he'd scream and yell and scare the daylights out of us. He's a very large person, and I'd give in just out of fear. Everything was my fault. It got to be the family joke."

Despite her husband's regular volcanic eruptions, Alice tried to hang on. "I had to overcome the generational thing, the idea that marriage was till death do you part, regardless of what happened. I was a doormat, if you want a term."

But finally she realized she needed to escape. "I knew I didn't want to live like this forever." So — slowly, carefully, and thoughtfully — Alice began negotiating her way out of her marriage.

She started her private divorce clock when their youngest child was eight years old. Alice knew that divorce can be devastating to young children, and she didn't think she could provide for them financially on her own. So she decided to tough it out until all the kids were out of high school.

She started taking steps to strengthen her position. She began setting her financial house in order to gain a clearer picture of their money situation. "I knew everything that was there." To make sure she would be able to meet her bills as a single woman, she began consulting a financial planner. She took quiet steps to document her husband's infidelity, gathering evidence to support her eventual divorce petition. And she began seeing a therapist, to help her "get up the courage to confront him with the divorce," she says. Finally, to prepare herself for her legal battle, Alice enrolled in a family law course at a paralegal institute, and eventually hired her professor to represent her in the divorce.

Her years of planning paid off when she finally announced the end of their marriage. Carefully "setting the table," she timed her announcement for the Christmas holidays, when all of her children would be home to support her. They anxiously waited in the kitchen as she called her husband into the living room. "I said, 'I need to talk to you, and I need to talk about our marriage.'" She confronted him about his mistress and told him: "You have this whole other life, and there is no point in going on anymore." By this time, she'd made sure there was no room for discussion; she told him she'd already filed legal papers and he would be served on the next business day. "I made it as short as possible," she says.

Her angry husband refused to move out of their house. Alice had no legal means to evict him, so for five uneasy months they continued to share living quarters. She slept downstairs, in a bedroom with a deadbolt on the door. "I locked myself in at night," she says.

The siege ended when her husband was invited to teach in Japan for a few months. During that time, a burglar broke into the house. Alice used the break-in as an excuse to get the locks changed — and conveniently forgot to send her estranged husband a key. When he returned to America, he packed up and moved out for good.

At first Alice had planned to sell their house and leave its unhappy memories behind. "That house had been a prison," she says. But after reviewing her finances and looking at alternatives, she thought better of it. "It was cheaper for me to stay," she realized. "It was way too small for the whole family, but it is just fine for me."

When the divorce settlement was finally approved, Alice ended up with half her husband's pension. She also got the better of their two cars and a jointly owned mutual fund. Because her husband's salary was triple her own, she was granted $1,000 a month in maintenance for three and a half years.

The divorce itself was not financially devastating, thanks to Alice's excellent research abilities and negotiation skills. She worked out a deal with her attorney, who agreed to let her do most of the prep work in return for a lower price. "I obtained the appraisers and arranged the documents in case it went to trial," she says. "I also made the financial budgets for the court and planner," she says. As a result, her legal bills came to only $5,000 — compared with an estimated $25,000 for her ex.

Now Alice is managing to get along on her modest salary. She doesn't have much of a financial cushion, and will probably need to keep working well into her seventies. But if things get really tight, she knows she can count on her children to help her. And since she's no longer receiving his checks, she doesn't have to deal with her husband anymore. "It's a bit harder, but I'm surviving," she says. These days, Alice says, "I'm not wealthy, but I'm happy. My children say how proud of me they are. Life is good."

Robin: Negotiating Her Way off Welfare

Robin Acree doesn't really like being called a good girl. "Why not phenomenal woman?" she asks.

She certainly didn't start out on the traditional good girl path. Pregnant at sixteen, she dropped out of school and got married. After three kids in four years, she started selling drugs to help make ends meet. "I didn't even know I had a problem," she remembers. Then she was arrested on drug charges and ended up spending sixty days in solitary confinement in a local jail. Soon after she was released from jail, she and her husband split. "I was in the projects with almost nothing," Robin says. "I realized I would have to negotiate for everything from that point on, whether it was a TV set, school supplies for my children, or Christmas presents. People used to tell me my biggest liability was my mouth. But it turned out that my biggest asset was my ability to negotiate."

Robin, whose children were seven, five, and two, managed to land a job as a kitchen assistant at a local restaurant and found a rent-subsidized apartment. But she soon realized that, between cab fare and baby-sitting expenses, she was losing money. "I was in the hole," she says. "I was trying to work, but it didn't make sense." She did some research and found that she would qualify for $342 a month in government assistance plus $200 in food stamps. Regretfully, she decided to quit working and go on welfare. "It's sad to say that was worth more than working," she says. "I didn't like not working, but I chose what was best for my kids."

That first year she was on welfare, Robin was barely scraping by. But she was determined to give her children a merry Christmas. She didn't have enough money to start a savings account, and she was pragmatic enough to admit that, if she started hoarding a Christmas fund in a jar at home, she wouldn't be able to resist raiding the piggy bank. So she convinced her local department store to relax its layaway policy for her. Normally customers were required to pay off their balances within sixty days. But Robin picked out some inexpensive clothes and a couple of Barbie dolls for her girls, and a My Buddy doll for her little boy. Then she talked the layaway supervisor into giving her six months to pay it off. "I was very matter-of-fact about it," Robin says. "I said, 'This is how much I can pay a month. How can we do this so I can buy these items?'"

As Robin struggled to keep her family afloat, she found that her brief jail term proved to be a blessing in disguise. The terms of her probation had required her to get professional counseling. Her therapist referred her to a vocational rehabilitation program. "I had to take some career aptitude tests," she says. "I was scared to death that they were going to say I had to study cosmetology or something like that. I couldn't possibly cut somebody else's hair."

But when Robin got her aptitude test results, "I was shocked when they told me I could go to college. They had to spend forty-five minutes convincing me that they didn't have my scores mixed up with someone else."

Through the rehabilitation program, Robin was eligible for tuition and childcare money. In 1989, at age twenty-seven, she enrolled in Moberly Area Junior College, forty-five minutes from her home in Mexico, Missouri. At first she paid a fellow student $3 a week to drive her back and forth. But when the ride was no longer available, she approached her credit union for a $300 loan, to buy a 1972 Chevy Impala. They turned her down. Under their credit guidelines, they didn't offer loans under $500, and they were uneasy about her repaying her loan with welfare money.

"I went to the president, and I wouldn't take no for an answer," Robin says. "I said rules are meant to govern things, but that doesn't mean they can't be broken, or at least flexed a little bit." She could have solved part of her problem by increasing the loan amount to $500, but Robin refused. "I didn't want to borrow more than I needed," she says. And she scoffed at the idea that it wouldn't be appropriate to use welfare funds to pay back a loan. "I reminded them that they didn't mind when I deposited my public assistance funds in their bank account." Her arguments overwhelmed the credit union's president. "I can be a really convincing advocate to get people to take a chance with me, to see that I'm worth a little bit of investment," Robin says proudly. She got her loan, and diligently paid back every cent.

After earning an associate's degree and an A average at Moberly, Robin applied to the University of Missouri at Columbia. The school accepted her, but the communications department put her on their waiting list. With her eligibility for a tuition reimbursement program running out, she pressed the dean for admission. "I said, 'I'm no kid. I've only got so much time to get my schooling done.' And I wouldn't go anywhere until he approved it. He didn't like that." Her persistence prevailed, and she got in.

At age thirty-three Robin landed a new job, as a local organizer for ROWEL, a welfare reform group based in St. Louis. Even with a monthly income of $1,500, she was nervous about living without the security of food stamps. But within five years, she doubled her salary by working her way up to a state-level organizing job.

With her professional career firmly established, Robin decided it was time to buy her own home. At first she asked her landlord to sell her the house she'd been renting. He asked for "way too much money," so she started looking elsewhere. After a year of fruitless searching, she came back to her landlord and successfully negotiated the price down below $20,000.

Then she had to negotiate a loan. Knowing that her credit history might frighten off a lender who didn't recognize her remarkable determination, Robin chose her lender carefully. "I didn't go to just any bank," she says. Instead she made an appointment with a loan officer who had worked beside her on a Habitat for Humanity project. "She had some history with me. She knew I was involved in the community, and that I was pretty persistent."

Robin qualified for a low-interest FHA loan, but the home inspections required by the program turned up some serious problems. The house needed a new roof and other costly repairs. Dauntless Robin just told her loan officer to add the repair expenses to the loan amount, pushing the mortgage dangerously close to the house's assessed value, and adding several new wrinkles to her loan officer's brow. "When she approved the loan, she said, 'Don't you let me down,'" Robin remembers. "And I didn't." Today Robin estimates that the house is worth $40,000. And because she's included a little extra with each monthly payment, she expects to pay off her mortgage in 2004.

Robin has been honing her bargaining skills in the political arena, with one very notable success. She and her coworkers scored a remarkable legislative victory by securing passage of a welfare reform bill opposed by the state's Department of Social Services. "It was the most empowering thing," Robin says with evident satisfaction. "They'd see our little heads peeping in their office windows. We'd go to each legislator and say, 'What will make you sign? Maybe we can get that for you.' And we'd warn them: 'If we do get what you ask for, we don't want to see you back out — because then we'd have to hold you accountable.' It was way cool."

Robin's remarkable advocacy skills have won her increasing recognition. She was recently invited to a national rights strategy session in Oakland, California, and she's very excited about working nationally and "taking my negotiating to another level."

But she's proudest of the work she's done for herself and her family. "More than anything else, I've negotiated for my dignity and my humanity." Through her honesty, courage, tireless effort, and extraordinary negotiating ability, she's triumphed against incredible odds. Now she takes strength from sharing her skills with other women and showing by her own example that "it can be done."

And she's drawn her line in the sand. "Some things are nonnegotiable," says Robin. "Nothing and nobody is going to break my spirit anymore."

Kathy: Negotiating Soup from a Stone

Kathy Allely was a reluctant advocate. A self-described "recovering shy person," she's soft-spoken and low-key, with rosy cheeks and a toothy smile.

But in 1980, when her daughter Rebecca was born fourteen weeks early, with a daunting array of medical problems, Kathy was forced to transform herself into a strong, competent negotiator. "I had a really hard time at first," she says. "I never was one to speak out in school. I was very shy. I think having my daughter cured me of that, because I had a lot to talk about. I just gradually found myself in situations where my passion overcame my shyness."

Her evolution began at her newborn daughter's bedside. For three months, Kathy sat beside her tiny daughter's incubator, trying to learn as much as she could about her daughter's condition and likely prognosis. "I read as much as I could about the kinds of medical needs she was having," she says. In the process she found that Alaska — her adopted home state — lacked the necessary technical equipment to perform one critical diagnostic test her baby needed.

"I had to negotiate my way out of the state," she says. At the time, she and her husband were just starting out, and they didn't have the money for a trip to an out-of-state hospital. So she asked Rebecca's pediatrician for help. "He knew what agony we were going through," she remembers. The doctor helped her to find an Oregon hospital that could perform the tests, and directed her to a state program that would cover their travel costs.

As Rebecca grew up, it became clear that she had substantial developmental problems. "Everything was significantly delayed," Kathy says. "She didn't walk until she was eighteen months old." Rebecca needed tons of special help, and Kathy became adept at finding that help for her. "I worked on becoming informed about what she needed, and then seeking out those people who could help me get those things for her. You know how it is with your kids — the love you have for them is so intense. I needed to make her life better."

Over time Kathy put her skills to work for the rest of Alaska's developmentally disabled children. "I had a mentor, who experienced a disability himself. He was doing a lot of advocacy work, and he sort of pulled me into it." She joined the Alaska Governor's Council on Disabilities and Special Education, and eventually chaired its health committee. Although trying to meet Rebecca's special needs while caring for her two younger girls was difficult, Kathy says, she felt called to volunteer. "It's probably something that was instilled in me from my own childhood, to leave the world better than it was when I got here. I think that's just something I have internally, that drives me."

Kathy was particularly interested in helping the parents of disabled children. "Parents shouldn't have to go through this alone," she says. "All those early years, we were really alone. None of the stuff that's in place now was available then. I saw this big void."

She was especially troubled that many Alaskan parents had to take their disabled children out of state to have their health problems evaluated. So the Governor's Council funded a study to determine Alaska's need for up-to-date diagnostic services. That study eventually led to the creation of Stone Soup Group, a collaboration of Alaskan parents, doctors, and state and private agencies aimed at improving services for families who have children with severe developmental disabilities.

"The project started as a collaboration of parents and providers who were determined to be innovative," says Kathy, now the organization's administrative director. "As this group came together, they began to see themselves as something akin to the Stone Soup fable, in which everyone throws a vegetable into the pot. None of us had all the resources needed, but we all had something to bring to the collective soup. So when it came time to incorporate, we couldn't think of a better name."

Getting a cluster of agencies and individuals to pool their re-sources and share can require some incredible negotiating. Kathy says the secret to Stone Soup's continued success is the group's tight focus on a shared goal. "I credit parents, staff, and our collaborators for their creativity and their willingness to come together — and stick together," she says. "Everyone has always considered the needs of families. We've kept that at the very heart of what we do."

Through her work on behalf of the state's disabled children, Kathy has become an expert at negotiating through the state bureaucracy — a skill that also has helped her gain access to the services Rebecca needs. Her biggest challenge came a few years ago, when Rebecca was about fourteen. "Our daughter had developed a lot of very challenging behaviors that were of great concern to us. It was a significant enough problem for her that we realized we weren't doing her any favors by keeping her at home. We needed to look for a very different kind of environment for her."

Kathy went to the state agency that oversees severely disabled children and asked for help. Their first offer was to put Rebecca in a therapeutic foster home, a suggestion Kathy firmly declined. "We didn't want to give her the message that she couldn't be part of our family anymore," she says. "We wanted a warm, loving, enriching environment for her." So Kathy did some intensive research and eventually found a program in Pennsylvania that seemed to fit her daughter's needs. Then she asked the state agency to pay Rebecca's tuition. At first she was turned down flat, even though it cost much less than the therapeutic foster home placement they had originally offered. But Kathy didn't give up. "I kept pressing until they listened." To prove that the Pennsylvania school was what their daughter needed, Kathy and her husband agreed to pay the $20,000 tuition for one year. But when Kathy showed how much progress Rebecca had made in that year, the state agency agreed to shoulder the program's costs.

"In the course of Rebecca's life, we have encountered so many professionals, and I've noticed that most of the people who go into this field are filled with passion and compassion," she says. "But there have been times we've encountered people in the system who are more rigid and bureaucratic." At those times, Kathy says, she's learned to be polite but persistent. "You have to pick your battles. You have to choose what is going to be important. And you have to plan for some rest time." There have been days when Kathy simply didn't feel like fighting. "You can't do it all the time. There were times I just couldn't find the energy. It wears you out. But then there were times I could pick up my strength and keep going."

CHAPTER 7

❧

BOY PLOYS

Beth has this one recurrent fantasy. In it, she's buying a new car. Of course, she's done all of her background research, and she bargains smartly and in good faith until she and the car salesman agree on a fair price. Then, just when it's time to sign the final papers, she announces: "I have to make a phone call." Leaving the astonished salesman in his seat, she ambles to the ladies' room, refreshes her lipstick, powders her nose, and pages idly through her Filofax.

After about five minutes, she returns to the salesman's desk with a sad look on her face. "I'm so sorry," she informs the salesman with an apologetic smile. "I talked to my mom, and she says she just can't approve that price. We're going to have to bring it down another $300. I sure wish there were something I could do, but Mom's the one who calls the shots around here."

When you're trying your best to put together a win-win negotiation, there's nothing more infuriating than an opponent who pulls out some stupid old ploy, some sneaky little trick designed to take you off guard and leave you vulnerable. Some are so well known as to be clichés — like the car dealer's old reliable: "This price is so low I'll have to ask my manager for special approval" (which, curiously enough, that mythical manager never grants). Others are so subtle that you may not consciously recognize them; you'll just feel a tight knot in the pit of your stomach as you sense that the negotiations are slipping out of your control.

It's frightening to walk into negotiations knowing that the people on the other side of the table may have attended seminars on how to use ploys to take advantage of naive suckers like us. But here's some reassurance: If you do all your homework and you come into a negotiation knowing your objectives and your bottom line, you're pretty well armed against most ploys. "If you have done your preparation, you have an idea of the worth of that transaction, and what you ultimately want," says Juliet Nierenberg, coauthor of *Women and the Art of Negotiating.* "If you keep your objectives in mind, it acts as a brake when you're about to do something stupid."

Nevertheless, it can be disconcerting the first time you encounter some of the ploys that are used to dupe good girls like us into paying more than we should and getting less than we deserve. So, as a vaccination, we're going to warn you about some of the most common gambits used to outmaneuver the opposition, and offer some effective counterstrategies. "If you can recognize something as a strategy, you can call their bluff, or ignore it," says Juliet. "Just recognizing it allows you to keep your cool and not be defeated."

But first, one word of warning: No matter how fiendishly effective some of these ploys may seem, it's a bad idea to rely on clever little stratagems to get what you want. It's one thing to set the table in a way that makes you most comfortable, so you'll feel strong and confident as you negotiate. It's quite a different matter to purposefully create an atmosphere designed to make your opponent anxious and ill at ease. The whole point to win–win negotiating is that you bargain in good faith, to make sure that all parties come away with something they value. "Strategies can be very dirty," Juliet says. "If you depend strictly on strategies, they can have the effect of antagonizing the opposition and destroying the climate of the negotiation. They can do a lot of harm." Even if it works once, the next time you sit down with those folks, they're going to be wary and distrustful — hardly the best attitude for a fruitful negotiation.

So if you're ever tempted to use some of these strategies, ask yourself what you're doing, and why. If you're waggling your finger and lowering your voice to grab the attention of some raging bull who's decided to throw a massive temper tantrum, then be our guest. But if you're telling a lie about your mother's upcoming surgery in an attempt to win your opponent's sympathy and hoodwink him into an unfair agreement — well, you won't be a good girl anymore, and we won't like you. Live with that if you can.

GENTLE PERSUASIONS

All right. Some of the strategies we've uncovered are going to startle you. (You won't believe how diabolical and dishonest some people can be.) To keep you from going into shock, let's start with some of the least offensive strategies you're likely to encounter.

The Silent Treatment

What does it mean when you ask for something and you get no response? Not a yes, not a no, not a maybe. Not even an "I'll have to think about it." Just a blank stare, or a deathly silence on the other end of the telephone line.

What does it mean? It means your opponent is playing one of the oldest tricks in the book — the silent treatment.

You see, silence makes most people nervous. And if you're nervous, chances are you'll start backing down, making concession after concession without even being asked. "If you are just quiet, the other side will negotiate themselves down," says Diane Bloem, a top-producing broker at Edina Realty in Edina, Minnesota. "It's really powerful."

Sometimes the silent treatment isn't a device. My friend Paul is a naturally quiet guy. He's not unfriendly; he just doesn't talk unless he thinks he has something to say. This personality trait served him tremendously well the last time he went shopping for a car. After the salesman had spent an hour running through the many safety benefits and high-performance features of this new sedan, he threw out a "low, low price." Paul, being Paul, stood there silently, mulling over whether he could afford it. After a minute or two of quiet, the salesman cracked. "Okay, how about $750 less?"

But all too often, the silent treatment is just a maneuver to get you to cave in. And it frequently works like a charm. Just ask my friend Amanda. Her mother-in-law is a prime practitioner of the art. Whenever her husband, Jeff, or his brothers did something that annoyed Mom, she'd shut up like an oyster, refusing to speak or make eye contact. In response, the boys would frantically try to regain her favor — clearing the table, doing their homework, or playing the piano.

After Jeff and Amanda got married, he tried the same tactic on her a few times. The trouble was, Amanda was brought up in a family where pouting was not allowed; if someone was quiet, that just meant they wanted to be left alone for a little while. So when her spouse clammed up, she'd leave the apartment and give him some quiet time. Pretty soon, Jeff realized that the silent treatment only works if there's someone else in the room.

Now that they have an adolescent daughter who seems to have inherited the family sulking gene, they've got their response down cold. "Honey, you seem to need a little time alone," they say in voices dripping with parental understanding. "We're going to Lalo's for dinner, and you can have the house to yourself." (You need to know that Lalo's is their daughter's very favorite restaurant on earth.) It's amazing how often the mere mention of enchiladas suizas is enough to bring their mute daughter back to life.

Whether you're dealing with a moody teenager or a wily insurance agent, you should never surrender to the silent treatment. If you have enough self-control, you can try being silent right back to them. (If you really feel devilish, you could hum. Amanda sometimes treats her daughter to "The Sounds of Silence.")

Unfortunately, most good girls couldn't withstand an uncomfortable pause if the fate of civilization depended on it. So opt out. Say, "I'll give you some time to think it over," and walk away. If there's no exit route, firmly change the subject. Talk about the weather, or that movie you saw last weekend.

Just don't let an uneasy silence force you into saying something contrary to your own best interest.

"You'll Have to Do Better Than That"

This phrase invites you to start bidding against yourself. Don't. Pam McDonough, Illinois's first female director of the state Department of Commerce and Community Affairs, runs into this one pretty regularly when she's trying to persuade corporations to set up shop in her state. When McDonough lays out the state's package of tax breaks and other assistance to a company, she's ready for that "you'll have to do better" line. She doesn't fall for it, because she knows it's really a ploy to make her sweeten her bid without waiting for a counteroffer — basically, to start bidding against herself. "Call their bluff and say no," she says. "Don't worry. If they're serious, they'll come back."

Sometimes this can be a perfectly acceptable good girl move. When you're presented with a set price, it's fine to ask, "Can you do better than that?" or "Do you have any sales coming up in the near future?" or "Are you running any special promotions or packages?" The invaluable *Unofficial Guide to Walt Disney World* claims that the reservationists at Disney hotels are instructed to mention special discounts only if you ask a direct question. One of its readers reported that, after the reservation clerk quoted a rate, he countered: "Are there any special rates or discounts for that room during the month of October?" As it turned out, there were. "For the price of one phone call, I saved $440," he crowed.

Think carefully when the other side demands a sweeter offer without throwing a little sugar in the jar himself. If, like Pam McDonough, you've done your homework and feel certain that you don't need to make further concessions, you can respond politely but firmly, "This is the best I can do." On the other hand, if you still have some wiggle room, then take this opportunity to signal your flexibility. Say something like, "Just how much better would I have to do to settle this now?"

Under no circumstances should you bid against yourself. Remember: You've made an offer and now it's his turn. He needs to give you a counterbid or proposal, which effectively puts some boundaries on what he's asking for. If you keep shooting in the dark, you're likely to hit your own foot.

Give Them a Taste

Here's a sweet little maneuver. As a young housewife, Debbi Fields had no college degree, no business experience, and no financial backers. So, not surprisingly, she had a hard time persuading bankers to bankroll her unconventional business idea: a walk-up cookie store. When she finally opened the doors of Mrs. Fields' Chocolate Chippery in Palo Alto, California, in 1977, it looked like the banks might be right. Her cookies sat all forlorn on the shelves, while shoppers walked right past her doors. "No one bought a single cookie," she recalled in a published interview.

Mrs. Fields figured she had nothing to lose. If customers weren't going to buy her mouthwatering goodies, she might as well give them away. "In desperation, I got the idea to walk outside and offer free samples to people passing by." Once they tasted her soft, chocolaty, freshly baked cookies, customers stormed into the shop to buy a bag to take home.

This is a highly effective tactic, used by lots of successful salespeople. Sometimes it alerts you to a product or service that is, in fact, something you'd really love. Just remember, the department store designer who encourages you to take that comfy dining room chair home on approval isn't just being nice. She knows that once you say yes to a free taste, it's hard to say no to the rest of the batch.

Be on guard against this one. You may have great sales resistance when it comes to the thousands of advertising messages that bombard you every day. You may be perfectly comfortable with hanging up on those annoying telemarketers who call during dinner. (Beth recently got a call from a fellow offering "vinyl protection services." "No, thank you," she trilled. "I don't have any vinyl that needs protection." Click.) But it can be difficult to turn down somebody who wants to give you something for nothing. "What harm can there be?" you think, as you pocket the free detergent sample, or read the free online book chapter, or send in the self-addressed, stamped envelope to get a thousand free stickers for your preschooler.

These savvy marketers aren't operating charities. They know that if you say yes to something small, you're likely to say yes to something bigger next time. (That's why those time-share marketers are so eager to fly you down to Florida for a free weekend, just to get you to listen to a two-hour sales pitch.) Unless you're really interested in a product or service, think twice before you bite.

Basically, before you accept that first free sample, ask yourself: Can I really eat just one cookie? If you can't, keep walking.

"I'll Have to Check with My Manager"

Of all the tricks of the negotiating trade, this one is probably the most notorious. You've just hammered out a deal with a car salesman, and you're ready to sign the papers and drive home. Then the salesman looks at the numbers and coughs nervously. "You know, I'm going to have to run this one past my manager," he says. The salesman then disappears for a few minutes and comes back with a sorrowful expression. "I'm so sorry," he says in a most sincere tone. "My manager won't approve this deal. We'll have to raise the price." What you're not supposed to know is that the salesman never talked to anybody. He just went in back, chatted with his colleagues for a few minutes, then straightened his tie, put on a sad face, and came back to gouge another $500 out of you.

This tactic flourishes outside car showrooms as well. The practice of citing a higher authority who's not currently available for comment but who definitely won't allow a particular concession occurs at all levels and has its legitimate applications. Parents love this one, in the form of "Darling, I'd love to let you go bungee-jumping, but your mother (or father) would never approve." It's a great way to hold the line in a negotiation without losing the goodwill of your opponent. It also lets you buy time while you try to figure out your fallback position.

But it's not so easy to fool little girls (and little boys) nowadays. The tactic is fairly simple to counter — as most eight-year-olds could tell you. When somebody invokes the opposition of an absent authority, whether it's the sales manager, Dad, or God, simply ask to speak directly to the boss. (This response worked really well for Martin Luther.) Make it clear you know exactly what's going on, and then refuse to negotiate with anyone who doesn't have the authority to enforce the deal. "Say, 'I prefer to deal with your manager,' and take the negotiation out of his realm," Juliet Nierenberg advises. "The salesman then has no recourse other than to change his tune, or else to let you speak to the manager."

QUESTIONABLE PRACTICES

As you've seen, most of the ploys above can be used both in straightforward, win-win, good girl negotiating and in that other kind. But now let's venture into more troublesome territory, with some crafty ploys most good girls would consider beneath them.

The Element of Surprise

Generally I love surprises. I like receiving little bouquets of violets, bestowed for no particular reason. I enjoy spur-of-the-moment lunch dates. I even think (although this hypothesis has not been tested) that I would appreciate a singing telegram. But I do not like being surprised in negotiations. I hate it when somebody pulls an unexpected little rabbit out of his hat and then expects me to come up with another carrot.

Kids are grand masters of this technique. If you have school-aged children, you've probably endured those lengthy negotiations over homework versus sleepovers. On Friday afternoon, you sit down and pore over your child's assignment notebook. "Okay," you say wearily. "If you finish your math problems and read your science chapter by 8:30 tonight, and if you practice your violin for an hour tomorrow morning, you may sleep over at Jonathan's house tomorrow night." Your child grumbles a bit but complies, and everything's peaceful until Sunday night — when the little wretch suddenly mentions that he has a social studies project that must be finished by Monday morning. "I forgot," says an unconvincing little voice. Once again you've been outmaneuvered by a miniature opponent — thanks to cunning use of the element of surprise.

Now obviously there are times when the unforeseen happens — the stock market tumbles, interest rates soar, the appraiser sets the house's value 15 percent below your bid, whatever. Those sorts of events take both sides by surprise, and you just have to reassess the situation and proceed from there. What I'm talking about here are deliberate attempts to unsettle or manipulate by springing something on you at the last minute. However, you may often find yourself unable to figure out whether your opponent is really dealing with an unanticipated change of events, or whether it's just a ploy to catch you off guard.

In either case, the best plan is to call a time-out. If you're reeling from shock, you can't think straight. So ask the other side to give you all the pertinent information, and then go somewhere quiet and peaceful until you can figure out what to do. Don't be intimidated by circumstances. Too often we try to swing at these curveballs. You feel as though you have no choice. You've taken the afternoon off for the closing, everybody's gathered around the table, the lawyers are all looking at their watches. Maybe the lack of flood insurance isn't that big a deal. How wet could it get?

Sweetheart, if you let yourself be taken by surprise, you're going to get soaked. So ask for fifteen minutes, or an hour, or whatever you need to assimilate this new information and come up with a thoughtful response. If this is truly a surprise to both sides, the other team may be grateful for a few minutes to brainstorm. And if they're pulling a fast one on you, your move to adjourn will give them a healthy scare.

There Must Be Some Misunderstanding

Ellen was bracing for the Great Family Holiday Fiasco. For about eleven months of the year, she loves living near both sets of parents. Her kids get to spend time with bunches of aunts and uncles, and there's always a family member willing to baby-sit on short notice. But from Thanksgiving through New Year's Eve, it's one massive ordeal. Ellen's mom is one of those mothers who take attendance at every holiday event; if Ellen is not present and accounted for, with all three little girls spruced up in their Christmas finery, she knows she can expect the emotional equivalent of coal in her stocking until Valentine's Day.

So in October last year, Ellen made a preemptive strike. She invited her mother out for a fancy little lunch; over dessert she gently tackled the upcoming holiday schedule. "It's too much to try to shuttle the girls back and forth to both families on Christmas Day," she said. "I thought this year you and Dad could come over to our house after the girls' church pageant on Christmas Eve. We'll open your gifts that night, and then we'll go to Tim's parents for Christmas Day."

"That sounds fine," her mother agreed. Whoosh! Ellen felt an overwhelming sense of relief, and was inspired to spend a little more than she should have on her mom's Christmas gift.

Then came Christmas Eve night. The girls sang like angels, and Ellen could barely see their aluminum foil halos through a haze of proud maternal tears. Afterward she set out the feast of roast duck and fresh cranberry sauce that she'd carefully prepared in advance. It was all wonderful — one of the best Christmases they'd ever had. As her folks were bundling up to leave, her mother gave her a hug and said, "Now, we'll expect you tomorrow around 4 o'clock."

Ellen's jaw dropped. "Mom, we talked about this," she gasped. "Tim's family is expecting us tomorrow."

"Ellen, you said you were going to Tim's for Christmas morning. I naturally assumed you'd be with us for Christmas night. I've invited everybody; your aunt Lillian is coming in from Milwaukee. They'll all be so disappointed if they don't see the girls. And truthfully, Ellen, Lillian hasn't been feeling too well. I don't know how many more Christmases she has left. If you don't want to come, I guess we'll have to get along without you. But we've all been looking forward to being together on Christmas night."

Ellen had just been hit with a classic ploy — the intentional misunderstanding. You've bargained in good faith, you've put together a win-win solution, and you're ready to close the deal. Then the rug gets pulled out from under your feet, as your opponent bats her eyelashes innocently and wonders why there's steam coming out of your ears.

As you can see, this one works beautifully on the home front. But it's also popular in a variety of workplace and commercial situations as well. Try reading these out loud in a sweet, puzzled little voice: "Oh, you meant you wanted *every* Thursday afternoon off?" "In this climate, we naturally assumed you'd want us to add undercoating." "I thought you understood that our quote for new windows didn't include the glass."

This tactic is tough to handle, because your crafty opponent usually waits until you're boxed in to spring it on you. Our old neighbor Shirley fell victim to a masterpiece of this kind. Her house desperately needed a new roof, so she carefully shopped around for the lowest price. But when the workers arrived, just after she'd left for work, they stripped off her still-functional garage roof and replaced it before she got home. When she complained, the roofing company owner explained that his guys simply misunderstood the order — they'd naturally figured she'd want that ugly old garage roof replaced. He then offered to remove the offending new roof, which would have left her garage open to the skies. Exasperated and outflanked, Shirley agreed to pay for the garage roof, too — and realized only later that the dishonest roofer was charging her 50 percent more per square foot for the garage job.

Shirley should have held her ground and called the city's consumer affairs office and the state attorney general. Since she hadn't signed a work order for the garage roof, she wasn't legally liable for the cost. But she didn't have the energy for a big fight. She also got scared when the roofer threatened to ruin her credit rating. So she gave up and paid the bill.

The best way to counter the intentional misunderstanding is to take advance action. Put everything in writing, with every definition carefully spelled out. Then make sure the person you're dealing with signs off at every important point.

That's what Ellen is doing this year. For New Year's, she gave her mom a beautiful new calendar. In it Ellen inked in her holiday schedule, and drew big red X's over the days she was spending with her in-laws. "I suppose she'll still find some way to misunderstand," Ellen says with a rueful grin. "But at least she'll have to be more creative about it."

Constant Interruptions

This ploy (Take that out of your mouth!) is very familiar (Could somebody answer the door?) to mothers (Can't you see that Mommy's talking on the phone?) of young (Why is the dog barking?) children who relentlessly (No, thanks, we're not interested in buying any aluminum siding) employ it to squeeze concessions (Look, everybody, Daddy's home!) out of their harried parents. It takes a tough-minded negotiator to hold her position when some fiendish little opponent decides to attack her at her most vulnerable point — that impossibly hectic hour just before dinner.

As you know, negotiating is stressful enough. But when you're constantly interrupted, it becomes almost impossible to concentrate on the business at hand. Some unscrupulous negotiators use that fact to their advantage, and purposely bombard their opponents with distractions. "This baiting can take many forms, from allowing phone calls and other business to interrupt the negotiation when someone else is speaking, to reading files or the newspaper," writes attorney Courtenay Bass in *The Woman Advocate*. "I have actually seen lawyers work on crossword puzzles while their opponents were speaking!"

If you've been careful to set the table properly, you shouldn't get caught by this one. But if you find yourself ducking shards of verbal shrapnel while you're trying to make your case, don't attempt to carry on regardless. Instead, address the problem calmly and directly, and request a new, quiet meeting time.

Let's Just Split the Difference

Consider the case of Gretchen and Joanne. After their second child was born, they put their Philadelphia condo on the market and found a house in a nearby suburb, with a good-sized gay community and a great school system.

They listed their condo for $225,000. A week or so later, they got a bid from Thomas, a single guy in his forties. Thomas's opening bid was $175,000, substantially below their expectations. After thinking it over for an hour, Gretchen and Joanne countered with $200,000. When Thomas came back at $186,000, they asked their broker to tell him that they weren't going any lower.

So Thomas pulled out this innocent-sounding ploy: "We're only $14,000 apart. Let's split the difference, and we'll have a deal."

"That sounds fair," Gretchen told Joanne. "Let's take it." Gretchen worked at home, and she was tired of cleaning up the place every time an agent wanted to show it to a prospective buyer. And besides, $193,000 was more than enough to pay off the mortgage and put a sizable down payment on their new house.

But Joanne, a former math major, wasn't so quick to acquiesce. She pointed out the "split the difference" fallacy. If they accepted $193,000, that would mean they had dropped their price by $32,000; Thomas had moved up only $18,000 from his initial offer. Suddenly, splitting the difference didn't sound so fair to Gretchen either. They decided to hold firm, and asked their real estate agent to tell Thomas why they weren't accepting his bid.

After a couple of days of looking at other condos on the market, Thomas came back with a new offer of $198,500, which they readily accepted. "We still gave up more than he did," Joanne says. "But I wasn't willing to fall for that 'let's just split the difference' thing."

Splitting the difference isn't always a bad option. If you threw out the first anchor, it might be okay. Just make sure you do the math. Don't let the other side set the anchor at an absurd spot then ask you to meet them in the middle. It may sound fair, but it's a cheap gimmick.

The Case of the Disappearing Negotiator

Corporate lawyer Linda Chaplik Harris once represented an entrepreneur who was selling his thriving business. "He came to the table with tremendous leverage," Linda recalls. But when the entrepreneur laid out his terms, the buyer's lawyer calmly announced that they had to think about it. Then he and the prospective buyer left the room.

That's when Linda's client started to sweat. The longer the buyer was gone, the more nervous he got. What was the buyer doing? Was he thinking of backing out? Could he be pursuing another deal? "I told him to cool it," says Linda, "but I saw my client melt." By the time the buyer walked back into the room, two hours later, Linda's client had completely lost his nerve. Despite her attempted intervention, he settled for substantially less than he should have. "Never underestimate what a good tactic that is," she warns.

Sometimes this one is legitimate. A new offer is on the table, and they want to talk it over privately. But remember that this move can also be used to throw you off balance and undermine your confidence. Either way, you shouldn't be rattled when the other side takes an unexpected break.

Keep in mind that not all negotiations proceed at a steady pace. "You've got to expect momentum to decrease and increase," Linda says. Don't get paranoid about every delay. Good girls are apt to think that a delayed response means no. An unexplained break in the action somehow triggers our internal tapes: "I shouldn't have asked for that much. I don't deserve it. They're not going to give it to me. They didn't really want me in the first place." It's incredibly hard to squelch that impulse to grab the phone and sweeten your offer. But don't let a delay scare you into bargaining against yourself.

This tactic has an even wilier cousin — the feigned walkout.

Linda remembers one of her first deals, when the buyer on the opposite side stormed out in a huff. "I was terrified," she recalls. She thought the deal was dead. But he returned, and the discussion proceeded — until they hit another snag and her hotheaded opponent stormed out again. Before the final agreement was signed, he had walked out seven times. "It got to be comical," she says.

This can also be a team sport, Juliet Nierenberg notes. One member of a team can explode and walk out in a huff, while the rest of his group feign horror. At that point you may be so intimidated by his outburst that you'll sign anything to get out before Frankenstein returns. In that case the other side will enjoy all the benefits of walking out without having to stay up past their bedtimes.

Juliet says the walkout can be "a very risky strategy. Suppose you want to make a very strong point, and let them know how dissatisfied you are. You might say, 'If the terms of this negotiation are not changed in five minutes, I'm leaving.' And after five minutes, you leave." But there's always the possibility that you may return to find the room empty and the deal dead.

The walkout, both authentic and feigned, is a very popular tactic in courtship negotiations. And quite frankly, it can work. When our friend Noreen grew tired of her true love Dwayne's unwillingness to walk down the aisle after two years of cohabiting in Chicago, she packed up and walked out — all the way back home to Baltimore. She got on with her life, and six months later she was starting to mend her broken heart with a perfectly nice young man. Then Dwayne heard about the other guy. The next day, he was at her doorstep with an engagement ring in his pocket. They've now been married for more than twenty-five years.

Don't threaten to walk out over trivial issues. Remember that you can only storm out once. Do it more often and your credibility dissolves. And make sure you have a BATNA in your back pocket in case negotiations don't resume.

When you're on the receiving end of a walkout, keep your temper. If your opponent returns without much coaxing, welcome him and get back to business. But if he starts to shuttle back and forth like a yo-yo, call him on it, gently but firmly: "We'll be more productive if we can stay at the table and keep working through the difficult issues, don't you think?"

Truth Lite

As that quintessential good girl Emily Dickinson once wrote: "Tell all the truth but tell it slant / Success in circuit lies."

In general, we believe honesty is the cornerstone of win–win negotiation. But you have to remember that there are all different kinds of truth. And the truth should not be confused with the whole truth or nothing but the truth.

Sometimes your opponent may reveal confidential information that supports his position in an honest effort to move you both toward a mutually acceptable agreement. For example, a home seller might show you a copy of his mortgage papers. But other times it's released in a strategic effort to stop you dead in your tracks. The litmus test is whether you're getting access to all the relevant information, and whether that information is open to negotiation. When an Estée Lauder exec brings out a profit and loss statement for an individual store to make his case to the owner, it's an honest tactic because he's willing to discuss the other line items on that sheet. If the retailer is being asked to boost the company's bottom line, it's only fair that she should have some input on whether the other expenses listed appear out of line.

That's why union negotiator Pat Harris refuses management's offers to let her look at the hospital's books, a move intended to underscore the institution's chronic cash shortage. Pat doesn't want to see the numbers unless she's offered a role in changing them. "There's no need for me to look unless you let me have a say in how you distribute the budget," she tells the hospital administrators. "Everyone else comes to you for more money, and you pay it. The paper towel vendor raises his price, and you pay it. But when we come, you find a reason not to pay. I'd be glad to go over the budget, but only if you let me decide how much is spent on paper towels and how much on salary."

Until she's offered a genuine chance to sharpen her pencil and squeeze some extra money for raises out of the hospital budget, she'd prefer not to see any confidential documents. "No one has ever said, 'Here are the books. Tell me how to better spend my money.'"

One Last Deal: Negotiating a Funeral

Imagine walking into a car dealership and saying, "I don't care what it costs. I only want the best for my family." Picture yourself handing your real estate agent a blank check and saying, "I just want it to be nice."

But when it comes time to negotiate the price of a funeral, that's exactly what most of us do. And it's costing us millions of wasted dollars every year.

Good girls are particularly vulnerable to unscrupulous funeral directors. Our soft hearts make us an easy target for any casket salesman who pats our hands and whispers, "I know you'd only want the best for your mother. I'll take care of everything."

From that point on, you're nothing but a big, juicy orange, ripe for the squeezing. That funeral director may have known you and your family for years. You may have gone through elementary school with his kids, and sat two pews away in church every Sunday. But when it comes to planning a funeral, it's strictly business. You're a prospective customer, and he's going to make a tidy profit from your grief.

It doesn't have to be that way. Just dry your tears for a second, and think about what's really important. Most likely, if you're a good girl, you were loving and dutiful throughout the life of this person you've just lost. You probably have some regrets, some unfinished business; we all do. But anyone who knows you knows how much you loved this person. You have nothing to prove, to yourself, to your friends and family, or (certainly) to the funeral home director. Your duty now is to yourself and your family. You'll do no one any good by overspending on a casket, gravestone, and funeral. That money could be put to much better use aboveground.

If you find yourself being pressured to spend needlessly on a family member's funeral, think back to the death of Princess Diana. Her funeral was easily the most expensive and elaborate any of us had ever seen, or probably ever will see. But when I think about it, the most moving and memorable part was Prince Harry's sweet little wreath of roses lying on the coffin, with just a card saying "Mummy."

To protect yourself from getting stiffed by your local mortician, here are a few tips to get you through this difficult time.

Negotiating a Funeral (cont.)

Don't do this alone.

The grave, as Andrew Marvell wrote, is a fine and private place. The funeral home is not. So while the funeral director may encourage you to come in with only your closest family members, now is the time to call in your best, toughest friends. You're going to need their emotional support and their unemotional bargaining skills.

On average, funerals cost $7,000 to $10,000. That's a lot of money — and much more than you need to pay for a nice, dignified funeral. That money could be a down payment on a condo for your oldest child, or it could serve as seed money for a scholarship program that would keep your loved one's memory alive for many years. It could also pay off a lot of debts that may have been left behind. You need someone at your side who's going to protect you from a funeral director's suggestion that your thrift cheapens the memory of the deceased.

Plan ahead.

Sometimes, of course, a death comes as a horrible surprise. But often we know in advance that a death is imminent. In that case, do yourself a favor and find out what you want and how much it's likely to cost, before you're overwhelmed by all the emotional turmoil caused by a family death. For straight information, call FAMSA (Funeral and Memorial Societies of America) or Funeral Consumers Alliance at 800-765-0107, or go to their joint Web site at www.funerals.org. These not-for-profit groups can put you in touch with a local society that can provide a list of low-cost mortuaries and educational materials on funeral planning. They also can provide ombudsman service if you think you've been ripped off. You can get a brochure on fair casket prices and other funeral costs by sending $2 and a large self-addressed, stamped envelope to the Good Shepherd Funeral Program, P.O. Box 939, Tempe, AZ 85280. The American Association of Retired Persons (601 E Street, NW, Washington, DC 20049) also offers a funeral guide.

Don't prepay.

This advice might seem contradictory. After all, taking care of your own funeral ahead of time seems like a great way to avoid burdening your family with arrangements and expense. That's why more than 1 million elderly people prepay for their own funerals, caskets, grave sites, and tombstones each year. But consumer advocates say lots of them get rooked. These plans are often nonrefundable or nontransferable — a real problem if the buyer has to move to another town. There also can be hidden fees charged to survivors, and the dead person isn't there to argue that those costs aren't valid. In the worst cases, the money simply vanishes. A 1995 *Consumers Digest* report found that $50 million in funeral prepayments had been stolen or lost. Instead, set up a special bank account or life insurance policy to cover your funeral costs, and talk candidly with family members about your funeral preferences.

Phone first.

Once you walk into a funeral home, you'll find it hard to walk out without buying something. To protect yourself, call the homes in your area and ask them to fax over a price list. If they refuse, cross them off the list. And for heaven's sake, don't tell them how much you're planning to spend!

Don't rush these decisions. It's usually okay to leave the body at the hospital for a little while until you've found a mortuary with fair prices.

Learn the ploys.

Always read the fine print — or have a friend read it for you. You need to make sure you're getting what you were promised, and that you're not paying for extras that you don't want, or that don't exist. One common markup is the added payment for using the funeral home parking lot. (Imagine if your grocery store charged you $200 for parking every time you came in to buy groceries!) If you find that you're being charged extra for "shelter of remains" or "use of lounge" or "additional funerary events," ask point-blank what the basic funeral home charge covers. From my perspective, a funeral home's basic fee should cover picking up the body, embalming it, and displaying it for visitation by friends and family until the funeral. If you're getting charged extra for any of those services, ask why.

If you're Catholic, Latino, African American, or Asian, know that the death industry is targeting you for a heavy sales pitch. That's because people in those categories tend to choose traditional, expensive funerals, while many white Protestants opt for cremations and memorial services.

Families who prefer cremation will be shown the body in a cheap cardboard box, designed to look so pitiful that an anxious relative is almost sure to

Negotiating a Funeral (cont.)

suggest, "Let's get something a little nicer." Funeral directors sometimes use that sad cardboard box to add about $1,400 to the cost of an average cremation.

Funeral home directors may mislead family members about state laws — for example, saying they're required to use an expensive grave liner or vault. In fact, they're not required by any state. Embalming is not routinely required either, FAMSA says, at least not when burial or cremation takes place within a day or two of the death.

Father Henry Wasielewski, a Catholic priest in Tempe, Arizona, has devoted his life to uncovering the sales tricks used by the funeral home industry. If you've got a strong stomach, read through his Web site at www.funerals-ripoffs.org. You'll be appalled by the scams reported by grieving family members.

Don't bury furniture.

You wouldn't take your mother's prized walnut sideboard and stick it in the ground. Then why on earth would you spend thousands of dollars on a gleaming oak casket with brass handles, only to bury it? When you're shopping for caskets, you need to know that most funeral homes display only their more expensive caskets in their showrooms. They boost their profits further through a "third-unit, target-merchandising system," Wasielewski reveals. Dejargoned, that means that they know most people will avoid the two cheapest caskets in the showroom. So you end up buying a casket you think is at the lower end, but you're really spending much more than you should.

There are some particularly unpleasant ploys used to get minority families to spend more on caskets. One industry insider says some funeral homes glue a cheap picture of the Virgin Mary inside the lid, then charge their Mexican Catholic customers hundreds more. Family members don't question these add-ons, in part because of the quasi-religious atmosphere inside the funeral home. As Wasielewski told *U.S. News & World Report,* "You don't sign the papers for a new car with Jesus staring down at you over the salesman's shoulder."

If you can't find a reasonably priced casket in your town, call Direct Casket (800-732-2753). They'll ship a good-quality, low-cost casket — just like the ones at the funeral home — to your mortuary within twenty-four hours. The funeral home will probably complain, but they cannot refuse or charge a handling fee for caskets bought elsewhere, nor can they demand that you be present for delivery.

Whatever you do, don't buy a protective-sealer casket.

Some funeral home directors will tell you that these caskets will protect your loved one from the elements for thousands of years. What they don't mention is that the sealed environments can be perfect breeding grounds for anerobic bacteria, which eat the body tissues and can produce explosive gases. *U.S. News & World Report* cited a Pennsylvania woman who sued the manufacturer when the casket seals burst, spewing goo all over her grandmother's mausoleum. (The company, which settled the claim, denied any wrongdoing.)

Consider this story of a brave and thoughtful family.

Before Supreme Court Justice Hugo Black died in 1971, he stressed to his family that he thought funerals should be "simple and cheap." But when his children (accompanied by two Supreme Court justices) went to a local funeral home to pick out a casket, the funeral director steered them to a beautifully crafted coffin made of expensive wood. Sure, it would cost thousands, but it would be a fitting resting place for a Supreme Court justice. Cost, the funeral salesman said, should really be no object.

Big mistake. That comment inspired Black's family and friends to honor the jurist's wishes and buy him the very cheapest casket available — a ghastly concoction covered with pink organza and pink satin bows, with a pink ruffled skirt around the bottom. As the salesman blanched, they started ripping off the fabric covering to reveal the "perfectly fine" plain pine box underneath, writes Josephine Black Pesaresi, the justice's daughter, in the Funeral Consumer Information Society of Connecticut newsletter. To appease the funeral director's injured feelings, they allowed him to clean up the resulting holes and glue residue — provided there was no extra charge for that service.

To further honor Black's memory, Dean Sayre of the National Cathedral asked the family to display the casket without a flag or flowers on top of it. "He wanted people to see that the cost of a coffin did not symbolize the abiding love of the living for the dead, nor did it reflect the stature of a man," Pesaresi says.

GOOD GIRLS DON'T

Now come the really slimy strategies, the ploys beloved of bottom-feeders who just get a big kick out of hoodwinking good girls like us. Well, don't let them. But don't follow in their foul footsteps either. These ploys are included for preventive purposes only.

My Wallet Belongs to Daddy

Imagine yourself confined in a bleak, windowless room, furnished only with a bare desk and a couple of rickety, uncomfortable chairs. You're trapped all alone with a mysterious spellbinder, who keeps insisting that you sign over 10 percent of your monthly income before he'll let you out the door.

Is this a cult indoctrination session? No, it's just some guy trying to sell you an overpriced piano.

Douglas Rushkoff, author of *Coercion: Why We Listen to What "They" Say,* calls this a textbook example of the "regression and transference" technique. In the "regression" mode, the salesman tries to confuse and intimidate until your inner child is vulnerable and exposed. "They put you in a room with fluorescent lights and no windows," Rushkoff says. "The car dealer will tell you, 'Sit here.' Then he'll talk about very complex financing." Pretty soon, you're trapped in an anxiety dream from second grade, where you haven't done your homework and you feel like you're about to wet your pants in front of the whole class.

Once you're feeling small, the canny salesman moves into the "transference" stage. He becomes the Big Daddy, the guy who knows everything and wants to take care of you. With your pulse racing and your mind spinning, you put yourself at the mercy of this ersatz father figure. But he has no mercy, Rushkoff says. "It's a hard, cold world out there."

This tactic always makes Beth think of the pitiless door-to-door vacuum cleaner salesman who preyed on her elderly grand-aunt Geneva. She and her husband, Harry, were living in a tiny house they could barely afford on their combined Social Security. Harry, in the end stages of emphysema with an oxygen tube up his nose, sat motionless while the salesman ran through the vacuum's many bells and whistles. Aunt Geneva was defenseless against the salesman's hard sell. At his command, she meekly signed the incredibly expensive purchase order. Later Beth inherited the vacuum and its many attachments. When she looked at the box full of gadgets, she just shook her head. "He even sold them the paint sprayer," she said in disbelief. "How much spray painting did he really think those two sick old people were planning to do?"

This type of coercion is almost guaranteed to work on frail, elderly, isolated consumers. But even healthy adults are susceptible. It doesn't take much to make most of us feel baffled and flustered, especially if we're caught in an unfamiliar, uncomfortable spot and bombarded with confusing information.

Don't let them do this to you. Pay attention to your emotional state, and protect yourself. "If you're feeling confused or disoriented, don't try to function and do something important there," Rushkoff says. "If someone's making you anxious, they're not your friend. Don't do business with them."

And if you're under duress from a salesman who won't leave your house, don't worry about being polite to this thief in friend's clothing. Go to the phone and dial 911. Tell them someone you don't know has entered your home and refuses to leave. When he hears those sirens approaching, he'll leave fast enough. After all, he's a criminal about to be caught in the act.

Good Cop, Bad Cop

A platinum blonde moll sits trembling in an interrogation room, unable to conceal her terror. A burly cop turns a blinding light in her face. "Listen, sister, we've got the goods on you. You've just bought yourself a one-way ticket up the river. And you won't need those fancy duds where you're heading. We've got a beautiful new wardrobe picked out for you, all in stripes. Stripes — get it, sister?"

A second police officer, younger and handsomer, interjects. "Hey, Sergeant. Lay off the kid. Can't you see she's scared to death? Now, Miss LaRue, let's turn off this bright light and get you a nice glass of cold water. Then I'd like you to tell me, in your own words, what happened the night Fast Eddie was shot."

This one happens a dozen times a night (at least it does if you live in a city with some good cable TV channels). It's a classic of the gangster movie genre — and it's also a classic negotiating device. One guy's mean and threatening. The other's nice and friendly. So which one is your friend?

Neither. Them guys are playin' you like a violin, angel face. Only them violin cases are full of machine guns. Get it, sister?

This strategy works beautifully whenever you make the mistake of negotiating before you do your homework. You're anxious, and you're not quite sure what you're getting into. So when the Bad Cop growls menacingly, you rush into the protective arms of the Good Cop, eager to cut a deal and get away from his threatening partner. That's exactly the plan. Their one-two punch is designed to knock you from your initial position and into their own ring, where the Good Cop's offer is the only game in town.

Psychologically this is a very powerful strategy, says Lisa, a lawyer who's also a former policewoman. "It works for a number of reasons," she says. "In the beginning, you're somewhat confused. Second, you really want something — whether you're trying to stay out of jail or trying to buy a house. You really want to believe the good cop, and you really want to avoid all the bad things the other guy is threatening. You, the victim, are anxious, fatigued, and vulnerable. They know all that. That's why it's so effective."

They don't actually need to have both cops on the premises to work this ploy against you. Edgar Dworsky, founder of Consumer World, a public-service consumer resource guide on the Internet, says this one is common in home maintenance scams. Suppose you see an ad for a carpet-cleaning service, offering three rooms for $69.95. You call the service, which sends over a "cleaning expert" (who's really a salesman). He looks at your carpets and shakes his head sadly. "I don't know why they're still pushing this method," he says. "It's just not as good as the new one." Then he dumps some dirt on your carpet, so he can demonstrate the difference. Sure enough, the new system works much better. However, it's much more expensive — about $500 for all three rooms. Seeing the shock in your face, the kindly cleaner heads for the phone. You hear him argue with his manager, until he comes back smiling. "I can do it for $195," he says proudly. You're so grateful to your champion that you pull out your checkbook. What you don't know, Dworsky says, is that you're still paying far more than you should. "Had you been in the know, that price is still outrageous."

There's one simple way to defend yourself from the good cop–bad cop ploy, Lisa says: "Remember that there is no good one." They're just two bad guys who have teamed up to take advantage of you.

If you find yourself flanked by a good cop–bad cop team, one option is to be direct and name it. Say something like, "I see that you're using the good cop–bad cop technique with me. Let's stop all this game playing and try to reach some mutually satisfying agreement." If that doesn't work, refuse to negotiate with the good cop. "Focus all your energies on turning the bad guy around to your point of view," advises Mark McCormack in *On Negotiating*. "If you can't do that, you haven't lost anything — because you won't do any better with his partner." Or better yet, walk out the door and find someone who's willing to negotiate with just the facts, ma'am.

Sign Now or the Deal's Off

Think back to one of those moonlit nights when you were a teenager. You were parked at Lookout Point, the stars were twinkling, and "your song" was playing on the radio. It was all so romantic. Then Joey got a little more persistent than usual. Make that a lot more persistent. All of a sudden, you found yourself in a world-class wrestling match, trying to fend off both his physical advances and his emotional barrage. "If you don't do it tonight, I won't love you anymore," he whispered. "It's now or never."

Well, we hope you slapped his face, jumped out of the car, and walked home. Because that kind of intense deadline is only used to pressure you into accepting a bad deal, without giving you time to consider what you're doing.

Obviously, there are lots of legitimate deadlines. Maybe you're moving to a different city and you need to be in your new house before the school year begins. Maybe you're the office manager and you need to have all the vacation requests in hand before you draw up the December schedule. Maybe you're heading the committee to build a new nursery school and you need all the contractors' bids in time to break ground on schedule. But when some fast-talker tells you his offer is only good until midnight tonight, that's usually a bad sign. "Ninety percent of the time, the timing is artificial," says executive Michele Hooper, who has negotiated several corporate buyouts. "If it goes beyond that, the world won't end."

One variation on this tactic is the phantom other buyer, the couple from California who seemed very interested in buying this house (or antique sofa, or Thoroughbred horse, or gift basket business). "In Boston that phantom buyer is always a professor at Tufts," muses Dworsky. The phantom is usually invoked to light a fire under a potential buyer who seems to be dragging her feet. Don't let the phantom scare you into making a deal that's not right for you.

"These situations are all bogus," says Lisa, the policewoman turned lawyer. "It's just a ruse." When someone attaches a pressure-cooker deadline to an offer, she says, "I'll put it in writing. I'll say, 'This acknowledges receipt of your offer,' and I'll just ignore the deadline, the part I know is not true. Then I tell my client, 'Don't take it if you don't want it. And if you do, it will still be there tomorrow. That's just a threat.'" When someone tries to pressure you into a decision, whether it's Joey in the backseat or James in the boardroom, don't sign before you've had time to think it over.

We Don't Have to Write This Down

National Health and Human Service Employees Union negotiator Pat Harris learned this one the hard way. After a particularly intense meeting ended with union reps and hospital administrators finally coming to an agreement, she didn't want to press further by asking them to put it all in writing right there and then. But when she saw the contract, drawn up by the hospital's attorneys, many of those hard-won concessions were missing.

At that moment she made a solemn vow: "No way will I ever walk away from a tense negotiation again without having something in writing." Now she jots down all the major agreements on a yellow legal pad and has her lead opponent sign it on the spot.

While some verbal agreements may be legally valid, they can be harder to enforce. Putting it in writing while you're at the table saves time and prevents misunderstanding later on. If the other side's attorneys have a fit at the idea of their client signing a handwritten document free of all legalese, you can compromise by making a photocopy of your informal deal memo and asking them to take a look at it before they leave.

Don't Worry About Little Me

Remember that nice salesman? The one who skipped his son's championship soccer game so he could sell you that beautiful bedroom set? Here's a news flash: That concerned dad is really a childless bachelor. And when he made that phone call, to let his wife know he wouldn't be home, he was really dialing the weather.

These guys have all got your number. When you walk into that showroom radiating naive sweetness, that salesman can just smell your vulnerability, like a T-rex sniffing a young hadrosaur scampering upwind. They know your weak spot: You're really, really nice.

So they set up a scenario to win your sympathy. They call home to let the little woman know they'll be late for dinner. They leave a message telling their daughter they'll try to see the last half of the school musical. They break away for a minute to tell Mom to put her birthday cake back in the refrigerator. It's an amazing coincidence; Beth says she has never bought a big-ticket item at a time that didn't conflict with a major family event on the salesperson's part.

There's no way you can negotiate effectively if you're envisioning a child's tearstained face looking hopefully toward the grandstand, only to see an empty seat where Daddy ought to be. So don't put yourself in this position. Don't try to sneak into the shop a half hour before closing; that immediately sets you up for the "I hope I don't miss the spelling bee" scenario. And whenever a salesperson wistfully mentions the family breakfast, lunch, high tea, lacrosse game, viola concerto, or synchronized swim meet that she's missing in order to serve you better, stop right there. Ask her for her card, set up a more convenient time, and go home.

Stand Back, Boys, She's About to Blow!

Things are getting intense. You're down to the wire, and you still need a few more concessions to put this deal together.

Then the guy on the other side of the table starts to get red in the face. Veins pop out on his forehead and neck. You can hear him breathing roughly. He's about to blow his stack, venting his venomous rage all over the room. What in heaven's name should you do now?

It's easy, says lawyer Lisa. Smile sweetly and hold your ground. "There are people who throw tantrums," she says. "It happens to lady lawyers all the time. Men try to intimidate you. It can be a very effective tool to use against professional women, because it's something they've never been trained to deal with. They equate that kind of rage with the boogie man."

The level of invective can be amazing. "One lawyer did say to me, 'Someday somebody's just going to kill you,'" Lisa remembers. "It was during a divorce situation, and I'm in the hallway, and there's this vociferous lawyer screaming at me, with his arms flailing. I just smiled and said, 'No, only the good die young.'"

Unfortunately, most of us don't have Lisa's incredible coolness. When voices rise and fists clench, we get stomachaches and will do just about anything to escape. Which is exactly why some educated adults behave this way; they know it works.

Figure out a way to neutralize the situation. Never engage in a screaming match; it's not likely to get you anywhere. "I never yell," Lisa insists. Instead, take a deep breath, then say, "I think things are getting a little heated here. I don't want this to degenerate. Why don't we take a break?" Then take a little walk — and if he follows you, head for the ladies' room. (If you're being pursued by a female ogre, you may have to be a bit more creative to shake her.) "Go make a phone call," Lisa says. "Do anything to get out."

Here's one more tactic that might help, Lisa adds. If you find yourself going up against an angry blowhard, "what I find very effective is to raise my index finger and go, 'No, no, no, no, no.' It really works with men. It brings them back to their school days, and gets their attention. I do it right when I want to make my most important point. I don't wear it out, but it does make people pause. And it gives me the break I need."

Fiddling with the Fine Print

At last, you've reached an agreement. All you have to do is sign the paperwork and everybody walks away with something valuable. So it's time to grab a pen and scribble your signature. Isn't it?

Not quite. You need to take adequate time to read through every word on those closely printed sheets. Because too often, the deal you're asked to sign doesn't match the deal you think you made.

"You'd be surprised," Lisa says. "They'll put a lot of mumbo-jumbo in there, with the secret sentence in the middle. The one-two punch is mixed somewhere in the boilerplate language that you would ordinarily overlook. That happens all the time."

Beth got a personal lesson in this when she leased her Honda minivan. Having done all her homework before negotiating the price of the car, she knew she was getting a good deal. Then the manager came in with piles of paperwork to sign.

As she looked over the sales agreement, Beth noticed that the price listed was $150 higher than she'd agreed to pay. When she pointed out the difference to the manager, he told Beth it was just a typing error and the difference in price would cost her only a couple bucks a month. "This is not the price we agreed to," she repeated. "It will take about fifteen minutes to retype it," he said. "Don't worry, I'll wait," she said with a thin smile. So he took the papers back to the office and returned with the proper price typed in.

"Who can absorb all this stuff?" Dworsky comments. "They know no one's going to take the time to sit and read this long, fine-print contract. So you need to say, 'I'm going to take this home tonight, and look it all over.' Don't feel pressured to sign right there on the dotted line."

Getting in the Driver's Seat: Car Leasing

If you're thinking about leasing a new car, think again.

While the lower up-front costs and monthly payments may seem attractive, leasing a personal car can be a questionable financial move. You're basically

Car Leasing (cont.)

renting a car for three or four years; at the end of that time, you've spent thousands of dollars without increasing your net worth. If you're really going to take that car down payment and buy college bonds, that's one thing. But if you're leasing because you're short on cash, you're probably buying trouble.

Whenever possible, bite the bullet and buy; four years later, you'll own a vehicle that's actually worth something — and you won't risk owing a car dealer hundreds for excess wear and tear and excess mileage charges.

Nevertheless, you may end up like our friend Ardis did, with a dying old car and not enough cash for a down payment on a new one. In that case, leasing may be your only option. But be smart: Some dealers have realized consumers have figured out the basic car-buying scams, so they've moved their ingenuity to the less familiar leasing department. "It's kind of disgraceful," says leasing expert Charles Hart. "A lot of times, I feel that the large car companies are participating in it, or at least tolerating this. I think that's shameful."

Certainly the dealerships have been capitalizing on their female (and male) customers' math anxieties, and have often aggravated the problem by using nearly impenetrable paperwork designed to obscure leasing scams. "It's a shame, but the laws up until recently have been very, very weak in terms of helping the consumer see what's going on," Hart says. While new regulations have forced dealerships to provide less confusing paperwork, that only helps educated consumers who know what to look out for.

To help you become that smart consumer, Hart's company, CHART Software, developed the program Expert Lease Pro (800-418-8450). "The program is designed to help the customer see what's going on and spot any hidden fees or funny business," he explains. The software is packaged with a listing of invoice and average retail prices, plus all the rebates and incentives currently being offered. Another helpful resource is Hart's Auto Leasing Resource Center, at www.leasetips.com.

Don't assume you're stuck because you signed a dishonest lease last week, or even last year. "We get a lot of people who experience leaser's remorse," Hart says. "After the fact, we've discovered they were totally screwed. In a few of those cases, we were able to coach them through getting out of it."

If the dealership isn't cooperative, you can seek restitution in the courts. Depending on what state you live in, your attorney general may not be much help, even though many of these leasing scams are against the law. But if you contact your local bar association for the name of an attorney experienced in automotive fraud, you can take the dealer to court.

To get a good deal on a lease, remember these tips:

Read the paperwork.

Read all of it very, very carefully. Take it home and add up all the numbers. Make sure the car price listed is the one you negotiated, and that you got full credit for your trade-in. This is the most common scam in auto leasing, and it's the one Ardis fell for. After a marathon negotiating session at the dealership, she just wanted to drive home in her great new car. So she didn't realize the dealership had quietly removed the trade-in from the lease paperwork, adding $500 to the cost of the new car. The dealer should be able to account for every penny on the lease form. Don't pay for options you didn't get. And don't be fooled by little terms like "acquisition fee" or "lease generation fee." That's dealerese for "We're adding $600 to the cost and we hope you don't notice." If they say the manufacturer insists on this fee, tell them to cut the price by that amount, or go find another dealer who will.

Don't be misled by the "money factor."

This one is a real honey. Although you pay interest on a lease — just as you would if you bought the car — the leases don't spell out the interest rate in normal percentage terms, such as "6.2 percent annually." Instead, they use a "money factor," which is written as a decimal starting with .OO. (We don't understand why either.) Basically, you can figure out the real interest rate by multiplying the money factor times 24.

A sneaky lease supervisor can use those numbers to confuse the heck out of you. Suppose the dealership is offering a 3.5 percent financing deal on new car purchases. You ask the lease guy if you can get 3.5 on the lease, too. He says sure — then gives you a money factor of .0035. You do the math. That's really an interest rate of .084 — or, in conventional terms, 8.4 percent annually. That ploy can cost you thousands of dollars over the life of the loan. And if you draw it to the leasing manager's attention, he can always claim it was an honest mistake. To protect yourself, ask the salesman to write down the money factor and the actual interest rate. Then recheck the paperwork yourself.

Car Leasing (cont.)

Don't compare leased apples with purchased oranges.

This one is devilishly effective, especially if you're just starting out or you've got a growing family and an overstretched budget.

Here's the scenario. You desperately need a car, but you just don't see how you can afford another car payment. The salesman, seeing the frustration in your eyes, offers to "run some numbers." So he tots up some impressive columns of figures, waves his magic wand, and presto! This dazzling new car will cost a whopping $520 a month to buy — but only $314 to lease.

If that sounds too good to be true, it is. The salesman produced that horrifying monthly cost for buying by inflating the interest rate and padding the purchase price. And that low, low lease cost doesn't include the extra charges you're likely to pay when you turn in your car — nor the hidden charges that the leasing department is planning to build into your paperwork (see above). If you went into a dealership planning to buy, don't let the salesman use this shell game to dazzle you into a lease that is not to your advantage. Chances are, he's not trying to save you money; he's trying to pick your pocket.

Get the terms you need.

If you're a carpool queen like us, you'll drive more miles than average, and you'll end up owing hundreds, even thousands, in extra mileage charges. Solve that problem up front by asking for more miles in your leasing agreement.

Beware the extended warranty.

This would seem like a "well, duh" situation. If you're entering a three-year lease and the manufacturer's warranty runs for three years, of course you don't need to extend it. But the salesman might try to talk you into it anyway, claiming you'll be sorry you didn't pop for the warranty if you buy the car at the end of the lease. But if you end up returning the car in three years, you'll have paid hundreds of dollars for absolutely nothing. We wouldn't do it. And we wouldn't sign a lease for longer than the manufacturer's warranty either. "The dealers know that if you want to lease for sixty months, you're either desperate or you don't know what you're doing," Hart warns.

Study for the final.

A lease actually requires two separate negotiations, one when you sign and one when you bring the car back. So before you return your now used car, review all your paperwork. (Of course you kept it all, including the original sticker. They're all legal documents, and they're important.) Do yourself a favor and have the car in tip-top condition when you bring it in. Don't let your dealer use a stray french fry under the backseat as evidence of excessive wear and tear. Check to see exactly what your original lease said — and don't forget the security deposit you paid up front. It's like a deposit on an apartment, and you should get it back. And for heaven's sake, don't wait until the last minute to decide what you're going to do about a new car. If you're desperate, you'll fall prey to the leasing vultures all over again.

CHAPTER 8

❦

IT AIN'T OVER TILL IT'S OVER
(And Even Then It May Not Be Over)

Cordia Harrington thought the deal was done. McDonald's had recruited this outgoing southerner, owner of three McDonald's restaurants, as part of the food giant's program to expand its relationships with women and minorities. So when Cordia expressed interest in opening a bun factory that would supply McDonald's restaurants in a multistate region, corporation executives paired her with two large food companies who had an established track record. As you may recall, she negotiated a wonderful deal and came away from the table delighted with her ample share of the pie. She set up her new company, Tennessee Bun, in Dickson, Tennessee.

At first she planned to start up gradually. Then came the great McDonald's Beanie Baby giveaway. The decision to give away the popular little beanbag toys with Happy Meals created an unprecedented influx of burger buyers, and they all needed buns. So Cordia had to hit the ground running; her spanking-new bakery pumped out a thousand buns a minute, twenty-four hours a day, during her first two weeks. "What a start-up we had!" she exclaims.

But when that promotion ended, demand eased up — too much, as it turned out. Cordia found that McDonald's orders were requiring less than half her top capacity. Those empty ovens worried her. Then Pepperidge Farm's buyers came calling, asking her to bake for them, too. To Cordia that sounded like a no-brainer. There was just one problem: She had promised she would move her buns nowhere but toward the golden arches.

Most good girls would have shrugged sadly and watched all that extra bread go flying out the window. After all, a deal is a deal. But Cordia couldn't let such a good opportunity go past without at least giving it her best shot. When her contacts at McDonald's vetoed the idea, she kept pressing. "I first met with severe resistance," she remembers. "Convincing them took many trips to their headquarters in Illinois. I explained that it would lower their overhead costs and make me stronger financially. I had to say it again and again."

As Cordia saw it, adding the Pepperidge Farm business was a win-win-win deal. She'd make more money, putting her bakery on a firmer footing. McDonald's would still get all the buns they needed, while substantially cutting their contribution to her overhead costs. And Pepperidge Farm would gain a great new supplier. Eventually she hammered those points home, and McDonald's gave the okay. "Now my business will more than double, and we're the lowest-price supplier for McDonald's anywhere," she says proudly.

A happy ending? Not yet. Cordia was just getting started. Soon after Pepperidge Farm signed on, the company asked her to freeze some of the bread before shipping. Unfortunately, Tennessee Bun just didn't have room to add freezer capacity. Cordia thought she was stuck — until one of her employees, who was listening to a local radio station, heard that Rich Products (a family-owned baked goods company in Nashville) had put its 60,000-square-foot plant up for sale. The energetic entrepreneur sprang into action. In less than a week, Cordia had checked out the facility and put in a bid. Her offer was low — hundreds of thousands of dollars lower than her nearest competitor's, she found out later. She knew she couldn't outbid her competitors. "I flat didn't have the money." But she did have some insights that her competitors lacked. Cordia had done her homework; her real estate broker had told her the Rich family was worried that a new owner might lay off many of their employees, most of whom were Laotian, Kurdish, and Filipino immigrants who might have trouble finding new jobs. So Cordia decided to negotiate "strictly on people." She didn't have the cash to boost her offer. But she could pledge to keep all the employees; she even promised to raise their wages by more than $1 an hour, to match what she was paying the workers at Tennessee Bun.

Once again Cordia closed the deal by underscoring the benefits to the other side. If they took her offer, they could be assured that their employees' jobs would be secure. "I said, 'You've got to decide what's important to you,'" she recalls. It worked. "Almost overnight they came back and accepted."

But Cordia knew it wasn't over yet. It was a big financial commitment, and she worried that something unexpected might scuttle the deal before closing. So bucking convention (and her real estate broker's advice), Cordia asked a representative of Mr. Rich to join her on the final walk-through. As it turned out, that unconventional move saved the whole deal.

When they got to the plant for the walk-through, Cordia's plant manager and engineer were fuming because key pieces of equipment were missing. "You automatically think the worst," she says. But with the seller's representative at her side, it was clear that he had no intention of cheating her. When she pointed out the missing items, he said he hadn't realized they were gone. To make up for the absent machines, he offered to leave much of the office furniture and equipment. He also agreed to foot the bill for repainting the factory, which it badly needed. "If he hadn't been there, we never would have closed," she says.

Just as they were about to sign, Cordia had an opportunity to be generous in return. She noticed that the contract mistakenly charged her a $5,000 fee usually paid by the sellers. But she had "mentally set aside surprise money," a smart tactic for easing the final stages of a big transaction. "If I have to leave $5,000 on the table somewhere to ensure we have a good relationship, it's worth it to me." That $5,000 investment in the Rich relationship has already paid off. "Rich's needs buns," she says, "and they called us for a quote."

DEALING FROM THE TOP OF THE DECK

As Cordia's experience shows, you can't fold up your bargaining table and pack it away in the attic once you've shaken hands, or even once you've closed the deal. An initial agreement rarely stands alone. Usually it ends up resembling one of those handkerchiefs magicians pull out of their top hats — each one tied to another in a seemingly endless string. New issues emerge, new alliances develop, new opportunities arise. That's why it's a bad idea to make an agreement that leaves a bitter aftertaste on either side. It can sour countless deals to come. "On the whole, it's not a good idea to take all of the marbles," says Catalyst president Sheila Wellington. "You can't leave people feeling trampled and destroyed. These things come back. You've got to be respectful."

Follow the example of Sue Rodin. She represents some of the hottest female athletes, including U.S. women's soccer team co-captain Julie Foudy and two of her teammates. Sports agents are notoriously tough dealmakers, but Sue thinks it's shortsighted to tread on toes today at the expense of tomorrow's relationships. "I always try to finish a deal so everyone feels that they've won, because that leads to other relationships," she says. "It's foolish to annoy people by insisting on getting as much as you can in every deal."

Sue's attitude won over John Hildenbiddle, formerly vice president of creative services for Champion International, a paper company in Stamford, Connecticut. John arranged athletes' appearances at schools for a company-sponsored academic program. While those may not sound like glamorous gigs, Champion paid its athletes decent fees, and the public appearances helped to build a fiercely loyal sports audience for the future. Thanks to Sue's fair-minded attitude John decided to work exclusively with Sue's clients. "A lot of agents are much tougher than they need to be," John says, "but she's such a pleasure to work with."

It can be hard for good girls to feel good about leaving a few dollars on the table for the other side. We're so used to being bamboozled that we can wind up feeling chronically exploited. After years of agreeing to bad deals because we're too nice to speak up for ourselves, we can turn to the dark side and become suspicious and unpleasant. We start to assume that everybody's trying to take advantage of us, and get so focused on scraping every last penny out of the deal that we forget why we came to the table in the first place. So if you find yourself reluctant to close a deal, even if you're getting most of what you asked for, step back and ask yourself whether you're getting a fair bargain. (If you've done all your homework, you'll know whether you're in the ballpark.) "Stop worrying about what the other person is getting," advises entrepreneur Susan DeFife. "What do you want? If you're getting it, it doesn't matter what the other side gets."

A they're-out-to-get-me attitude almost scuttled the deal when my friend Elaine put her house on the market. Thanks to record low interest rates, a moderate price tag, and some recently improved curb appeal (real estate–speak for new stucco), she sold it for her asking price in less than two hours.

Good news, right? Well, that speedy sale made Elaine think she could have done even better if she'd held out for more. She didn't stop to think about how horrible it would have been trying to keep the house scrupulously clean twenty-four hours a day. She certainly didn't consider the extra mortgage interest and property taxes she'd wind up paying if her wait for a better offer took six months or more. Instead, she brooded as she read the real estate section, and fretted when she heard neighbors gossip about soaring home prices. Basically, she worked herself into a complete state of seller's remorse.

Then came a minor snag; the home inspector found a family of squirrels in her attic. Removing her unwelcome tenants would cost about $350. Elaine refused to pay. Having convinced herself that the buyers had taken base advantage of her good nature by paying full price for her house, she wasn't going to give up one more cent. She insisted that since she hadn't known the squirrels were there, they weren't her responsibility. If the new owners weren't animal lovers, that was their problem. She relented after a week, but she almost lost the sale because the buyers — not surprisingly — were so offended by her attitude. So for $350, she nearly lost a $150,000 sale (which, incidentally, was a very fair price).

We know it's easy to go nuts when you're trying to close a major transaction. That's why it's so critically important to keep sight of your goals. To maintain your focus, write those goals down on paper and carry that sheet with you constantly. A memo reading, "I want to sell my house and get settled in my new job by September 1," might have helped Elaine to realize that her $350 rodents were a nonissue in the context of a very good deal.

Martha Furst, the mustard maker, relies on an opposite strategy. As the closing nears, she writes down all the "true deal-breaking issues" that might arise. If a problem comes up that's not on her list, she ignores it. That way, she says, "you don't get distracted by issues of lesser importance." Whether you accentuate the negatives or the positives, the result is the same: You zoom in on what's important and don't let minor issues scuttle a deal that's basically right for you.

Keep that piece of paper handy when you're talking to your advisers, both paid and amateur. Real estate brokers, attorneys, accountants, and your uncle Louie all may offer important insights and information. But in the end, it's your call.

Winner's Curse

It doesn't happen often. But sometimes a perfect deal magically appears on the table. You can see from forty paces that this agreement works for everybody. "Yes," you want to shout. "Yes! Absolutely! No further discussion required! Hand me a pen!"

Stifle yourself. While the mutual benefits of this agreement may be crystal-clear to you, an overenthusiastic response might leave the other side wondering if they gave away more than they bargained for.

Remember Ingrid, the editorial assistant who cried when she didn't get promoted? After a year at another magazine, she wanted a raise. Doing her homework, she learned that the going rate for editors at her level ranged from $35,000 to $75,000. She was currently making $30,000, and friends advised her not to overreach. But Ingrid decided to go for broke and ask for $40,000.

To buttress her case, Ingrid put together a list of all she'd accomplished over the past year. Then she practiced her speech, first in front of the mirror, then for her older sister. "I was so psyched to go in and make this argument." But when she went into her boss's office to make her case, he told her he didn't have time to listen. He just wanted to know how much she wanted. When she stammered out her salary request, the editor said, "Okay. Fine."

Success at last — until she went home and announced the big news. "My older sister told me, 'If he said okay just like that, it means you left money on the table.' I told her, 'You just spoiled my entire accomplishment.' I think my sister was probably wrong. But I have done some second-guessing since then." Her distracted boss had broken one of the cardinal rules of negotiating: Don't jump at the first offer, even if it's exactly what you'd had in mind. Let the other side know you're taking them seriously (and not taking them to the cleaners). If you say yes too fast, the other side may stay up nights wondering whether they might have gotten even more.

Ingrid's boss could have done her a big favor — and shut up Sis — if he'd spent a few minutes explaining that her 33 percent request was exactly what he'd had in mind. By getting to yes with such lightning speed, he actually took some of the joy out of her terrific raise. "I know this type of thing happens in the business world every day," Ingrid says. "But it was a big event to me." A little more empathy on her boss's part would have made her great deal feel even more wonderful.

MOVING THINGS ALONG

Focus on closing the deal from the moment you sit down at the table. Obviously, you need to put together a smart deal that makes sense for you, and you should never feel compelled to accept a bad bargain just because you've invested so much time and effort in negotiating. But remember that a good-enough deal that closes is better than a great deal that dissolves. At any point, you may run into obstacles that can sabotage fruitful negotiations. Arm yourself with strategies to help you over some common hurdles.

Be ready to ask that basic question: "Do we have a deal here?" It's amazing how often we do our homework, listen carefully, make our best case, and then — nothing. Timidly, we stand around digging our toes into the sand, trying to act nonchalant and waiting for the other guy to pull out his checkbook. "You need to learn how to close a conversation," says entrepreneur Melissa Moss. "When interests have been met and further discussion would not be productive, you need to make an offer."

You may put off asking for a commitment because you fear rejection. Most people don't want to hear a no. But if you don't ask, you may miss your chance to turn a maybe into a yes. Beth once gave her Girl Scout troop a tutorial in this during cookie sale season. She had arranged for them to sell cookies in a busy bank lobby one Saturday morning. The girls looked just adorable in their little green uniforms. They smiled hopefully at the passing bank patrons, who averted their eyes from the carefully arranged boxes of cookies. Within half an hour, the discouraged girls were asking to go home. But Beth decided they needed a lesson in smart salesmanship. So she ordered the girls to approach each patron personally, smiling and asking, "Would you like to buy some Girl Scout cookies?" "Make them say no to you," Beth advised. The girls balked at the idea of courting so much rejection. But Beth knew it would take a heart of stone to say no to such sweet, earnest little girls. The tactic worked beautifully. Looking down into those fresh, turned-up faces, most grown-ups couldn't resist digging into their pockets and buying a box or two.

Sometimes, as the Girl Scouts learned, all you have to do to close the deal is ask. But when you run into some initial resistance, you can't give up. Sandra Pesmen, the "Dr. Job" columnist, says she's learned that a good negotiator goes to work when she hears the word "no." "The minute you hear no, you know your sales call has begun," she says. "That's your real starting point."

That first no can signal that you haven't fully explained the deal's benefits to the other side. You need to remind them of what you have to offer, and what they stand to lose if you can't reach an agreement. Don't make them feel bullied; just lay out the likely consequences if they let this deal slip away. Cordia Harrington used this technique masterfully in her talks with McDonald's. Instead of focusing on how much she wanted to take on a new customer (and how resentful she'd feel if she missed this great opportunity), she stressed how much a revised agreement would benefit the fast-food giant. If they insisted on holding her to the exclusive deal, they'd wind up paying more for buns than they needed to.

This is an effective tactic on the home front, too. When California teacher Yvonne Tanielian, thirty-four, opted to stay home after the birth of her first child, she found that a day of intense mothering was far more exhausting than eight hours spent corralling a classroom of adolescents. But her husband figured that since she was at home all day, she could handle the domestic front without his help. Most of us might resort to threats, complaints, and tears when confronted with an unhelpful husband. But Yvonne was smarter. Having studied win-win dealmaking at the Program for Young Negotiators, a Harvard-affiliated project for middle-school teachers, she figured out a way to make her husband realize he'd benefit from getting off the couch and helping around the house. "I told him if I had to cook, give her the bath, and then do the dishes I'd be so tired I wouldn't have any time for him. So helping would meet my interests — and his." She offered him a deal he couldn't refuse: If he'd do the dishes while she gave the baby her bath, they'd have a quiet half hour together after their daughter went to sleep. Every evening since, her husband has willingly rolled up his sleeves and headed toward the kitchen sink.

FIGHTING FOOT-DRAGGING

Sometimes a deal can get gummed up by minor, unimportant details. Most of us have endured those endless meetings where one

Getting the Most out of a No

No matter how hard you try, some deals just won't close. Despite your best persuasions and most insightful strategies, there are people who wouldn't recognize a good deal if it jumped in their lap, kissed them on the cheek, and whispered, "Win-win, baby," in their ear. "Some deals just don't work," says entrepreneur Susan DeFife. Rather than try to force a deal, she advises, "step back." In politics, particularly, deals fall through for no good reason. "Just because it makes sense doesn't mean it'll happen," sighs Pam McDonough, director of the Illinois Department of Commerce and Community Affairs.

When the other side walks away from a proposal that makes perfect sense for both sides, don't explode into righteous indignation. Instead, keep the lines of communication open; if it's possible, offer your opponents an open invitation to come back to the table if they change their minds. Someday they just might surprise you and show up.

In the meantime, try to save face — your opponent's and your own. There are plenty of pleasant ways to end a round of negotiations without a deal. If you're the one who decided to back off, be as gracious as possible. "You could put the project on hold," suggests Susan Onaitis, author of *Negotiate Like the Big Guys.* "End with something upbeat, like, 'I sure hope we can do business in the future.' If you end up walking away, you don't want it necessarily to be forever."

Former Del Monte executive Fran Lent, who started Fran's Healthy Helpings, a line of healthy frozen meals for kids, tries to make the most of every deadlock by looking ahead. "You can't always satisfy the other side," she says. But she's found that even negotiations that don't pan out can offer her some insight into future opportunities. For example, when a grocery store chain rejects her line for lack of available freezer space, she tries to find out when another product might be winnowed out. "If they're going to have more room in the next five months, we regard that as a positive thing. Even if we don't get an account the first time, the door's open for the next time."

person decides to fixate on the most minor points. Suppose you're the board president of a local charity, planning the spring benefit. You're tiptoeing delicately between last year's event chairman (a well-intentioned control freak) and a committee member who's still upset that her brother-in-law (who owns a hot dog stand) was not asked to cater the event. For this event to succeed, you'll need everyone's enthusiasm and wholehearted commitment. But every time you make a little progress, your detail-obsessed colleague starts trying to "pin things down" — raising such life-or-death issues as what flavors of cream cheese to serve with the miniature bagels. If you don't intervene, you'll be there all night. Worse, you'll frustrate half of your members right off the committee. So tell everyone to put down their pencils and turn their attention to the big picture. Wait until you have agreement on a few major points, then set a time to come back and fine-tune.

Sue Rodin uses this technique to get her clients' contract talks moving ahead. She tries to strike a generalized agreement in principle, postponing the chore of hammering out highly technical contract language. "Can't we just get this done today, verbally?" she says. Once they have a basic agreement, it's much easier to put the details in place.

Remember that some people are just naturally averse to making commitments. My friend Lucy's father is notoriously skittish when it comes to making advance plans, thus driving Lucy's mother out of her mind. "What do you mean, you don't know if you're free for dinner with the Johnsons on Saturday?" she fumes. "Are you afraid the Commissioner will turn on the Batsignal and call you to save Gotham City?"

But clever Lucy has learned how to outwit her dad. Knowing that the idea of committing to a particular plan makes her father overwhelmingly anxious, she asks for a tentative commitment: "Dad, could you pencil me in for the twenty-fourth? If anything comes up you can let me know." By offering her dad the option of backing out, she gives him the comfort zone he needs. If you sense that the other person feels unreasonably anxious about committing to a particular point, can you ask for a tentative agreement that can be rescinded later if need be? That may free him up to work with you toward a mutually acceptable deal.

You can reduce anxiety levels by keeping your objectives modest at first. Kids' food maven Fran Lent tries to start small with new business partners. "It's much better to accomplish something simple together and have a success early on, rather than bite off more than you can chew," she observes. Those first negotiations set the stage for more ambitious deals later on.

The judicious use of deadlines can sometimes keep talks moving forward. Whenever she sits down to negotiate, Fran says, she always has a specific date in mind — even if it's just the date of the next meeting. "Nail down the next time you'll meet and what you'll accomplish in the meantime," she suggests. Otherwise, your open-ended talks can stretch on indefinitely. If deadlines start to slip, Fran asks for another meeting to find out what's going wrong. If her prospective partners are too overworked to give her deal the attention it needs — which is often the case — she tries to figure out how to ease their burden. "We ask them, 'What can we do to offload work from you? Or to make your life simpler?'" By setting reasonable deadlines and helping out, she creates a friendly, cooperative atmosphere that advances her own cause tremendously.

But remember that patience is a virtue. Don't set arbitrary deadlines that create needless stress for the other side. Sometimes you just have to sit tight. "I've had to work against my own impatience," admits Melissa Moss, named one of *Fast Company* magazine's "rising stars." "Sometimes you really do have to give time for the other side to think things over, or to come back with a new proposal, or to accommodate your requests."

UNLOCKING DEADLOCK: THREE STRATEGIES

Deadlock is, of course, the biggest threat to any deal. So if your opponent slams the door, here are three of the best strategies for prying it open again.

Strategy No. 1: Buy Time

If you have kids, you've probably endured some long rainy afternoons trapped with a couple of bored little cranks. Tempers shorten, voices rise, and pretty soon everyone's in tears.

Exasperated, you separate the combatants. "Okay, everybody, time out!" After ten or fifteen minutes of quiet time in their rooms, they're usually ready to be a bit more civilized. And you've had a minute to regain your composure and come up with a few nonviolent activities to keep them pleasantly occupied until dinner.

The same strategy works with adults, too. Just like a good parent, a skilled negotiator knows that a strategic separation can dampen the flames of a heated exchange. When tempers flare and talks stall, consider a time-out. That can be a tough call, especially when you're facing a deadline. But pushing on ahead despite weariness and battle fatigue can be counterproductive.

Olympia Snowe, the moderate Republican senator from Maine, was one of the few Washington politicians whose stature was enhanced during the Clinton sex scandal, thanks to her negotiating skills. As the Senate trial loomed, Democrats and Republicans were deadlocked over procedural matters. The Republicans had enough votes to carry the issue and force the Democrats to call a long string of witnesses to the stand. But Snowe feared that if the Republicans muscled the issue through, voters would never forgive them for using the Senate chambers to stage a sideshow aimed solely at embarrassing the president. She believed a bipartisan solution was the only way to keep the voters' respect. So she proposed that the warring legislators sleep on it and meet the following day. By the next morning, they had seen the light. Both parties agreed on rules for the trial, ultimately calling only three key witnesses.

Time and distance also can give you a little perspective in those less weighty confrontations that can sometimes make everyday life seem like a battle. Beth relearned this basic principle recently when a women's magazine sent her to cover a trade show at Chicago's sprawling McCormick Place.

Her editor somehow got the times confused, and the show's unsympathetic public relations people told her she'd just have to wait three hours for the exhibit floor to open. Peeved, Beth was ready to throw a full-scale fit and go home. Then she realized that one executive she had to interview was appearing at a brunch on the far side of the convention center, more than half a mile away. If she sprinted, she just might get there in time.

Despite her best power walking, Beth arrived just as the housekeeping staff was clearing away the coffeepots. So she had to head back to the public relations office. That mile-plus hike gave her a chance to simmer down and come up with a solution: She called one of the exhibitors on his cell phone. He rescued her from the pressroom and gladly escorted her onto the exhibit floor. So that unexpected time-out saved her story, and burned up a few extra calories, too.

Strategy No. 2: Do Something Unexpected

Judith was getting fed up. After years of working as her partner both at work and at home, her husband, Mark, had retired from the New York art gallery they had opened together. Judith, who continued to work full-time, reasonably assumed that her husband would use some of his increased leisure time to help more around the house. He didn't.

Repeated requests for some extra domestic help fell on conveniently deaf ears. Finally, Judith says, "I had to put my foot down."

To get her husband's attention, Judith came up with an unexpected Plan B: She wrote him a letter, putting all her hurt feelings in writing. "I don't have energy enough to do everything," she wrote. "You need to help me." He took it very seriously. Her decision to put it in writing underlined how deeply she felt. "It's not like I write him a letter every day."

Mark agreed to do his part. And for the next few months, he carried Judith's letter in his pocket every day. "It helped remind him."

Strategy No. 3: Check with the Experts

You say tomayto. He says tomahto. Who's right?

That's an easy one. You just look it up in the dictionary.

Unfortunately, most disputes aren't that easy to resolve. But the basic principle, of resolving a difference of opinion by turning to an objective, reliable outside source, is a good one. And very often, you'll be able to find an informed third party who can help you and the other side figure out what's fair.

For example, suppose you're trying to sell your seven-year-old Toyota Camry. You're asking $10,000. The guy next door says he's not willing to pay more than $5,000. Stalemate.

To move the negotiations along, drive your neighbor to your local library and check out a copy of the *Kelley Blue Book,* the leading guide to fair-market car values. You may still haggle over whether your car is in "excellent" or "good" condition, but at least you'll have an objective starting point.

Sometimes bringing in outside standards makes it easier to back down if you've painted yourself into a corner. When you've been clinging to your position through hours of tough negotiations, it can be hard to say, "I was wrong." But if you come up with some objective standards, you can probably bring yourself to admit, "I was misinformed."

Strategically, resorting to expert information can also help you to cover yourself later if someone questions your negotiating skills. Obviously, we want you to be confident in your own judgment. But if you've got to explain to your boss why you couldn't coax your fabric suppliers into meeting your target price, it helps to pull out that *New York Times* story reporting that a below-average cotton crop was sending wholesale prices into the stratosphere.

MORE THAN YOUR FAIR SHARE

When you're trying to figure out how to coax a recalcitrant opponent to give up a fair piece of the pie, you'd probably just roll your eyes at the problem of getting more than you deserve. But believe it or not, one of these days someone's going to offer you more than your share. And you'd better think twice before you jump at this unexpected chance to even up your lifetime score.

Take a good hard look at the whole situation. Do you have a long-term relationship with the person who's making this extraordinary offer? If your boyfriend offers to take your dirty clothes to the Laundromat, he's trying to be a nice guy. Let him. When someone's obviously trying to do you a favor, say thank you and accept graciously.

However, it's a different story when innocent little Jacqueline is about to barter her mother's prized milk cow for your handful of magic beans. It is immoral, unethical, and sometimes illegal to take advantage of someone who obviously has no idea that she's giving away the store. We don't care how many bad deals you've made in the past, or how often you've let some city slicker take advantage of your girlish naïveté; trying to even up the score by gouging someone else is simply wrong.

Very often, it's also dumb. Think about those bad deals you've been suckered into in the past. How did you feel once you realized you'd accepted a salary offer 15 percent below the going rate? Did it make you want to work longer and harder? Probably not. Instead, you began revising your resumé on company time. In the long run, your employer would have been better off to just pay you a fair wage. "You want an outcome both sides can live with," says Scholastic's Deborah Forte. "If they can't, you will have a problem moving forward."

There's one notorious woman lawyer — let's call her Cruella — who operates a real sweatshop. She hires lawyers who are desperate for work — younger attorneys whose law firms have suddenly imploded, or just-divorced women who are parachuting back into the workforce. Cruella hates to share the wealth, so she pays about two-thirds of the standard wage, just enough to lure in the desperate. Then she inflicts a mandatory six-day, sixty-hour workweek, paying no overtime. The work conditions are so horrendous that the firm's annual staff turnover rate nears 100 percent; lawyers stay there only until they can find a more humane employer. At the end of the fiscal year, Cruella congratulates herself on keeping her payroll costs incredibly low. She ignores the heavy cost of finding and training new staff. Nor does she consider the added revenues she could rake in if she offered some incentives for workers to stay with the firm and bring in new clients.

Think back to childhood when you convinced your baby sister to trade all her little dimes for your great big nickels and pennies. Once she realized how she'd been had, she vowed to get even. When you walked into your room and saw that she'd colored all over your David Cassidy posters, you realized those dimes weren't such a bargain after all. As grown-ups, we sometimes forget those early lessons in the importance of good-faith negotiating. We're brainwashed into believing that losers deserve what they get; that's why we're so ashamed to admit we've made bad deals. But I still have faith in that basic good girl principle: What goes around comes around. Don't let your desire to win undermine your sense of fair play.

FUTURE SHOCK

Okay. You're sprinting toward the finish line. You've settled the major principles, you've worked out the details, and you're ready to sign.

Not so fast, sweetheart. Before you sign anything, fast-forward yourself a few months, or even a few years. Are you confident that your opponent will stick to the agreement? Don't let your enthusiasm blind you to dark clouds on the horizon. You may be incredibly proud of yourself for holding your ground and forcing your jerk ex-husband to pay his fair share in child support. But what happens if he quits his job in a huff? You can't afford to go months without his support check. Sit down with your lawyer and walk through all the worst-case scenarios, to make sure you're covered.

Ask whether you're likely to change your mind about this agreement in the months to come. That can be emotionally difficult. When you're still floating on the euphoria of putting together a win-win agreement, you don't want to let the air out of your balloon by thinking of all the things that can go wrong. My friend Gail says her husband has had to coach her into thinking about the endgame whenever she enters a new business relationship. "Before you get in, you have to figure out how you're going to get out," she says. That's not an optimistic good girl approach. But thinking about how and why you'd break off a relationship can help you to figure out whether a deal will make sense in the long run. "It's a hard world out there, and there are no guarantees. You have to know what you can live with."

You also should agree in advance about what to do if the deal breaks down somewhere along the line. If it's a personal dispute, is there a friend or relative you both trust? If it's a professional matter, perhaps a local judge or official in a trade organization can help you resolve the issue. If you can settle on an arbitrator or mediator before disputes arise, it's one less thing to argue about later.

ONE MORE THING

After hours, days, or even weeks, you've finally got this thing nailed down. You're ready to call it a day and turn out the lights when your opponent casually announces, "There's just one more thing. . . ." Should you (a) tear up the agreement and storm out of the room? (b) punch him in the nose? or (c) sigh, fold your hands, and listen patiently to what he has to say?

Although it's enough to make you pull your hair out in clumps, it's actually quite common for a new issue to hit the table just when you think you've got a deal. "It's very frustrating," says attorney Linda Chaplik Harris. "But sometimes there are legitimate issues that come up."

When she runs into one of those eleventh-hour "just one more thing" situations, Linda puts the request to the empathy test. If she were sitting on the other side of the table, she asks herself, "would I feel this needs to be addressed?" If the answer is yes, Linda forces herself to try to work something out. But if the answer is no, she doesn't hesitate to refuse to negotiate any further. At that point, she insists, "you have to say, 'This has got to stop.'"

WRITE IT DOWN!

Movie mogul Samuel Goldwyn once said: "A verbal agreement isn't worth the paper it's written on." Legally that's not quite the case. But it's certainly easier to enforce a deal that's written and signed. That's why sports agent Sue Rodin wastes no time in converting verbal pledges to written agreements, first preparing deal memos, then following them up with formal contracts.

The deal memo is a critical document, so be certain it sets out the deal's basic points clearly and correctly. Make sure your side prepares the memo. That gives you control over timing and wording. But to avoid problems later on, some experts recommend reviewing the memo with your opponent before you send it over. It's so easy to misunderstand each other, especially in the heat of an emotional give-and-take. Ask directly: "Is that what you agreed to? Has anything been left out?" That way when your memo arrives, there won't be any ugly surprises.

A Few Words About Contracts

I have a confession to make: I hate looking at contracts. I can't stand reading through all those pages and pages of legal details. It's so stressful to read those grim paragraphs setting out the penalties that will be inflicted if I fail to meet my obligations, and which court will resolve any lawsuits related to this deal. After a page or two, I just want to close my eyes and sign.

However, I've learned the hard way that I can't let my anxieties rule when it comes to contracts. So I consciously set aside a quiet time to read over each and every sentence, and I make sure there's someone to explain what all those legal phrases mean in real-life terms. I've had to overcome my good girl fear of asking stupid questions; when it comes to contracts, it's absolutely true that the only stupid question is the one you were too shy to ask.

No matter who prepares a contract, even if it's your own trusted lawyer, READ IT CAREFULLY. Even the best lawyer can miss something, and you're the one who will have to bear the consequences if you sign a contract without noticing the land mine buried in section four, paragraph B.

Be especially careful if the negotiations have been adversarial. Confusing footnotes, hidden charges, and intentional omissions are all ways in which the other side may try to take advantage of an unsuspecting good girl. Double-check all the dates. A "typographical error" could turn 2001 into 2010; that might mean you'd end up waiting an extra nine years for the last payment.

Watch out for sins of omission. Terry Frishman, a New York City–based marketing consultant, ran into this when she was reviewing a contract for a benefit dinner. Terry had persuaded the owner of a fashionable restaurant to give her a break on the price, since the dinner's high-profile guests were likely to draw lots of favorable publicity. But when the restaurateur faxed her the contract, the agreed-upon price didn't include the cost of wine, even though their verbal agreement had covered both food and wine.

Terry knew that if her client had to foot the wine bill, her good deal would quickly ferment into an expensive fiasco. So she summoned her courage, picked up the phone, and politely pointed out the error. To her relief, the owner acknowledged the error and agreed to fix it right away. "If I hadn't noticed that detail, it would have resulted in a big price increase," she says. "You've got to follow through so no balls drop."

A Few Words About Contracts (cont.)

Attorney Linda Chaplik Harris occasionally spots errors that benefit her side of the table. After weighing her client's interests, she usually decides to come clean, on the principle that doing the right thing generally pays off. "In the vast majority of cases, you gain enormous credibility and respect," says Linda. "It may be intangible, but it's an immeasurable benefit."

GOING BACK TO THE WELL

Once you've signed a contract, you're stuck, right?

Wrong. Contracts are written in ink, not chiseled in stone. Too often, good girls assume that a bad deal is irreparable once it's put on paper. But you shouldn't let a contract keep you from asking for better terms. It might be an uphill battle, but you could find that the other side is more flexible than you realized.

Beth and I have been living through this one for the past year or so, as we've been working on this book. Originally, I intended to do most of the work myself, with Beth contributing ideas and the occasional joke. So we drew up a contract that gave me the bigger chunk of the book advance. But as the months passed, it seemed as though I was living through a suburban version of the ten plagues of Egypt: head lice, chicken pox, a basement flood, you name it. As the deadline grew nearer, I realized I needed help, bad. So I called Beth with a frantic cry for assistance. Since she's my friend, she offered both empathy and sympathy. "I'll do whatever I can, and we'll work out the money later," she said. (And isn't that a classic good girl offer?) Eventually, despite some stressful times and brief misunderstandings, we agreed to a 50-50 split. We both ended up happy with our deal, and — more important — with our book.

It was hard to admit, even to a friend, that I needed help. Deep within my good girl brain, I guess I was afraid that she'd refuse to pitch in, or that she'd take advantage of my plight and make some exorbitant demands. Before I made that call, I wish I had taken a minute to imagine how I'd feel if I were on the other end of the line. Obviously, if my friend and business partner needed help, I'd be more than happy to tear up the old contract and come up with a new deal that made sense for both of us.

Going back to the well makes you feel like you made a mistake the first time. You underestimated how much time something would take. You were overly optimistic about costs. You didn't foresee a change in the market, or the weather, or whatever it is that has made this deal stop working for you. Well, listen — nobody's perfect. People make mistakes every day. You don't have to live with last year's bad decision forever. If the people on the other side are fair and honorable, they'll be willing to listen to your concerns, and they well may agree to help you out.

THE HEART OF COMPROMISE

Sometimes this feels like a hard, cold world. No matter what you want — whether it's a raise, or a new car, or simply a husband who'll pick up his own dirty underwear — it can seem as though you're beset by opposition at every turn. It's easy to believe that your winning ways and warm heart render you defenseless, and that goodness has no real value in the current marketplace.

Well, it's not true. Yes, our society too often rewards the victors and punishes the vanquished, regardless of their personal merits. But many of us — more than you know — are finding that making trade-offs is a highly effective and surprisingly rewarding way to move through life. Surrounded by winners and losers, we're learning to celebrate the beauty and balance of the tied score.

Sports fans sometimes complain that "a tie is like kissing your sister." That's true, on a much more profound level than they realize. Negotiating a fair, win-win agreement is a lot like kissing your sister or brother; it's a way to confirm and nourish a relationship that benefits both parties.

If you've worked hard to put together a mutually beneficial agreement and you've traded concessions of equal value with your opponent, you've probably wound up with something that looks quite different from what you originally imagined. But your new solution often has an elegance all its own.

Take the case of Maria, a hospital administrator in Minneapolis. She's a warm, funny woman who gives thoughtful care to every aspect of her job. When she asked for a raise last year, her supervisor explained that he didn't have the budget to meet her request. But he wanted to acknowledge her exceptional performance. So he offered her extra time off instead — an additional 20 days of paid vacation. At first Maria wasn't thrilled by the offer; she really wanted the extra cash. But she realized that her supervisor was doing the best he could. So she accepted graciously. Putting the best possible spin on the deal, she figured it would give her some days free to attend her daughters' school concerts, repaint the master bedroom, and even — luxury of luxuries — spend a couple of days at home all by herself, doing absolutely nothing.

Sadly, that's not how it worked out. Instead, her beloved father got very sick. So she used her vacation time to fly home and spend a week with him — a week that turned out to be his last. At that point, her supervisor's compromise seemed divinely inspired. And who's to say it wasn't?

ONE GOOD DEAL DESERVES ANOTHER

When you've put the finishing touches on a good deal, you deserve more than a pat on the back. It's time for a party. So call somebody up — maybe even your opponent — and celebrate. It doesn't have to be fancy. But your victory celebration should be rewarding enough to inspire you to keep on negotiating, anytime you get the chance. After Beth and I hashed out our book contract, we celebrated with decaf and chocolate muffins. We'd earned it.

Don't deny yourself if your deal wasn't quite as good as you'd hoped. "I still make mistakes," admits Irma Elder, the seventy-something master car dealer. If Irma can stumble occasionally and still rev up her motor to try again, so can we. And we should reward ourselves for that, too.

Then promise yourself to keep trying. Read another book on negotiating. Take a course in it, if you can. Practice, practice, practice.

If I sound overly bright-eyed and optimistic, it's because I've spent the last year talking to scores of women who have used their negotiating skills to get ahead, to make a difference, to right wrongs, and to change the world. Sure, some people will always try to take you for a ride; a few will succeed. But if you're prepared, you'll find that you'll slowly start to make more good deals — and learn to walk away from the bad ones.

Look, this isn't easy stuff. It's hard for us to ask for what we want, to look somebody else straight in the eye and say, "I'm worth more than this. So make another offer." But if you're prepared, if you're informed, and if you truly believe in your own value, you can be a good girl and a good negotiator. That means that the next time you sit down to try to get what you deserve, you won't be ruled by your fears and anxieties. Instead, you'll know what you want and why you want it, which is the strongest place to start. And if you use the full force of your creativity, intelligence, perceptiveness, and perseverance — not to mention your natural goodness — you will succeed.

CHAPTER 9

❧

GOOD GIRLS —
THE NEXT GENERATION

Nora and Angela weren't trying to claw their way into the corner office. All these two young sisters wanted was a warm, dry, secure place to call home.

When they were in junior high, their mother's drug problem led to the family's eviction from their apartment. So she moved herself and the two girls into the broken-down family car.

The sisters were afraid to ask anyone for help, for fear of being separated and placed in foster homes. When their sympathetic teachers figured out the situation, they agreed not to report the family's plight to social service authorities. Instead, they put the girls in touch with a local center for homeless families, which kept close tabs on their whereabouts and provided a place to bathe.

Their teachers also made sure that the girls had enough to eat, even if that meant treating them to lunch at McDonald's. Everyone agreed it was all very sad, but there didn't seem to be anything anyone could do. It didn't occur to anyone that the girls themselves might have the fortitude and ability to find a new home. That is, it didn't occur to anyone but the girls.

By a tremendous stroke of good fortune, the girls were students in a special class on negotiating. Their teacher had trained at Harvard's Program for Young Negotiators, which is dedicated to spreading the use of win-win conflict resolution and problem-solving skills in schools. In the class, the students were asked to set goals they could achieve during the ten-week course, brainstorm about possible roadblocks, and develop action plans to get around them. The teacher hoped the class would equip her students to deal with the challenges of adult life. But her straightforward advice inspired Nora and Angela to negotiate their way off the streets.

The girls' basic strategy was simple: They would target the resident managers of big apartment buildings in their neighborhood. In a classic negotiator's stance, they put themselves in their opponent's shoes. What would an apartment manager be willing to trade? Working with their teacher, the girls developed a proposal: In return for a break on the rent, they would offer to live in vacant apartments until they were leased, then clean them up for the new tenants. That meant the girls and their mother would have to move from unit to unit, but at least they'd have a permanent address. To sweeten the deal, they also offered to pick up trash and tend to the grounds.

In rehearsing their pitch, they came up with a serious problem — Angela's quick temper. Quite frankly, they were afraid that rejection might provoke Angela to hit an uncooperative apartment manager. So they repeatedly ran through their scenario; if a manager refused, they would politely say, "Thank you for your time," and leave. After one afternoon of multiple refusals, Angela reported back to her teacher: "You'd be so proud of me. I didn't slap 'em once!"

Finally their resolution paid off and they got to yes. A manager who ran a building two blocks away from school agreed to make a deal, cutting the rent in half in return for their cleaning services. Although they changed apartments several times, the girls kept a roof over their heads until the end of the school year, when the family moved in with a relative in another town.

Negotiating can't solve every problem and save the world; even the most optimistic good girl has to admit that hard truth. But it's incredibly exciting to think about what it would mean to our society if every girl learned to negotiate as skillfully and effectively as Angela and Nora.

A WIN-WIN FUTURE

The basic concepts of negotiating aren't new to us. For centuries, women have been using their bargaining skills to break through barriers, brainstorm solutions to difficult problems, and fend for themselves and their families. But we still haven't managed to get the equal treatment we deserve. Pamela McCorduck, author of *The Futures of Women: Scenarios for the 21st Century,* smiles ruefully when she thinks about her first job as a women's studies professor. When she signed on in 1971, she thought the successes of the women's movement would soon make her department obsolete. Thirty years later, she's still waiting. "I'm not saying it's not better," she says. "But the golden age has not arrived."

It will be up to future generations of good girls to bring that golden age into reality. So we need to equip our daughters to negotiate a better world for themselves in the coming century. Fortunately, there are some signs that we may be handing down a much stronger bargaining position to our daughters and granddaughters. Thanks to a number of relatively new laws and legal decisions, women are protected from some of the most outrageous acts of workplace discrimination. And some basic feminist principles, such as equal pay for equal work, are now so widely accepted they're even supported by the "I'm not a feminist, but" crowd.

The next generation will also have the advantage of following in the footsteps of the "ice breakers," thousands of women who dedicated their lives to breaking new ground, personally and professionally. Tomorrow's women will be able to walk swiftly down paths that were rocky and difficult for their mothers and aunts.

The challenge for the next few generations will be learning to balance their hard-won independence with the needs of their communities. "In my family we refer to people with OLW or 'own little world' syndrome," says Jessica Lipnack, co-CEO of the consulting firm NetAge and coauthor of *Virtual Teams: Reaching Across Space, Time, and Organizations with Technology.* "That's the guy who pulls into the parking space you've been waiting for. They put their needs ahead of everybody else's."

In rearing two daughters, Jessica, now fifty-two, says she's tried to help them balance compassion and competitiveness. "It's a tricky thing, raising girls who stand up for themselves in a healthy way without being selfish," she acknowledges. But in some ways, she believes her daughters' generation will have an easier time learning to balance their own needs with those of their family, friends, employers, or community. "We were at the cutting edge, trying to bust through," she says. "But my daughters have seen a different model. They have seen women do what needs to be done in a caring and loving way."

"If You Do That Again, I'll Kill You": Negotiating with Your Children

A few years ago, Beth was involved in a long, complicated, high-stakes negotiation with an incredibly tough opponent. The person on the other side was uncompromising, focused, persistent, persuasive — and she didn't want to use the big-girl potty.

At first Beth basically ignored the issue, not wanting to turn the process into a pitched battle with her strong-willed younger daughter, Claire. "She'll use the potty when she's good and ready," Beth said confidently.

But with Claire's third birthday looming, Beth felt stumped. Then, while sketching out plans for a family vacation, she had an idea. "Claire, how would you like to go to Disney World and see Mickey?" she asked. Claire's eyes lit up like firecrackers. "Let's go now!" she shrieked.

"Not so fast," replied her wily mother. "I'm not sure, but I don't think they allow diaper babies in Disney World. So we can't go until you start using the potty like a big girl."

It was a real dilemma, and Claire took several months to resolve it. Like any crack negotiator, she started out by doing some basic research. She asked all her little friends if Disney World was really, really fun, and she spent several hours reviewing the Disney vacation tape her mother just happened to leave in the VCR. Before sitting down for final negotiations, she reviewed her fallback position. "Mommy," she asked. "Do they let diaper babies go to Kiddieland?"

After due consideration, Claire agreed to try a pair of big-girl underpants (with Minnie Mouse on them, of course). In a few short weeks, she was completely out of diapers — and her mother, a good-faith negotiator, booked the family's tickets to Orlando.

Win-Win for Short People

While trading diapers for Disney World may sound a bit extreme, it was really a classic case of win-win negotiating. If only every parent-child interaction were so simple. Unfortunately, it's hard for children to realize that what felt like mean, heartless parental decisions ("No, you can't skip your uncle's funeral to go to a rock concert") were really win-win calls, helping them to grow into kind, considerate, thoughtful adults.

It's tough for any parent to stand firm in the face of a child's disappointment or distress. But it's especially rough for us good girls. We're so anxious to be

Negotiating with Your Children (cont.)

liked in our everyday encounters that we tend to fold up like origami swans at the slightest hint of conflict. So you can imagine how hard it is for us to draw a line in the sandbox when we're facing the little people we love most.

It doesn't help that we've been indoctrinated by all those warm, fuzzy visions of motherhood. When you think of the perfect mom, you probably don't imagine a litigator or a labor union representative. Instead, you envision someone gentle and generous, someone unfailingly kind and giving.

But in reality, a good mother needs to be a great negotiator. It takes real bargaining savvy to resolve the dozens of little household conflicts that arise each day. And if you learn to use your dealmaking skills effectively at home, you'll ease many of the strains that crop up in even the happiest families.

Some tenderhearted good girls may worry that forcing their children to negotiate for what they want will make them feel overwhelmed, or even unloved. Well, don't worry; most kids are born with a tremendous array of bargaining tools. You'll be doing them a huge favor if you help them to build on those natural skills, so they'll be able to negotiate effectively for themselves when they go off on their own into the wide world.

Don't worry if unenlightened outsiders accuse you of bribing your children into good behavior. Think about it for a minute. Why do people get up and go to work every day? Because it's the nice thing to do? Because it makes their mommies happy? No — because they're getting regular paychecks. As adults, we expect some form of compensation for most of the things we do in life — if not money, then thanks and appreciation. It makes sense to give kids tangible reasons to get with the parental program.

If you think of child rearing as a twenty-year exercise in negotiating, you'll probably find it much easier to keep your emotions in check the next time you go head-to-head with your little darling. You wouldn't go into a tailspin if one of your employees came into your office and announced: "I need to leave early on Thursdays for the next six months." You'd start using your good girl assets to come up with a win-win solution to her problem.

It's really the same deal when your nine-year-old pitching sensation walks into the kitchen and declares: "I'm dropping out of softball." Your first impulse may be to turn purple and scream, "No kid of mine is going to be a quitter!" But if you recognize this as the beginning of a negotiating session, you can stay calm, put your listening skills and empathy to work, and come up with a deal that works for you and your child.

The Home Office

You'll have more success in negotiating with your kids if you approach these deals the way you would at work. (In fact, developmental psychologist Lois W. Hoffman, author of *Mothers at Work: Effects on Children's Well-Being,* has found that mothers who are employed outside the home seem to have an easier time negotiating with their kids, possibly because they have more experience in making deals in the workplace.)

Start out by laying down some ground rules. You wouldn't allow your employer to follow you into the bathroom and start talking about your upcoming raise. So don't let your kids try to negotiate their allowances while you're in the shower.

Instead, set the table, just as you would in a more formal session. Let your kids know that an ambush will result in an automatic no. If they want you to consider their requests, they'll have to set up a mutually convenient time to talk. This may sound overly formal, but basically, what it means is that they have to wait until you've toweled off and put your clothes on. Don't let them ensnare you into a discussion of an important point when they're bouncy and energetic and you're tired and distracted.

Similarly, don't agree to negotiate with a child who's angry or abusive. You wouldn't allow a professional colleague to berate you; don't reward that behavior in your child. When your kid starts whining and screaming, simply explain that there are some voices your ears just can't hear, and walk out of the room. And if you find yourself losing your own cool, call a time-out. Retreat to the bathtub, or take a walk. Don't let yourself get stressed into making an agreement you can't live with long-term.

Once you've agreed on a time and a place, open your ears and shut your mouth. That's not easy for many mothers. A child's request for a later bedtime or an extra cookie can trigger an old script from your own childhood. Suddenly, you hear your mother's what-happens-when-you-eat-too-many-cookies lecture pouring out of your mouth. Admittedly, it may be a darn good lecture, and perfectly suited to the occasion. But before you embark on your mom's well-polished tirade, make sure you have all the necessary information. Maybe your son gave his cookie to his baby sister to keep her from crying when the dog ate hers. "Letting the child give his side of the story is very important," Hoffman says. "When that kid hits the teenaged years, it will be very helpful to have a good history of communication."

You wouldn't want to work for a boss who shouted "Hell, no!" before you could even finish your question. And strategically it's a bad idea to automatically say no before you have the whole picture; if you have to backpedal later, it gives your children the message that Mom's no really means maybe.

Smart Love

Once you're clear on the situation, bring your empathy into play to find some win-win options.

Take the example of the pitcher who wants to drop out of softball on the eve of the championships. A half hour of quiet, sensitive listening may elicit some thought-provoking reasons behind that decision. Maybe (heaven forbid) his coach is whispering abusive comments into his players' ears. Or maybe it's something simple. If a particular after-school cartoon is the hot topic of conversation on the school playground, your busy little athlete may feel left out of the loop. Children are usually pretty clear about what they want, but they don't have an adult grasp of all the available options. As a parent, you may be able to expand the pie and come up with a settlement your child never imagined.

Make sure you're taking your child's age and abilities into account. In a baby-sitting crisis some years ago, Beth found herself forced to take her two-year-old into a business meeting. "If you sit here quietly for ten minutes," Beth promised, "we'll go out and get ice cream as soon as I'm finished." It was so touching to see how hard little Madeline tried. Every few minutes, she whispered, "Is it ten minutes yet?" Beth, inspired by her daughter's strenuous efforts, wrapped up the meeting in record time, then declared, "Let's go get our ice cream!" Beth's adult colleague intervened, saying, "She didn't hold up her end of the deal. She wasn't quiet for ten minutes." "That's very true," Beth replied. "But she doesn't know what a minute is, and she can't count to ten."

Try to have a few canned responses ready before tough questions arise. I ran into one of these personally a few months ago, when my twelve-year-old son opened a conversation with the dreaded words: "Mom, if I tell you something, do you promise not to do anything about it?" Eager to share my son's confidence, I agreed. But after he gave me the details of a situation involving a schoolmate, I realized the other child's parents needed to hear this story. Trapped by my unthinking promise of confidentiality, I had to persuade Ben to release me from my vow of silence. Now when I hear, "Mom, if I tell you something . . . ," I'm ready with this well-thought-out answer: "I really love hearing about your life, and I can usually keep it completely confidential. But if I think another adult really needs this information, I'll have to share it. But I'll never do that without letting you know." If he's unwilling to confide under those conditions, I say, "I'm always here if you change your mind."

Don't forget to call on Team Good Girl — which in this case should definitely include your spouse. Children excel at using the divide-and-conquer ploy; when Mom says no, they go to Dad for a second opinion. "You need to collaborate with your partner," advises Barry G. Ginsberg, Ph.D., director of the Center for Relationship Enhancement in Doylestown, Pennsylvania.

Other parents can be your allies as well. The best way to combat a child's plaintive wail of "Everybody else gets to watch R-rated movies" is to get on the phone and check it out. There's strength in numbers, and other parents may be relieved to hear they're not the only puritans in the neighborhood.

Brace yourself for some stormy responses when you can't reach a mutual agreement. "Pick what's really important to you and stand your ground," Ginsberg says. "If they don't like it, you'll just have to cope with that."

But don't be afraid to give in once in a while. Obviously, some things — such as wearing seat belts or doing homework — are nonnegotiable. But my friend Doreen, the mother of two young teenagers, says she occasionally shocks her kids by allowing them to skip a half day of school or attend a rock concert. "If they're sure the answer will always be no, they'll stop asking," she reasons. "This way, they ask for permission because they know there's a tiny chance that I'll say yes."

You and your child won't be able to find a win-win answer to every problem. That's okay — and it's okay for you to make the wrong call once in a while. Parenting is incredibly difficult, and it takes decades to find out whether you're doing it right. So listen to your own heart and conscience, and make the choices that seem right to you. And when you think you've made a mistake, admit it. I have great respect for people who are willing to take responsibility for their bad decisions, and are open enough to apologize and figure out a way to make amends. Most children are equally impressed when their parents have the guts to acknowledge their mistakes.

In the short run, negotiating with children is much more time-consuming than simply laying down the law. But over the years, you'll find that negotiating family life yields tremendous benefits. "You really have to take time for talking and negotiating," Hoffman believes. "It doesn't always bring the quickest

Negotiating with Your Children (cont.)

solution, but it's important for your long-range goal of helping your child see this as a reason-based world."

You can actually start negotiating with infants. "It's something you can do pretty early in the game," Hoffman says. "When you negotiate with a child in a peaceful voice, even if she doesn't get the full grasp of what you're saying, you set up a style that you don't scream and you don't shout."

Like all parenting skills, learning to negotiate with your children requires a lot of work and patience. But if you stay calm and focused on your long-term goals, you may end up, as Beth did, with a five-year-old who sat down, looked her mother in the eye, and said, "Mom, my skating lessons are not working for me."

"Come into my office," Beth replied, trying desperately to keep a straight face. "I think we can work something out."

NEW AGE NEGOTIATORS

So what exactly can we do to nurture nimble negotiators for the New Age? Here are some suggestions.

➜ *Enroll more girls — and boys — in negotiating courses.*

The Harvard-based Program for Young Negotiators has trained teachers in thirty-five schools nationwide, and independent evaluators have found that a significant number of these teachers' students came away from their negotiating class with enhanced self-confidence and improved skills. Denisha Shaw, a graduate of the course, says the middle-school program's benefits have followed her into high school. "I used to blame others when we had a disagreement," Denisha says. "Now it helps me look at the other point of view. It's not only about me. Even when me and my sister are arguing, I think, 'What might she be thinking?'"

→ *Make your baby-sitter bargain for her pay.*

Here's a scene familiar to anyone who's ever hired a teenaged baby-sitter. At the end of a lovely (and much-needed) evening out, you're standing in your hallway getting ready to drive the baby-sitter home. As you pull out your wallet, you ask, "How much do I owe you?" She looks vaguely away. "Oh, I don't know," she murmurs. "Whatever you think." Too often, your decision on her wages depends less on her work performance and more on how much cash you have in your purse. But don't waste this perfect opportunity for bargaining education. Your baby-sitter is a service provider, just like the carpet cleaners or the car repair person. So decide on a fee in advance, just as you would with any other vendor. Force her to name her price — it's good practice for her.

→ *Forget about baby-sitting; lend Jennifer your lawn mower.*

The more skills you have, the stronger your negotiating stance. So why would you limit your daughter's options before she even reaches high school? Take a look at "Past the Pink and Blue Predicament: Freeing the Next Generation from Sex Stereotypes," a study published in 1992 by Girls Incorporated, a national organization dedicated to inspiring girls to be "smart, strong, and bold." The study found that 58 percent of eighth-grade girls earn money baby-sitting, compared with 6 percent of boys. But 27 percent of the boys were doing yard work for their neighbors — which "pays a heck of a lot more per hour," notes Heather Johnston Nicholson, director of research for the Indianapolis-based group. Only 3 percent of the girls were out there with rakes, mowers, and snow shovels, even though a little outdoor labor probably could have doubled their incomes.

Teaching your daughter to handle those traditionally boy-dominated chores does more than give her a little extra folding money, Heather says. It drives home the idea that girls don't have to content themselves with lower-paying jobs just because they seem more "feminine." While you're at it, Heather says, teach your sons to cook and do laundry. If they're comfortable in the domestic realm, they'll be more likely to shoulder their fair share of the household labor when they grow up.

→ *Help her think big.*

When she learns to write her name, tell her to write it in great big letters. That piece of advice comes from Joline Godfrey, founder of Independent Means and editor of *No More Frogs to Kiss: 99 Ways to Give Economic Power to Girls.* If that seems trivial, consider this: How many insurance companies are named after John Witherspoon? He signed the Declaration of Independence, too — but John Hancock's signature was much, much bigger.

Encourage your daughter to think big in other ways. When your adolescent talks about a career choice, expand on it. If she says she wants to be a doctor, introduce her to neurosurgery, or challenge her to do a little research on the National Institutes of Health. Help her to take risks and stretch herself. If she likes to sing, haul her downtown to audition when the local opera house needs a children's chorus. Maybe she won't get in, but the experience of trying out for the big leagues will let her know that her horizons can be very broad indeed.

→ *Admit your own mistakes.*

"If I had tried for them dinky singles, I could have batted around .600," claimed Babe Ruth. Instead, the mighty Bambino swung for the fences and ended up hitting 714 home runs, with a lifetime batting average of .342. But Babe Ruth's audacity had a price: In his 8,399 appearances at the plate, he struck out 1,330 times.

Those are great statistics to tell kids. When boys hear about Babe's boldness at the plate, they understand that it's okay to make a mistake if you're giving it your very best. Well, girls need to hear about a few strikeout queens, too. So tell her about some of the bad calls you've made, and make sure she hears other successful women talk about their missteps. "Ask your mentor about her mistakes," advises Denver contractor Barbara Grogan. "If she says she doesn't have any, get a new mentor. Successful people are failing all the time. What's special about successful people is that they keep stepping up to the plate."

→ *Sign her up for sports, and tell her to play to win.*

Chicago Tribune sports reporter Bonnie DeSimone watches female athletes up close. "I'm envious of these women," she says. "What I have observed, on the elite level especially, is that they learn they can compete for a position, and beat out a teammate who might also be a friend, and still have a relationship. Women are usually worried about being pushy, or abrasive, or making someone angry. But in sports, you can beat someone. That doesn't mean you're not going to be liked. It just means you won your spot. The skills and attitudes they've learned through high-level competitive sports translate extremely well into the business world. These are things I had to learn on the job in my twenties and thirties, and these girls learned them as teenagers."

➙ *Put a sword in her hand.*

All right, this one may seem a little over the edge. But when Beth's daughter started taking fencing lessons, she tapped into a vein of tough competitiveness that stunned everyone. Even play-fighting can give girls a sharper edge. Dawn Alden is the founder of Babes with Blades, a Chicago-based performance group conceived to give female actors an opportunity to showcase their training and talent in stage combat. Dawn says the onstage duels also provide hands-on training in win-win encounters. "You have to work together," she says. "At the same time you want to win, you have to look out for their safety. That means adjusting to their body type and individual strength and weaknesses."

When she comes off the stage after a performance, Dawn says, "there is an amazing rush. We feel like gods!" That translates into a feeling of power even when she doesn't have her trusty broadsword in her hand. Thanks to her years of stage combat, Dawn says, "I know I'm more apt to speak up and stand my ground. I know I'm more willing to fight."

➙ *Give her plenty of opportunities to win — and lose.*

For her book *See Jane Win: The Rimm Report on How 1,000 Girls Became Successful Women,* child psychologist Sylvia Rimm surveyed one thousand "successful, satisfied" women about their upbringing. The positive childhood experience most frequently cited by the women was "success in competition." Too often, we bend over backward in encouraging girls to share the spotlight and give the

Rehearsing for the Tough Ones

It's one thing to shake your head and sigh when your thirteen-year-old daughter can't bring herself to ask the prevailing wage for snow shoveling. It's quite a different case when she doesn't have the skills to escape a potentially dangerous situation.

Your daughter needs to know how to make a quick but graceful getaway when she's confronted with a drunk driver or a vial of cocaine. Too often, girls are pressured into making choices that go against their upbringing and their own good sense because they don't know how to say no.

So start on this early. Try watching a movie or TV show together, and discuss the choices that the characters make. Recently one mother and teen daughter were watching *Dead Poets Society,* a movie about a teenaged boy who kills himself because his father is pressuring him to become a doctor. The mother asked her daughter if she could think up any other ways to solve the problem of an overly pushy parent. "Sure, Mom," the daughter said with a big smile. "I'd just flunk out."

Come up with some what-if situations and brainstorm about possible options. My friend Julia has been helping her fifteen-year-old daughter deal with Suzy, who has suddenly gone seriously boy-crazy. Julia's daughter, Lizzie, is keenly uncomfortable with her friend's sexy new persona, but she's not ready to end their ten-year friendship. To keep Lizzie from getting trapped by Suzy's bad judgment, Julia has come up with some open-ended situations. "What would you do if Suzy met some boys and wanted you to go with her in their car?" she asked one day. Lizzie initially said she'd go with her, because otherwise Suzy would be left alone and vulnerable. After some calm discussion, Julia convinced her that it would be better to let Suzy go on her own. Most likely, Suzy wouldn't make such a foolhardy move if she knew she'd be going solo. And if she did go, at least Lizzie would know what had happened to her. "I'd write down the license plate number," Lizzie said firmly.

Talk about your own experiences. Remember, your daughter didn't know you when you were a tongue-tied adolescent. So unearth some of those painful teen disasters buried deep in your memory. Tell her about that awful double-date you spent chattering nervously away in the front seat while your friend and the other boy steamed up the back windows.

Don't restrict yourself to stories with simple morals and happy endings; she needs to know that you've made some decisions you regret, and that you'll still love and respect her even if she makes an unwise choice. But don't just swap stories. Develop a plan that makes it easy for her to get out of a bad situation. Make sure she's got your pager number, and devise a distress code, so she won't have to go into specifics in front of her friends. She'll just know that if you see your pager flashing 911, you'll be there to pick her up within ten minutes. Make sure she's got a Plan B, so that if she can't reach you, there's always a relative or neighbor on call.

Help her to rehearse some snappy comebacks. Role-playing through some of these situations can actually be fun. Tell her the story of that goofy teacher who advised girls in sexual situations to suddenly sit up and demand a hamburger. A more up-to-date option might be, "Oh, goodness, my beeper just went off!" (Stress that this one is just as effective if she's not wearing a beeper.) One of Beth's high school friends managed to avoid drugs and alcohol and keep her friends in stitches with this routine: Whenever she was offered a joint or a can of beer, she'd say, "I have to ask my mom." She'd disappear from the room for a minute, then return with a downcast expression on her face. "I'm sorry," she'd moan. "Mom says no."

If you can come up with lines your daughter is comfortable saying, and she hears herself saying them out loud, she'll be ready when she really needs to use them.

---

other kids a chance. Don't try so hard to avoid raising a jerk that you end up rearing a dishrag instead. "Girls often feel competitive but they may not admit it," Rimm writes. "Winning builds confidence; losing builds character."

→ Let her know it's okay to say no — even to you.

Don't raise a girl who can't say no. "I was a forty-year-old professor of political science before I realized that I didn't have to say yes to an invitation just because I didn't have anything else to do," admits Heather of Girls Incorporated. It's a pleasure having a daughter who's friendly and agreeable. When somebody asks if your teenaged daughter can baby-sit, or play her violin, or coach a Pee-Wee girls softball team, it makes you feel all warm inside when you hear her respond, "Sure, I'd love to!" However, Heather thinks too much agreeableness can be unhealthy. Like their mothers, today's girls are "socialized to please everybody," she says. And now they have more people to please than ever before.

In addition, many girls — especially the daughters of working moms — are assigned a substantial load of family duties, including after-school childcare for younger siblings. While accomplishing some household chores helps to give a child a sense of competence and responsibility, too much can leave a girl feeling overloaded and desperate. "It's a lot for a girl to cope with," Heather says. "Give girls a break." If your daughter tells you she can't watch her little sister next Thursday afternoon, don't explode. Instead, ask her for help in finding another baby-sitter, and give her a day off.

It's also important to make sure her brother is doing his fair share. When both parents work outside the home, one study found, teenaged girls spend an average of ten hours a week doing chores; their brothers put in only three hours. So take a look at the family workload and make sure it's equitable.

→ Encourage her to negotiate for herself.

The best gift you can give your daughter is a chance to practice bargaining on her own behalf. "I think it's important to share these difficult issues with your kids, to let them know why you have to struggle to find your way through," says Charlotte Lyons, author of *Mothers and Daughters at Home*. "This is the kind of stuff we talk about a lot at the dinner table. We've told them to negotiate their own deals with their teachers, that we're not going to solve all their problems for them. You have to start when they're little to increase your kids' confidence, which ultimately helps them to be able to demand fair treatment in life."

Stop a second to ponder before you charge in and take up the cudgels on her behalf. If she thinks her French teacher is grading her unfairly, ask your daughter whether she can resolve the problem on her own. If she needs some help, you might suggest that she put all her assignments in order and make an appointment to present them to the teacher, along with a plan to do some extra-credit work. She needs to know you're in her corner, but you have to let her fight some of her own battles.

⇢ *Think twice before you call her a "good girl."*

It's hard not to call your sweet little petunia a good girl, especially when she's just turned somersaults — real or figurative — to make you happy. But beware of reinforcing the very behavior that has sometimes hampered your own success. It's so sweet to see your little angel sharing her Halloween candy with her cousin, or energetically picking up all the toys so that she and her sister can go to the zoo. But remember that your spontaneous outburst — "What a good girl!" — may actually be encouraging her to sacrifice her own pleasure to win praise, or to shoulder an unfair part of the burden.

We're not trying to stamp out the qualities that make good girls so good; learning to share and to help are necessary for the moral development of any child, male or female. Just be careful to give her equal praise when she holds her ground and sticks up for herself, even when her robust self-defense stirs up a noisy hornet's nest of sibling conflict. It's wonderful that you're raising a good girl. Just make sure she knows she's going to be a great woman.

Got some more good ideas? We'd love to hear them. To share your stories, tips, and mistakes — or to see a list of resources — go to www. goodgirlsguide.com.

BIBLIOGRAPHY

❧

Acuff, Frank L. *How to Negotiate Anything with Anyone, Anywhere in the World.* New York: AMACOM Books, 1997.

Ainsworth-Vaughn, Nancy. *Claiming Power in Doctor-Patient Talk.* Oxford, England: Oxford University Press, 1998.

Barbara, Dominick A. *The Art of Listening.* Springfield, Ill.: C. C. Thomas Publishers, 1958.

Bazerman, Max H., and Margaret A. Neale. *Negotiating Rationally.* New York: Free Press, 1992.

Butler, Carol A., and Dolores D. Walker. *The Divorce Mediation Answer Book.* New York: Kodansha International, 1999.

Chapman, Jack. *Negotiating Your Salary: How to Make $1,000 a Minute.* Berkeley, Calif.: Ten Speed Press, 1996.

Cohen, Herb. *You Can Negotiate Anything.* New York: Bantam Books, 1982.

Crawford, Susan Hoy. *Beyond Dolls & Guns: 101 Ways to Help Children Avoid Gender Bias.* Portsmouth, N.H.: Heinemann, 1995.

Cross, Carla. *Buyer Beware: Insider Secrets You Need to Know Before Buying Your Home.* Chicago, Ill.: Dearborn Financial Publishing, 1998.

Engel, Peter. *Negotiating.* New York: McGraw-Hill, 1996.

Fezler, William, and Eleanor S. Field. *The Good Girl Syndrome: How Women Are Programmed to Fail in a Man's World — And How to Stop It.* New York: Macmillan, 1985.

Fisher, Roger, and Scott Brown. *Getting Together: Building a Relationship That Gets You to Yes.* New York: Penguin Books, 1988.

Fisher, Roger, William Ury, and Bruce Patton. *Getting to Yes,* 2d ed. New York: Penguin Books, 1991.

Glink, Ilyce R. *100 Questions Every First-Time Home Buyer Should Ask.* New York: Random House, 2000.

Godfrey, Joline. *No More Frogs to Kiss: 99 Ways to Give Economic Power to Girls.* New York: HarperBusiness, 1995.

Goldsmith, Joan, and Kenneth Cloke. *Resolving Conflicts at Work: A Complete Guide for Everyone on the Job.* San Francisco: Jossey-Bass, 2000.

Goleman, Daniel. *Working with Emotional Intelligence.* New York: Bantam Books, 1998.

Hoffman, Lois W., and Lise M. Youngblade. *Mothers at Work: Effects on Children's Well-Being.* Cambridge: Cambridge University Press, 1999.

Irwin, Robert. *Tips & Traps When Negotiating Real Estate.* New York: McGraw-Hill, 1995.

Kolb, Deborah M., and Judith Williams. *The Shadow Negotiation: How Women Can Master the Hidden Agendas That Determine Bargaining Success.* New York: Simon & Schuster, 2000.

Kozicki, Stephen. *Creative Negotiating.* Holbrook, Mass.: Adams Media Corporation, 1998.

Koren, Leonard, and Peter Goodman. *The Haggler's Handbook: One Hour to Negotiating Power.* New York: W. W. Norton, 1991.

Lewicki, Roy J., David M. Saunders, and John W. Minton, eds. *Negotiation: Readings, Exercises, and Cases,* 3d ed. New York: Irwin/McGraw-Hill, 1999.

Lewicki, Roy J. and Joseph Litterer. *Negotiation.* Homewood, Ill.: Richard D. Irwin, 1985.

Lyons, Charlotte. *Mothers and Daughters at Home: 35 Projects to Make Together.* New York: Simon & Schuster, 2000.

Maccoby, Eleanor Emmons, and Carol Nagy Jacklin. *The Psychology of Sex Differences.* Stanford, Calif.: Stanford University Press, 1974.

McCormack, Mark H. *On Negotiating.* Los Angeles, Calif.: Dove Books, 1995.

Mackay, Harvey. *Swim with the Sharks Without Being Eaten Alive,* reissue ed. New York: Ballantine Books, 1996.

Margulies, Sam. *Getting Divorced Without Ruining Your Life.* New York: Simon & Schuster, 1992.

Martin, Judith. *Miss Manners' Guide to Excruciatingly Correct Behavior.* New York: Atheneum, 1982.

Mendelson, Cheryl. *Home Comforts: The Art and Science of Keeping House.* New York: Scribner, 1999.

Nierenberg, Gerard I. *The Art of Negotiating.* New York: Pocket Books, 1981.

Nierenberg, Juliet, and Irene S. Ross. *Women and the Art of Negotiating.* New York: Barnes and Noble Books, 1997.

Obst, Lynda. *Hello, He Lied, and Other Truths from the Hollywood Trenches.* Boston: Little, Brown, 1996.

Onaitis, Susan. *Negotiate Like the Big Guys: How Small and Midsize Companies Can Balance the Power in Dealing with Corporate Giants.* Los Angeles: Silver Lake, 1999.

Pinkley, Robin, and Gregory Northcraft. *Get Paid What You're Worth.* New York: St. Martin's Press, 2000.

Pipher, Mary. *Reviving Ophelia: Saving the Selves of Adolescent Girls.* New York: Ballantine Books, 1995.

Post, Emily. *Etiquette.* New York: Funk & Wagnalls, 1922.

Rickard, Jacqueline. *Complete Premarital Contracting: Loving Communication for Today's Couples.* New York: M. Evans and Co., 1993.

Rimm, Sylvia B. *See Jane Win: The Rimm Report on How 1,000 Girls Became Successful Women.* New York: Crown Publishers, 1999.

Rushkoff, Douglas. *Coercion: Why We Listen to What "They" Say.* New York: Riverhead Books, 1999.

Schaffzin, Nicholas Reid. *Negotiate Smart.* New York: Random House, 1997.

Shapiro, Ronald M., and Mark A. Jankowski with James Dale. *The Power of Nice: How to Negotiate So Everyone Wins — Especially You!* New York: John Wiley & Sons, 1998.

Shister, Neil. *10-Minute Guide to Negotiating.* New York: Alpha Books, 1997.

Snyder, Jean MacLean, and Andra Barmash Greene, eds. *The Woman Advocate.* Chicago: Section of Litigation, American Bar Association, 1996.

Thompson, Leigh. *The Mind and Heart of the Negotiator.* Upper Saddle River, N.J.: Prentice-Hall, 1998.

Ury, William. *Getting Past No: Negotiating Your Way from Confrontation to Cooperation.* New York: Bantam Books, 1993.

Walsh, Mary Roth, ed. *Women, Men, and Gender: Ongoing Debates.* New Haven, Conn.: Yale University Press, 1997.

Webb, Martha. *Dress Your House for Success: 5 Fast, Easy Steps to Selling Your House, Apartment, or Condo for the Highest Possible Price!* New York: Crown Publishers, 1997.

Weintraub, Pamela, Terry Hillman, and Elayne J. Kesselman, Esq. *The Complete Idiot's Guide to Surviving Divorce,* 2d ed. Indianapolis, Ind.: Alpha Books, 1999.

Whitfield, Eileen. *Pickford: The Woman Who Made Hollywood.* Lexington, Ky.: University Press of Kentucky, 1997.

Whittelsey, Frances Cerra, and Marcia Carroll. *Women Pay More (And How to Put a Stop to It).* New York: New Press, 1995.

INDEX